IDIOT AMERICA

DOUBLEDAY

NEW YORK LONDON TORONTO

SYDNEY AUCKLAND

IDIOT AMERICA

＊

How Stupidity Became a Virtue
in the Land of the Free

CHARLES P. PIERCE

DD

DOUBLEDAY

Copyright © 2009 by Charles P. Pierce

All Rights Reserved

Published in the United States by Doubleday, a division of
Random House, Inc., New York.
www.doubleday.com

DOUBLEDAY and the DD colophon are registered trademarks of
Random House, Inc.

Book design by Elizabeth Rendfleisch

Library of Congress Cataloging-in-Publication Data
Pierce, Charles P.
Idiot America : how stupidity became a virtue in the Land of the Free /
by Charles P. Pierce. — 1st ed.
p.   cm.
1. United States—Politics and
government—1989—Philosophy.
2. Stupidity—Political aspects—United States. I. Title.
JK275.P378 2009
973.93—dc22   2008046604

ISBN 978-0-7679-2614-0

PRINTED IN THE UNITED STATES OF AMERICA

1 3 5 7 9 10 8 6 4 2

First Edition

To the memory of John Doris, Ph.D.,
lifelong teacher, lifelong student

Where can a heretic,
Where can a heretic,
Where can a heretic call home?

—CHRIS WHITLEY

Contents

PART IV
MR. MADISON'S LIBRARY

Dinosaurs with Saddles (August 2005)

There is some art—you might even say design—in the way southern Ohio rolls itself into the hills of northern Kentucky. The hills build gently under you as you leave the interstate. The roads narrow beneath a cool and thickening canopy as they wind through the leafy outer precincts of Hebron, a small Kentucky town named, as it happens, for the place near Jerusalem where the Bible tells us that David was anointed the king of the Israelites. This resulted in great literature and no little bloodshed, which is the case with a great deal of Scripture.

At the top of the hill, just past the Idlewild Concrete plant, there was an unfinished wall with an unfinished gate in the middle of it. Happy, smiling people trickled in through the gate on a fine summer's morning, one minivan at a time. They parked in whatever shade they could find, which was not much. They were almost uniformly white and almost uniformly bubbly. Their cars came from Kentucky and Tennessee and Ohio and Illinois and from as far away as New Brunswick, in the Canadian Maritimes. There were elderly couples in shorts, suburban families piling out of the minivans, the children all Wrinkle Resistant and Stain Released. All of them wandered off, chattering and waving and stopping every few steps for pictures, toward a low-slung building that seemed to be the most finished part of the complex.

Outside, several of them stopped to be interviewed by a video crew. They had come from Indiana, one woman said, two impatient toddlers pulling at her arms, because they had been homeschooling their children and they'd given them this adventure as a field trip. The whole group then bustled into the lobby of the building, where they were greeted by the long neck of a huge, herbivorous dinosaur. The kids ran past it and around the corner, where stood another, smaller dinosaur.

Which was wearing a saddle.

It was an English saddle, hornless and battered. Apparently, this was a dinosaur that performed in dressage competitions and stakes races. Any dinosaur accustomed to the rigors of ranch work and herding other dinosaurs along the dusty trail almost certainly would have worn a sturdy western saddle. This, obviously, was very much a show dinosaur.

The dinosaurs were the first things you saw when you entered the Creation Museum, the dream child of an Australian named Ken Ham, who is the founder of Answers in Genesis, the worldwide organization for which the museum is meant to be the headquarters. The people here on this day were on a special tour. They'd paid $149 to become "charter members" of the museum.

"Dinosaurs," Ham said, laughing, as he posed for pictures with his honored guests, "always get the kids interested."

AiG is dedicated to the proposition that the biblical story of the creation of the world is inerrant in every word. Which means, in this interpretation, and among other things, that dinosaurs co-existed with humans (hence the saddles), that there were dinosaurs in Eden, and that Noah, who certainly had enough on his hands, had to load two brachiosaurs onto the Ark along with his wife, his sons, and his sons' wives, to say nothing of the green ally-gators and the long-necked geese and the humpty-backed camels and all the rest.

(Faced with the obvious question of how Noah kept his 300-by-30-by-50-cubit Ark from sinking under the weight of the dinosaur couples, Ham's literature argues that the dinosaurs on the Ark were young ones, who thus did not weigh as much as they might have.)

"We," announced Ham, "are taking the dinosaurs back from the evolutionists!" And everybody cheered.

This was a serious crowd. They gathered in the museum's auditorium and took copious notes while Ham described the great victory won not long before in Oklahoma, where city officials had announced a decision—which they would later reverse, alas—to put up a display based on Genesis at the city's zoo so as to eliminate the discrimination long inflicted upon sensitive Christians by the statue of the Hindu god Ganesh that decorated the elephant exhibit. They listened intently as Ham went on, drawing a straight line from Adam's fall to our godless public schools, from Charles Darwin to gay marriage. He talked about the great triumph of running Ganesh out of the elephant paddock and they all cheered again.

The heart of the museum would take the form of a long walkway down which patrons would be able to journey through the entire creation story. The walkway was in only the earliest stages of construction. On this day, for example, one young artist was working on a scale model of a planned exhibit depicting the day on which Adam named all the creatures of the earth.

Adam was depicted in the middle of the delicate act of naming the saber-toothed tiger while, behind him, already named, a woolly mammoth seemed on the verge of taking a nap.

Elsewhere in the museum, another Adam, this one full-sized, was reclining peacefully, waiting to be installed. Eventually, he was meant to be placed in a pool under a waterfall. As the figure depicted a prelapsarian Adam, he was completely naked. He also had no penis.

This seemed to be a departure from Scripture. If you were willing to stretch Job's description of a "behemoth" to include baby *Triceratops* on Noah's Ark, as Ham did in his lecture, then surely, since he was being depicted before his fall, Adam should have been out there waving unashamedly in the paradisiacal breezes. For that matter, what was Eve doing there, across the room, with her hair falling just so to cover her breasts and her midsection, as though in a nude scene from some 1950s Swedish art-house film?

After all, Genesis 2:25 clearly says that at this point in their lives, "the man and the woman were both naked, and they were not ashamed." If Adam could sit there courageously unencumbered while naming the saber-toothed tiger, then why, six thousand years later, should he be depicted as a eunuch in some family-values Eden? And if these people can take away what Scripture says is rightfully his, then why can't Charles Darwin and the accumulated science of the previous hundred and fifty–odd years take away the rest of it?

These were impolite questions. Nobody asked them here by the cool pond tucked into the gentle hillside. Increasingly, amazingly, nobody asked them outside the gates, either. It was impolite to wonder why our parents had sent us all to college, and why generations of immigrants had sweated and bled so that their children could be educated, if not so that one day we would feel confident enough to look at a museum full of dinosaurs rigged to run six furlongs at Aqueduct and make the not unreasonable point that it was batshit crazy, and that anyone who believed this righteous hooey should be kept away from sharp objects and their own money. Instead, people go to court over this kind of thing.

Dinosaurs with saddles?

Dinosaurs on Noah's Ark?

Welcome to your new Eden.

Welcome to Idiot America.

* * *

THE title of this book very nearly was *Blinking from the Ruins,* and it very nearly was merely a tour of the extraordinary way America has gone marching backward into the twenty-first century. Unquestionably, part of the process was the shock of having more than three thousand of our fellow citizens killed by medievalist murderers who flew airplanes into buildings in the service of a medieval deity, and thereby prompted the United States, born of Enlightenment values, to seek for itself the medieval remedies for which the young country was born too late: Preemptive war. Secret prisons. Torture. Unbridled, unaccountable executive power. The Christian god was handed Jupiter's thunderbolts, and a president elected by chance and intrigue was dressed in Caesar's robes. People told him he sounded like Churchill when, in fact, he sounded like Churchill's gardener. All of this happened in relative silence, and silence, as Earl Shorris writes, is "the unheard speed of a great fall, or the unsounded sigh of acquiescence," that accompanies "all the moments of the descent from democracy."

That is why this book is not merely about the changes in

the country wrought by the atrocities of September 11, 2001. The foundations of Idiot America had been laid long before. A confrontation with medievalism intensified a distressing patience with medievalism in response, and that patience reached beyond the politics of war and peace and accelerated a momentum in the culture away from the values of the Enlightenment and toward a dangerous denial of the consequences of believing nonsense.

Let us take a tour, then, of one brief period in the new century, a sliver of time three years after the towers fell. A federally funded abstinence program suggests that the human immunodeficiency virus can be transmitted through tears. An Alabama legislator proposes a bill to ban all books by gay writers. The Texas House of Representatives passes a bill banning suggestive cheerleading at high school football games. And the nation doesn't laugh at any of this, as it should, or even point out that, in the latter case, having Texas ban suggestive cheerleading is like having Nebraska ban corn.

James Dobson, a prominent Christian conservative spokesman, compares the Supreme Court of the United States with the Ku Klux Klan. Pat Robertson, another prominent conservative preacher man, says that federal judges are a greater threat to the nation than is Al Qaeda and, apparently taking his text from the Book of Gambino, later sermonizes that the United States should get on the stick and snuff the democratically elected president of Venezuela. And the nation does not wonder, audibly, how these two poor fellows were allowed on television.

The Congress of the United States intervenes to extend into a televised spectacle the prolonged death of a woman in Florida. The majority leader of the Senate, a physician, pronounces a diagnosis from a distance of eight hundred miles, relying for his information on a heavily edited videotape. The majority leader of the House of Representatives, a former exterminator, argues against cutting-edge research into the use of human embryonic stem cells by saying "An embryo is a person. . . . We were all at one time embryos ourselves. So was Abraham. So was Muhammad. So was Jesus of Nazareth." Nobody laughs at him, or points out that the same could be said of Hitler, Stalin, Pol Pot, or the inventor of the baby-back rib.

And finally, in August 2005, the cover of *Time*—for almost a century, the clear if dyspeptic voice of the American establishment—hems and haws and hacks like an aged headmaster gagging on his sherry and asks, quite seriously, "Does God have a place in science class?"

Fights over evolution—and its faddish camouflage, "intelligent design," a pseudoscience that posits without proof or method that science is inadequate to explain existence and that supernatural sources must be studied as well—roil through school boards across the country. The president of the United States announces that he believes that ID ought to be taught in the public schools on an equal footing with the theory of evolution. And in Dover, Pennsylvania, during one of these controversies, a pastor named Ray Mummert delivers the line that ends our tour and, in every real sense, sums it up.

"We've been attacked," he says, "by the intelligent, educated segment of our culture."

And there you have it.

Idiot America is not the place where people say silly things. It is not the place where people believe in silly things. It is not the place where people go to profit from the fact that people believe in silly things. That America has been with us always— the America of the medicine wagon and the tent revival, the America of the juke joint and the gambling den, the America of lunatic possibility that in its own mad way kept the original revolutionary spirit alive while an establishment began to calcify atop the place. Idiot America isn't even those people who believe that Adam sat down under a tree one day and named all the dinosaurs. Those people pay attention. They take notes. They take time and spend considerable mental effort to construct a worldview that is round and complete, just as other Americans did before them.

The rise of Idiot America, though, is essentially a war on expertise. It's not so much antimodernism or the distrust of the intellectual elites that Richard Hofstadter teased out of the national DNA, although both of those things are part of it. The rise of Idiot America today reflects—for profit, mainly, but also, and more cynically, for political advantage and in the pursuit of power—the breakdown of the consensus that the pursuit of knowledge is a good. It also represents the ascendancy of the notion that the people we should trust the least are the people who know best what they're talking about. In the new media age, everybody is a historian, or a scientist, or a preacher, or a sage. And if everyone is an expert, then nobody is, and the worst thing you can be in a society where everybody is an expert is, well, an actual expert.

This is how Idiot America engages itself. It decides, en masse, with a million keystrokes and clicks of the remote control, that because there are two sides to every question, they both must be right, or at least not wrong. And the words of an obscure biologist carry no more weight on the subject of biology than do the thunderations of some turkeyneck preacher out of the Church of Christ's Own Parking Structure in DeLand, Florida. Less weight, in fact, because our scientist is an "expert" and, therefore, an "elitist." Nobody buys his books. Nobody puts him on cable. He's brilliant, surely, but no different from all the rest of us, poor fool.

How does it work? This is how it works. On August 21, 2005, a newspaper account of the intelligent design movement contained this remarkable sentence:

"They have mounted a politically savvy challenge to evolution as the bedrock of modern biology, propelling a fringe academic movement onto the front pages and putting Darwin's defenders firmly on the defensive."

"A politically savvy challenge to evolution" makes as much sense as conducting a Gallup poll on gravity or running some-one for president on the Alchemy party ticket. It doesn't matter what percentage of people believe that they ought to be able to flap their arms and fly: none of them can. It doesn't matter how many votes your candidate got: he's not going to be able to turn lead into gold. The sentence is so arrantly foolish that the only real news in it is where it appeared.

On the front page.

Of the *New York Times*.

Consider that the reporter, one Jodi Wilgoren, had to com-pose this sentence. Then she had to type it. Then, more than likely, several editors had to read it. Perhaps even a proofreader had to look it over after it had been placed on the page—the *front* page—of the *Times*. Did it occur to none of them that a "politically savvy challenge to evolution" is as self-evidently ridiculous as an "agriculturally savvy" challenge to Euclidean geometry would be? Within three days, there was a panel on the topic on *Larry King Live,* in which Larry asked the following question:

"All right, hold on, Dr. Forrest, your concept of how you can out-and-out turn down creationism, since if evolution is true, why are there still monkeys?"

And why, dear Lord, do so many of them host television programs?

Part I

＊

THE AMERICAN WAY OF IDIOCY

CHAPTER ONE

The Prince of Cranks

Ralph Ketchum sits on the porch of his little house tucked away on a dirt lane that runs down toward a lake, pouring soda for his guest and listening to the thrum of the rain on his roof. He has been talking to a visitor about the great subject of his academic life—James Madison, the diminutive hypochondriac from Virginia who, in 1787, overthrew the U.S. government and did so simply by being smarter than everyone else. American popular history seems at this point to have de-volved into a Founding Father of the Month Club, with several huge books on Alexander Hamilton selling briskly, an almost limitless fascination with Thomas Jefferson, a steady stream of folks spelunking through George Washington's psyche, and an HBO project starring the Academy Award winner Paul Giamatti as that impossible old blatherskite John Adams. But Madison, it seems, has been abandoned by filmmakers and by the writers of lushly footnoted doorstops. He also was a mediocre president; this never translates well to the screen, where all presidents are great men.

"There are two things that make Jefferson superior to Madison in the historical memory," says Ketchum. "One was Jefferson's magnetism in small groups and the other was his gift for the eloquent phrase. Madison has always been a trailer in that way because, well, he writes perfectly well and, occasionally, manages some eloquence. Occasionally."

Madison was not a social lion. In large gatherings, Ketchum writes, people often found him "stiff, reserved, cold, even aloof and supercilious." He relaxed only in small settings, among people he knew, and while discussing issues of which he felt he had command. "He therefore seldom made a good first impression," writes Ketchum, "seldom overawed a legislative body at his first appearance, and seldom figured in the spicy or dramatic events of which gossip and headlines are made." Madison thought, is what he did, and thinking makes very bad television.

However, for all his shyness and lack of inherent charisma, Madison did manage to woo and win Dolley Payne Todd, the most eligible widow of the time. Ketchum points out that the Virginian came calling having decked himself out in a new beaver hat. (The introductions were made by none other than Aaron Burr, who certainly did get around. If you're keeping score, this means that Burr is responsible for the marriage of one of the authors of the *Federalist* and the death of another, having subsequently introduced Alexander Hamilton to a bullet in Weehawken.) "He did win Dolley." Ketchum smiles. "He had to have something going for him there."

Ketchum's fascination with Madison began in graduate school at the University of Chicago. His mentor, the historian Stuart Brown, encouraged Ketchum to do his doctoral dissertation on Madison's political philosophy. Ketchum finished the dissertation in 1956. He also spent four years working as an editor of Madison's papers at the University of Chicago. He began work on his massive biography of Madison in the mid-1960s and didn't finish the book until 1971.

"Partly," Ketchum says, "the hook was through my mentor, Stuart Brown, and I think I absorbed his enthusiasm, which was for the founding period in general. He said that he thought Madison had been neglected—my wife calls him 'the Charlie Brown of the Founding Fathers'—and that he was more important, so that set me to work on him."

Madison was always the guy under the hood, tinkering with the invention he'd helped to devise in Philadelphia, when he improved the Articles of Confederation out of existence. "You can see that in the correspondence between them"—Jefferson and Madison. "Madison was always toning Jefferson down a little bit. Henry Clay said that Jefferson had more genius but that Madison had better judgment—that Jefferson was more brilliant, but that Madison was more profound."

We are at a dead level time in the dreary summer of 2007. A war of dubious origins and uncertain goals is dragging on despite the fact that a full 70 percent of the people in the country don't want it to do so. Politics is beginning to gather itself into an election season in which the price of a candidate's haircuts will be as important for a time as his position on the war. The country is entertained, but not engaged. It is drowning in information and thirsty for knowledge. There have been seven years of empty debate, of deliberate inexpertise, of abandoned rigor, of lazy, pulpy tolerance for risible ideas simply because they sell, or because enough people believe in them devoutly enough to raise a clamor that can be heard over the deadening drone that suffuses everything else. The drift is as palpable as the rain in the trees, and it comes from willful and deliberate neglect. Madison believed in self-government in all things, not merely in our politics. He did not believe in drift. "A popular government," he famously wrote, "without popular information, or the means of acquiring it, is but a prologue to a tragedy or a Farce, or perhaps both." The great flaw, of course, is that, even given the means to acquire information, the people of the country may decline. Drift is willed into being.

"I think we are nowhere near the citizens he would want us to be," Ketchum muses. "It was kind of an idealism in Madison's view that we can do better than that, but it depends, fundamentally, on improving the quality of the parts, the citizens. I think he would be very discouraged."

Madison is an imperfect guide, as all of them are, even the ones that have television movies made about them. When they launched the country, they really had no idea where all they were doing might lead. They launched more than a political experiment. They set free a spirit by which every idea, no matter how howlingly mad, can be heard. There is more than a little evidence that they meant this spirit to go far beyond the political institutions of a free government. They saw Americans—white male ones, anyway—as a different kind of people from any that had come before. They believed that they had created a space of the mind as vast as the new continent onto which fate, ambition, greed, and religious persecution had dropped them, and just as wild. They managed to set freedom itself free.

Madison himself dropped a hint in *Federalist* 14. "Is it not the glory of the people of America," he wrote, "that whilst they have paid a decent regard to the opinions of former times and other nations, they have not suffered a blind veneration for antiquity, for custom, or for names, to overrule the suggestions of their own good sense, the knowledge of their own situation, and the lessons of their own experience?"

Granted, he was at the time arguing against the notion that a republic could not flourish if it got too big or its population got too large. But you also can see in his question the seedbed of a culture that inevitably would lead, not only to Abraham Lincoln and Franklin Roosevelt and Ronald Reagan, but to William Faulkner, Jackson Pollock, and Little Richard. A culture that moves and evolves and absorbs the new. Experiment, the founders told us. There's plenty of room here for new ideas, and no idea is too crazy to be tested.

* * *

EARLY on the sparkling morning, the golf carts, newly washed, sit gleaming in a row along one side of the parking lot. There's a faint and distant click, the sound of the day's first drives being launched down the shining fairways. Inside the clubhouse of the small public course along Route 61 just outside Minneapolis, two elderly gentlemen are just sitting down for breakfast when someone comes in and asks them if they know how to get to the old lost town. They think for a minute; then one of them rises and points out the window, past the dripping golf carts and off down Route 61, where the winding road runs toward the Mississippi River.

"As I recall," he says, "when my grandfather took me out there when I was a kid, it was down that way, right on the riverbank. It's all grown over now, though, I think."

A dream lies buried in the lush growth that has sprung up on the banks of the great river. In 1856, a dreamer built a city here; the city failed, but the crank went on. He went into politics. He went off to Congress. He came home and he farmed on what was left of the land from his city, and he read. Oh, Lord, how he read. He read so much that he rediscovered Atlantis. He read so much that he discovered how the earth was formed of the cosmic deposits left by comets. He read so much that he found a code in Shakespeare's plays proving that their author was Francis Bacon. His endless, grinding research was thorough, careful, and absolutely, utterly wrong. "It is so oftentimes in this world," he lamented to his diary in 1881, "that it is not the philosophy that is at fault, but the facts." They called him the Prince of Cranks.

Ignatius Donnelly was born in Philadelphia, the son of a doctor and a pawnbroker. He received a proper formal education, and after high school found a job as a clerk in the law office of Benjamin Brewster. But the law bored him. He felt a stirring in his literary soul; in 1850, his poem "The Mourner's Vision" was published. It's a heartfelt, if substantially overcooked, appeal to his countrymen to resist the repressive measures through which the European governments had squashed the revolutions of 1848. Donnelly wrote:

> *O! Austria the vile and France the weak,*
> *My curse be on ye like an autumn storm.*
> *Dragging out teardrops on the pale year's cheek,*
> *adding fresh baseness to the twisting worm;*
> *My curse be on ye like a mother's, warm,*
> *Red reeking with my dripping sin and shame;*
> *May all my grief back turned to ye, deform*
> *Your very broken image, and a name,*
> *Be left ye which Hell's friends shall hiss and curse the*
>   *same.*

As one historian gently put it, the poem "was not critically acclaimed."

Donnelly also involved himself in Philadelphia's various fraternal and professional organizations, as well as in its tumultuous Democratic politics. By 1855, he'd developed a sufficient reputation for oratory that he was chosen to deliver the Fourth of July address at the local county Democratic convention in Independence Square.

However, for the first—but far from the last—time in his life, Donnelly's political gyroscope now came peculiarly unstuck. Within a year of giving the address, he'd pulled out of a race for the Pennsylvania state legislature and endorsed his putative opponent, a Whig. The next year, he again declared himself a Democrat and threw himself into James Buchanan's presidential campaign. Buchanan got elected; not long afterward, Donnelly announced that he was a Republican.

By now, too, he was chafing at the limits of being merely one Philadelphia lawyer in a city of thousands of them, many of whom had the built-in advantages of money and social connections that gave them a permanent head start. He'd married Katherine McCaffrey, a young school principal with a beautiful singing voice, in 1855. He wanted to be rich and famous. Philadelphia seemed both too crowded a place to make a fortune and too large a place in which to become famous. And, besides, his mother and his wife hated each other. (They would not speak for almost fifteen years.) He was ready to move. Not long after he was married, Donnelly met a man named John Nininger, and Nininger had a proposition for him.

The country was in the middle of an immigration boom as the revolutions of the 1840s threw thousands of farmers from central Europe off their land and out of their countries. Nininger, who'd made himself rich through real estate speculation in Minnesota, had bought for a little less than $25,000 a parcel of land along a bend in the Mississippi twenty-five miles south of St. Paul. Nininger proposed that he himself handle the sale of the land, while Donnelly, with his natural eloquence and boundless enthusiasm, would pitch the project, now called Nininger, to newly arrived immigrants. Ignatius and Katherine Donnelly moved to St. Paul, and he embarked on a sales campaign that was notably vigorous even by the go-go standards of the time.

"There will be in the Fall of 1856 established in Philadelphia, New York, and other Eastern cities, a great Emigration Association," Donnelly wrote in the original Statement of Organization for the city of Nininger. "Nininger City will be the depot in which all the interests of this huge operation will centre." Donnelly promised that Nininger would feature both a ferry dock and a railroad link, making the town the transportation hub between St. Paul and the rest of the Midwest. To Nininger, farmers from the distant St. Croix valley would send their produce for shipment to the wider world. Nininger would be a planned, scientific community, a thoroughly modern frontier city.

"Western towns have heretofore grown by chance," Donnelly wrote, "Nininger will be the first to prove what combination and concentrated effort can do to assist nature."

Eventually, some five hundred people took him up on it. In time, Nininger built a library and a music hall. Donnelly told Katherine that he wasn't sure what to do with himself now that he'd made his fortune. In May 1856, he waxed lyrical to the Minnesota Historical Society about the inexorable march of civilization and the role he had played in it. At which point, approximately, the roof fell in.

It was the Panic of 1857 that did it. The Minnesota land boom of the 1850s—of which Nininger was a perfect example—had been financed by money borrowed from eastern speculators by the local banks. When these loans were called in, the banks responded by calling in their own paper, and an avalanche of foreclosures buried towns like Nininger. The panic also scared the federal government out of the land-grant business, which was crucial to the development of the smaller railroads. When the Nininger and St. Peter Railroad Line failed, it not only ended Nininger's chance to be a rail hub but made plans for the Mississippi ferry untenable as well.

Donnelly did all he could to keep the dream alive. He offered to carry his neighbors' mortgages for them. He tried, vainly, to have Nininger declared the seat of Dakota County. The town became something of a joke; one columnist in St. Paul claimed he would sell his stock in the railroad for $4 even though it had cost him $5 to buy it. Gradually, the people of Nininger moved on. Ignatius Donnelly, however, stayed. In his big house, brooding over the collapse of his dream, he planned his next move. He read widely and with an astonishing catholicity of interest. He decided to go back into politics.

Donnelly found himself drawn to the nascent Republicans, in no small part because of the fervor with which the new party opposed slavery. In 1857 and again in 1858, he lost elections to the territorial senate. In 1858, Minnesota was admitted to the Union, and Donnelly's career took off.

The election of 1859 was the first manifest demonstration of the burgeoning power of the Republican party. Donnelly campaigned tirelessly across the state; his gift for drama served him well. He allied himself with the powerful Minnesota Republican Alexander Ramsey, and in 1859, when Ramsey was swept into the governorship, Donnelly was elected lieutenant governor on the same ticket. He was twenty-eight years old. Contemporary photos show a meaty young man in the usual high collar, with a restless ambition in his eyes. He found the post of lieutenant governor constraining and, if Ramsey thought that he was escaping his rambunctious subordinate when the Minnesota legislature elected him to the U.S. Senate in 1862, he was sadly mistaken. That same year, Ignatius Donnelly was elected to the House of Representatives from the Second District of Minnesota.

For the next four years, Donnelly's career was remarkably like that of any other Republican congressman of the time, if a bit louder and more garish. After the war, he threw himself into the issues surrounding Reconstruction, and he worked on land-use matters that were important back home. He also haunted the Library of Congress, reading as omnivorously as ever. He began to ponder questions far from the politics of the day, although he took care to get himself reelected twice. Not long after his reelection in 1866, however, his feud with Ramsey exploded and left his political career in ruins, in no small part because Ignatius Donnelly could never bring himself to shut up.

It was no secret in Minnesota that Donnelly had his eye on Ramsey's seat in the Senate. It certainly was no secret to Ramsey, who had long ago become fed up with Donnelly, and who was now enraged at his rival's scheming. One of Ramsey's most influential supporters was a lumber tycoon from Minneapolis, William Washburne, whose brother, Elihu, was a powerful Republican congressman from Illinois. In March 1868, Donnelly wrote a letter home to one of his constituents in which he railed against Elihu Washburne's opposition to a piece of land-grant legislation.

On April 18, Congressman Washburne replied, blistering Donnelly in the *St. Paul Press*. He called Donnelly "an office-beggar," charged him with official corruption, and hinted ominously that he was hiding a criminal past. In response, Donnelly went completely up the wall.

By modern standards, under which campaign advisers can lose their jobs for calling the other candidate a "monster," the speech is inconceivable. Donnelly spoke for an hour. He ripped into all Washburnes. He made merciless fun of Elihu Washburne's reputation for fiscal prudence and personal rectitude. Three times, the Speaker of the House tried to gavel him to order. Donnelly went sailing on, finally reaching a crescendo of personal derision that made the florid sentiments of "The Mourner's Vision" read like e. e. cummings.

"If there be in our midst one low, sordid, vulgar soul . . . one tongue leprous with slander; one mouth which is like unto a den of foul beasts giving forth deadly odors; if there be one character which, while blotched and spotted all over, yet raves and rants and blackguards like a prostitute; if there be one bold, bad, empty, bellowing demagogue, it is the gentleman from Illinois."

The resulting campaign was a brawl. The Republican primary was shot through with violence. Ultimately, Ramsey County found itself with two conventions in the same hall, which resulted in complete chaos and one terrifying moment when the floor seemed ready to give way. Donnelly lost the statewide nomination. He ran anyway and lost. By the winter of 1880, after losing another congressional race, Donnelly lamented to his diary, "My life had been a failure and a mistake."

Donnelly went home to the big house in what had been the city of Nininger. Although he would flit from one political cause to another for the rest of his life, he spent most of his time thinking and writing, and, improbably, making himself one of the most famous men in America.

During his time in Washington, on those long afternoons when he played hooky from his job in the Congress, Donnelly had buried himself in the booming scientific literature of the age, and in the pseudoscientific literature—both fictional and purportedly not—that was its inevitable by-product. Donnelly had fallen in love with the work of Jules Verne, especially *Twenty Thousand Leagues Under the Sea,* which had been published to great acclaim in 1870, and which features a visit by Captain Nemo and his submarine to the ruins of a lost city beneath the waves. Donnelly gathered an enormous amount of material and set himself to work to dig a legend out of the dim prehistory. From the library in his Minnesota farmhouse, with its potbellied stove and its rumpled daybed in one corner, Ignatius Donnelly set out to find Atlantis.

It was best known from its brief appearances in *Timaeus* and *Critias,* two of Plato's dialogues. These were Donnelly's jumping-off point. He proposed that the ancient island had existed, just east of the Azores, at the point where the Mediterranean Sea meets the Atlantic Ocean. He argued that Atlantis was the source of all civilization, and that its culture had established itself everywhere from Mexico to the Caspian Sea. The gods and goddesses of all the ancient myths, from Zeus to Odin to Vishnu and back again, were merely the Atlantean kings and queens. He credited Atlantean culture for everything from Bronze Age weaponry in Europe, to the Mayan calendar, to the Phoenician alphabet. He wrote that the island had vanished in a sudden cataclysm, but that some Atlanteans escaped, spreading out across the world and telling the story of their fate.

The book is a carefully crafted political polemic. That Donnelly reached his conclusions before gathering his data is obvious from the start, but his brief is closely argued from an impossibly dense synthesis of dozens of sources. Using his research into underwater topography, and using secondary sources to extrapolate Plato nearly to the moon, Donnelly argues first that there is geologic evidence for an island's having once been exactly where Donnelly thought Atlantis had been. He then dips into comparative mythology, arguing that flood narratives common to many religions are derived from a dim memory of the events described by Plato. At one point, Donnelly attributes the biblical story of the Tower of Babel to the Atlanteans' attempt to keep their heads literally above water.

He uses his research into anthropology and history to posit a common source for Egyptian and pre-Columbian American culture. "All the converging lines of civilization," Donnelly writes, "lead to Atlantis. . . . The Roman civilization was simply a development and perfection of the civilization possessed by all the European populations; it was drawn from the common fountain of Atlantis." Donnelly connects the development of all civilization to Atlantis, citing the fact that Hindus and Aztecs developed similar board games, and that all civilizations eventually discover how to brew fermented spirits. The fourth part of the book is an exercise in comparative mythology; Donnelly concludes by describing how the Atlantean remnant fanned out across the world after their island sank. He rests much of his case on recent archaeological works and arguing, essentially, that, if we can find Pompeii, we can find Atlantis. "We are on the threshold," he exclaims. "Who shall say that one hundred years from now the great museums of the world may not be adorned with gems, statues, arms and implements from Atlantis, while the libraries of the world shall contain translations of its inscriptions, throwing new light upon all the past history of the human race, and all the great problems which now perplex the thinkers of our day!"

Harper & Brothers in New York published *Atlantis: The Antediluvian World* in February 1882. It became an overnight sensation. The book went through twenty-three editions in eight years, and a revised edition was published as late as 1949. Donnelly corresponded on the topic with William Gladstone, then the prime minister of England. Charles Darwin also wrote, but only to tell Donnelly that he was somewhat skeptical, probably because Donnelly's theory of an Atlantean source for civilization made a hash of Darwin's theories. On the other hand, Donnelly also heard from a distant cousin who was a bishop in Ireland. He deplored Donnelly's blithe dismissal of the biblical accounts of practically everything.

The popular press ate Donnelly up. (One reviewer even cited

Atlantis as reinforcing the biblical account of Genesis, which showed at least that Donnelly's work meant different things to different people.) The *St. Paul Dispatch,* the paper that had stood for him in his battles against Ramsey and the Washburnes, called Atlantis "one of the notable books of the decade, nay, of the century." Donnelly embarked on a career as a lecturer that would continue until his death. He got rave reviews.

"A stupendous speculator in cosmogony," gushed the *London Daily News.* "One of the most remarkable men of this age," agreed the *St. Louis Critic.* And, doubling down on both of them, the *New York Star* called Donnelly "the most unique figure in our national history."

CHAPTER TWO

The War on Expertise

This is a great country, in no small part because it is the best country ever devised in which to be a public crank. Never has a nation so dedicated itself to the proposition that not only should people hold nutty ideas, but they should cultivate them, treasure them, shine them up, and put them right up there on the mantelpiece. This is still the best country ever in which to peddle complete public lunacy. In fact, it's the only country to enshrine that right in its founding documents.

After all, the founders were men of the Enlightenment, fashioning a country out of new ideas—or out of old ones that they'd liberated from centuries of religious internment. The historian Charles Freeman points out that "Christian thought . . . often gave irrationality the status of a universal 'truth' to the exclusion of those truths to be found through reason. So the uneducated was preferred to the educated, and the miracle to the operation of the natural laws."

In America, the founders were trying to get away from all

that, to raise a nation of educated people. But they were not trying to do so by establishing an orthodoxy of their own to replace the one at which they were chipping away. They believed they were creating a culture within which the mind could roam to its wildest limits because the government they had devised included sufficient safeguards to keep the experiment from running amok. In 1830, in a letter to the Marquis de Lafayette, James Madison admitted: "We have, it is true, occasional fevers; but they are of the transient kind, flying off through the surface, without preying on the vitals. A Government like ours has so many safety valves . . . that it carries within itself a relief against the infirmities from which the best of human Institutions can not be exempt." The founders devised the best country ever in which to go completely around the bend. It's just that making a living at it used to be harder work.

* * *

SLOWLY, but with gathering momentum, the realization is dawning on people that we have lived through an unprecedented decade of richly empowered hooey. At its beginning, Al Gore was vice president of the United States. He was earnest to the point of being screamingly dull. He was interested in things like global climate change and the potential of a mysterious little military project called Arpanet which, he believed, could be the source of the greatest revolution in communications—and, thus, in the dissemination of knowledge—since Gutenberg set his first line of type. Gore had the rhetorical gifts of a tack hammer. In 2000, he ran for president. He lost because of some jiggery-pokery in Florida and because of a Supreme Court decision that was so transparently dodgy that its own authors did everything except deliver it in a plain brown envelope. But he was beaten, ultimately, by nonsense.

He was accused of saying things he didn't say, most especially about that curious little initiative that subsequently blossomed into the Internet. He told jokes that people pretended to take seriously. His very earnestness became a liability. His depth of knowledge was a millstone. (On one memorable occasion, a pundit named Margaret Carlson told the radio host Don Imus—and that would have been a meeting of the minds, if they hadn't been two short—that she much preferred picking at Gore's fanciful scabs to following him into the thickets of public policy, where a gal might trip and break her glasses.) By comparison, George W. Bush was light and breezy and apparently forgot during one debate that Social Security was a federal program. In fact, his lack of depth, and his unfamiliarity with the complexities of the issues, to say nothing of the complexities of the simple declarative sentence, worked remarkably to his advantage. As Jimmy Cagney's George M. Cohan said of himself, Bush was an ordinary guy who knew what ordinary guys liked. That was enough.

This was not unprecedented. Adlai Stevenson's archness and intellectualism failed twice against the genial Kansas charm of Dwight Eisenhower, but at least the latter had overseen the largest amphibious invasion in human history and the triumphant destruction of European fascism. Bush had no similar accomplishments, nor did he accrue any during his eventful first term in office. Nevertheless, four years later, at the end of August 2004, a Zogby poll discovered the critical fact that 57 percent of the undecided voters in that year's election would rather have a beer with George Bush than with John Kerry.

The question was odd enough on its face, but a nation to which it would matter was odder still. Be honest. Consider all the people with whom you've tossed back a beer. How many of them would you trust with the nuclear launch codes? How many of them can you envision in the Oval Office? Running a

Cabinet meeting? Greeting the president of Ghana? Not only was this not a question for a nation of serious citizens, it wasn't even a question for a nation of serious drunkards.

By the end of the second term, and by the writing of this book, the hangover was pounding. The nation was rubbing its temples, shading its eyes, and wondering why its tongue seemed to be made of burlap. Al Gore had moved along, putting his tedious knowledge of global climate change into a film that won him an Academy Award, a Grammy, and, ultimately, a share of the Nobel Peace Prize. He also wrote a book called *The Assault on Reason.* "Faith in the power of reason," he wrote, ". . . was and remains the central premise of American democracy. This premise is now under assault."

The national hangover seems to be moving into that moment when the light feels less like daggers in your eyes, and regret and guilt start flooding in to replace the hammers that have ceased to pound inside the head. This is that moment in the hangover in which you discover that your keys are in your hat, the cat is in the sink, and you attempted late the previous night to make stew out of a pot holder. Things are in the wrong place. Religion is in the box where science used to be. Politics is on the shelf where you thought you left science the previous afternoon. Entertainment seems to have been knocked over and spilled on everything. We have rummaged ourselves into disorder. And we have misplaced nothing so much as we have misplaced the concept of the American crank, with dire consequences for us all.

The American crank is one of the great by-products of the American experiment. The country was founded on untested, radical ideas. (The historian Gordon Wood argues that it was in the provinces, in America and in Scotland, that the ideas of the Enlightenment grew most lushly.) The country's culture was no different from its politics. It ran wild, in a thousand different directions. More than anything else, the American crank is simply American, first, last, and always.

The American crank stood alone, a pioneer gazing at the frontier of his own mind the way the actual pioneers looked out over the prairie. American cranks fled conventional thinking for the same reasons that people fled the crowded cities of the East. They homesteaded their own internal stakes. They couldn't have found the mainstream with two maps and a divining rod and, truth be told, they didn't care to look for it anyway.

For example, largely because of the play and film *Inherit the Wind,* William Jennings Bryan has come down to us as a simple crank, but there never has been anything simple about the American crank. In his biography of Bryan, Michael Kazin describes the endless woodshedding that Bryan did in and around Nebraska, including an almost inhuman campaign schedule in his first run for Congress. He wasn't moving the country. The country was moving toward him, long before he electrified the Democratic National Convention in 1896 with the "Cross of Gold" speech that made him famous. "Bryan was using his talent . . . to signal the arrival of a new era," writes Kazin. The establishment politicians of the time had a name for Bryan and the people who rallied to his call; they called them the "money cranks."

American cranks did not seek out respectable opinion. It had to come to them. It adapted to the contours of their landscape, or they simply left it alone. If it did so, that was fine, and if in doing so it put some money into their pockets, well, so much the better. Very often, it was the cranks who provided the conflict by which the consensus changed. They did so by working diligently on the margins until, subtly, without most of the country noticing, those margins moved. As the margins moved, the cranks either found their place within the new boundaries they'd helped to devise, or moved even further out, and began their work anew. That was their essential value. That was what made them purely American cranks. The country was designed to be an ongoing and evolving experiment. The American crank sensed this more deeply than did most of the rest of the country.

The American crank was not necessarily a nerd or a geek, although some cranks certainly are. The American crank was not necessarily an iconoclast, a demagogue, or a charlatan. That's merely what some cranks do for a living. At bottom, the American crank's greatest contribution to the country is to provide it with its living imagination. All of our cranks did that—the sidewalk preachers and the sellers of patent medicines, always in the market for suckers and a quick getaway; populist politicians and old men singing the blues on a sharecropper's porch as the sun fell hotly on the Delta and on Huck Finn's raft.

American cranks always did their best work in the realm of the national imagination. They were creatures of it, and they helped create a great deal of it. They wandered out to its far borders and they mapped its frontiers. They took risks in creating their vision of the country, and the biggest risk they took was that everything they believed might be the sheerest moonshine. They acknowledged that risk. They lived with it. They did not insist on the approbation of the people living in the comfortable center of the country. They did not yearn, first and foremost, for the book deal, or for the prizes, or to be the chairman of the department. Without this nagging, glorious sense of how far they've strayed from the mainstream, American cranks simply become noisy people who are wrong. To win, untested, the approval of the great masses, whether that's indicated by book sales or by, say, conventional political success, is to make American cranks into something they never should be—ordinary. The value of the crank is in the effort that it takes either to refute what the crank is saying, or to assimilate it into the mainstream. In either case, political and cultural imaginations expand. Intellectual horizons broaden.

The crank is devalued when his ideas are accepted untested and unchallenged into the mainstream simply because they succeed as product. The more successful the crank is in this latter regard, the less valuable he is to America. There is nothing more worthless to the cultural imagination than a persistently wrong idea that succeeds despite itself.

The failure of Idiot America is a failure of imagination or, more specifically, it is a failure to recognize the utility of the imagination. Idiot America is a bad place for crazy notions. It neither encourages them nor engages them. Rather, its indolent tolerance of them causes the classic American crank to drift easily into the mainstream, whereupon the cranks lose all of their charm and the country loses another piece of its mind.

The best thing about American cranks used to be that, if they couldn't have the effect they desired, they would stand apart from a country that, by their peculiar lights, had gone completely mad. Not today. Today, they all have book deals, TV shows, and cases pending in federal court. One recalls the lament of Paul Newman's ace con artist Henry Gondorff in *The Sting:* "There's no point in being a grifter if it's the same as being a citizen."

It is, of course, television that has enabled Idiot America to run riot within modern politics and all forms of public discourse. It's not that there is less information on television than there once was. In fact, there is so much information that "fact" is now defined as something believed by so many people that television notices their belief, and truth is measured by how fervently they believe it. Just don't be boring. And keep the ratings up, because Idiot America wants to be entertained. In the war on expertise that is central to the rise of Idiot America, television is both the battlefield and the armory. "You don't need to be credible on television," explains Keith Olbermann, the erudite host of his own nightly television show on the MSNBC cable network. "You don't need to be authoritative. You don't need to be informed. You don't need to be honest. All these things we used to associate with what we do are no longer factors."

Further, television has killed American crankhood by making it obsolete. Because television has become the primary engine of validation for ideas within the culture, once you appear on television, you become a part of the mainstream so instantly that your value as an American crank disappears, destroyed by respectability that it did not earn. Because it's forced neither to adapt to the mainstream nor to stand proudly aloof from it, its imaginative function is subsumed in a literal medium. Once you're on television, you become an expert, with or without expertise, because once you're on television, you are speaking to the Gut, and the Gut is a moron, as anyone who's ever tossed a golf club, punched a wall, or kicked a lawn mower knows.

The Gut is the roiling repository of dark and ancient fears. It knows what it knows because it knows how it feels. Hofstadter saw the triumph of the Gut coming. "Intellect is pitted against feeling," he writes, "on the ground that it is somehow inconsistent with warm emotion. It is pitted against character, because it is widely believed that intellect stands for cleverness, which transmutes easily into the sly or the diabolical." If something feels right, it must be treated with the same respect given something that actually is right. If something is felt deeply, it must carry the same weight as something that is true. If there are two sides to every argument—or, more to the point, if there are people willing to take up two sides to every argument—they both must be right or, at least, equally valid.

Dress it up and the Gut is "common sense," which rarely is common and even more rarely makes sense. It often comes down to assessing what Everybody Knows, even though Everybody might be as false as blue money to the truth of things. The Gut is as destructive to the value of the American crank as television is. While television undermines the crank by making the crank instantly respectable, the Gut destroys him by forcing him into the procrustean bed of commercial salesmanship. Time was when the American crank forced the mainstream into a hard choice. It could come to him, engage him on his own terms, and be transformed; or it simply could leave him alone. The Gut changes the equation by adding the possibility that the crank can be a part of the mainstream without effecting any change in it. The component of imagination is gone. The crank then becomes simply someone with another product to sell within the unimaginative parameters of the marketplace; his views are just another impulse buy, like the potato chips near the cash register. The commercial imperatives of the Gut restrict the crank's ability to allow his ideas to grow, lushly and wildly, to their fullest extent, and they deprive us of the crank's traditional value. In exchange, the Gut becomes the basis for the Great Premises of Idiot America.

We hold these truths to be self-evident.

The First Great Premise: Any theory is valid if it sells books, soaks up ratings, or otherwise moves units.

In her book, *The Age of American Unreason,* Susan Jacoby mercilessly lampoons the very American notion that, because there are two sides to every question, both deserve respect and both must, in some way, be true. The Gut tells us that this is only fair, and we are a fair people, after all. All one has to do is muster an argument with enough vigor, package it well, and get enough people to buy both the idea and the product through which it is expressed. The more people buy, the more correct you are. The barriers that once forced American cranks to adapt or withdraw—or even merely to defend—their ideas all have fallen. It is considered impolite to raise them again, almost un-American, since we are all entitled to our opinion.

"The much lionized American centrists, sometimes known as moderates," Jacoby writes, "are in no way immune to the overwhelming pull of belief systems that treat evidence as a tiresome stumbling block to deeper, instinctive 'ways of knowing.' "

Two of America's best-selling authors present a good case study in what Jacoby is talking about. In 2008, a conservative writer named Jonah Goldberg shook up the best-seller list with the publication of his *Liberal Fascism: The Secret History of the American Left from Mussolini to the Politics of Meaning*. Apparently written with a paint roller, Goldberg's book is a lugubrious slog through a history without reliable maps, a pre-Columbian wilderness of the mind where, occasionally, events have to have their hearts ripped out of all context and waved on high to the pagan god of the unblinking sun.

The book is little more than a richly footnoted loogie hawked by Goldberg at every liberal who ever loosely called him a fascist. In that capacity, if not as history, it is completely successful. There are people who too blithely toss around the concept of fascism. Some of his gibes at liberalism are funny. If he had stuck with them, Goldberg would have stood as tall and as proud as any American crank before him. He even would have made just as much money.

Alas, his vengeful turgidity insisted on the conventional historical validity of its central premise—namely, that fascism is, and always has been, a phenomenon of the political left. Before Goldberg happened upon it, this provocative theory had eluded almost every serious student of fascism, including Mussolini. At one point, though, Goldberg seems confused about whom he's arguing with, and he winds up quarreling with the voices in his head:

> It is my argument that American liberalism is a totalitarian religion, but not necessarily an Orwellian one. It is nice, not brutal. Nannying, not bullying. But it is definitely totalitarian—or "holistic," if you prefer—in that liberalism today sees no realm of human life that is beyond political significance, from what you eat to what you smoke to what you say. Sex is political. Food is political. Sports, entertainment, your inner motives and outward appearance, all have political salience for liberal fascists. Liberals place their faith in priestly experts who know better, who plan, exhort, badger, and scold. They try to use science to discredit traditional notions of religion and faith, but they speak the language of pluralism and spirituality to defend "nontraditional" beliefs. Just as with classical fascism, liberal fascists speak of a "Third Way" between right and left where all good things go together and all hard choices are "false choices."

This is an altogether remarkable bowl of word salad, containing morsels of almost every tasty treat from the All U Can Eat buffet at the Hofstadter Café. Especially piquant is that passage about "priestly experts" and about how liberals—or liberal fascists—use science to discredit traditional religion, as though, somewhere in a laboratory, physicists are studying the faintest echoes of the big bang and thinking, at first, not of the Nobel Prize and the nifty trip to Stockholm, but, rather, "Bite me, Jehovah!"

The general does not improve at all when it moves into the specific. Goldberg asserts that Woodrow Wilson—admittedly, a hopelessly overrated president—was nothing less than "the twentieth century's first fascist dictator."

Glorioski.

It seems that Wilson was a Progressive, and Goldberg sees in the Progressive movement the seedbed of American fascism which, he argues, differs from European fascism, especially on those occasions when he needs it to differ because he has backed up his argument over his own feet. Anyway, Wilson brought the country into World War I. Therefore, Progressives love war.

Of course, Wilson's evil scheme was briefly derailed by a filibuster in the Senate in 1917. The filibuster was led by men who'd come from the same Progressive politics that had produced Wilson, most notably Robert La Follette of Wisconsin. It was so effective that Wilson memorably fumed against the tactics of "a small group of willful men" and fought for (and won) a change in the Senate rules that provided for the cloture system we have today. Every person involved in this episode—which involved no less important an issue than whether the United States would slide toward a war—was a Progressive. Caught in his astonishing assertion about Wilson, Goldberg deals with the filibuster by not dealing with it at all. This is no longer the admirable cri de coeur of a valuable American crank. It's just a long-winded explication of an idea that's wrong.

What Goldberg is to political history, Mitch Albom is to eschatology. Albom's first breakthrough was *Tuesdays with Morrie,* an altogether unobjectionable stop-and-smell-the-roses memoir concerning his weekly conversations with a dying college professor. From these talks, the author learns valuable lessons about dealing with his fellow human beings.

Not content with passing along life lessons from real people, Albom branched out into the afterlife with *The Five People You Meet in Heaven,* a brief meditation on the great beyond that is what Dante would have written had he grown up next door to the Cleavers. It is the story of Eddie, who dies unexpectedly in an accident on the job at an amusement park. Eddie finds himself in heaven, which looks very much like the amusement park he has left behind. He first encounters the Blue Man, who explains to him what heaven is all about. The Blue Man, it turns out, is a guy who died of a heart attack after the youthful Eddie ran out in front of his car chasing a ball. In his life, Eddie was not aware that this had happened. The Blue Man explains that, even though he's in heaven, Eddie's not getting off that easily. He is handed the kind of emotional ab-crunching that the three spirits gave Ebenezer Scrooge one Christmas Eve.

> There are five people you meet in heaven. . . . Each of us was in your life for a reason. You may not have known the reason at the time, and that is what heaven is for. For understanding your life on earth . . . People think of heaven as a paradise garden, a place where they can float on clouds and laze in rivers and mountains. But scenery without solace is meaningless. This is the greatest gift that God can give you: to understand what happened in your life. To have it explained. It is the peace you have been searching for.

This makes Rick Warren read like St. John of the Cross. Compare it, for example, to the description of the New Jerusalem wrought by the half-crazed author of Revelation, who never sat on Oprah's couch and never got a movie deal—and who, it should be noted, has had his work pillaged without proper credit in recent times by movie directors and by best-selling Christian authors who turn Jesus into one of the X-Men:

> And the building of the wall thereof was of jasper stone, but the city itself pure gold, like to clear glass. And the foundations of the wall of the city were adorned by precious stones. The first

foundation was jasper; the second, sapphire; the third, a chalcedony; the fourth, an emerald; the fifth, sardonyx; the sixth, sardius; the seventh, chrysolite; the eighth, beryl; the ninth, a topaz; the tenth, a chrysoprasus; the eleventh, a jacinth; the twelfth, an amethyst. And the twelve gates are twelve pearls, one to each, and every several gate was one of several pearl. And the street of the city was pure gold, as it were transparent glass.

Now, that's a heaven worth dying for.

By contrast, Albom's heaven sounds more than anything like the old Catholic notion of Purgatory. And it's made up entirely of other people—which, as you may recall, was Sartre's precise description of hell. Albom's writing doesn't have any more to do with actual theology than Goldberg's does with actual history.

The one thing they have in common is that they both were genuine phenomena. They sold wildly well. This immediately worked to immunize both authors from the carping of those who saw no logical connection between organic food and the Nuremberg rallies, or who resisted a vision of Paradise in which you spent eternity being as bored with your relatives as you were in life. It was the way his book sold that liberated Goldberg to dismiss as "trade-guild historians" even those critics who had dedicated their lives to the study of the very history he tossed blithely into his Mixmaster. For his part, Albom has developed a lucrative second career as an "inspirational" speaker, charming audiences of suburbanites with a vision of heaven not overly different in its banality from the one presented at the Creation Museum, where that eunuch Adam lounges around the Garden of Eden.

Goldberg and Albom are both cranks. There is much to admire in a culture that can produce—and, indeed, reward—

their work. There was a time in which they would have had to build their own personal soapboxes; their success would have depended on how their work bent itself to the general marketplace of ideas, and the marketplace to their work. Instead, their sales have brought their ideas into the mainstream whole and undigested. These works are products, purely and completely. Goldberg's target audience is made up of those conservatives who see themselves beset on all sides by powerful liberal elites. Albom's comprises an anxious nation hungering for a heaven with roller coasters. This quest for conventional credibility devalues an American crank, and the more loudly the crank insists on it, the less valuable he is to the rest of us.

Which leads us, inevitably, to the Second Great Premise: Anything can be true if someone says it loudly enough.

Television sells. It sells notions as well as potions. It validates people and their ideas as surely as it does baldness cures and male-enhancement nostrums. Television is the primary vehicle through which America first misplaced its cranks, to the everlasting detriment of both America and the cranks. Commercial idiocy, for example, once required the deft mixing of noxious ingredients and the purchase of a stout wagon. It also required a keen eye, on the lookout for large groups of dissatisfied consumers carrying pine rails and hempen ropes. Political idiocy required tireless work at the grass roots, endless nights haranguing exhausted, half-broke, fully drunk farmers about how you and they were being played by easy money, eastern bankers, and the Bilderberg group. When your theory finally swept the nation—invariably, it would be described as doing so "like a prairie fire"—nobody gave a thought to how many hours you spent honing your pitch out in the dark places where the cold winds do blow.

And religious idiocy—where, often, commercial idiocy and

political idiocy came together to be purified, sanctified, and altogether immunized against the ridicule they all so richly deserved—required at least a loud voice and a busy street corner. The Mormons picked up and moved west. The Millerites gathered on a hill—more than once—and waited vainly for the world to end. There was a certain work ethic involved that, even leaving God out of the whole business, sanctified religious idiocy through the sheer physical effort people were willing to put in on its behalf. You try to carve a thriving state out of the bleak Utah desert.

Once upon a time, then, peddling your idiocy for profit was an up-by-the-bootstraps activity, embarked upon only by those brave souls strong enough to withstand the possibility that, sooner or later, in a country that valued knowledge and progress and innovation as much as this one did, someone was going to discover a virus or invent a steamboat, thereby making a crank's entire public career vanish.

Television changed every part of this dynamic. Idiocy can come to the nation wholly and at once and, because idiocy is almost always good television, it can remain a viable product long after the available evidence and common sense has revealed it to be what it is. Television is the sturdiest medicine wagon, the biggest grange hall, the busiest street corner. And it is always open for business. Get your ideas on television—or, even better, onto its precocious great-grandchild, the Internet, where television's automatic validation of an idea can be instant and vast—and it will circulate forever, invulnerable and undying. The ideas will exist in the air. They will be "out there," and therefore they will be real, no matter what reality itself may be. Reality will bend to them, no matter how crazy they are.

The sheer inertial force created by the effort people are willing to put behind the promulgation of what they believe to be true leads inevitably to the Third Great Premise: Fact is that which enough people believe. Truth is determined by how fervently they believe it.

On September 11, 2001, Ed Root of Coopersburg, Pennsylvania, was returning to the United States with his wife after a trip to Europe. Midway over the Atlantic, it struck Root as odd that they hadn't yet been given their customs declaration cards. He asked the flight attendant about it, and she told him not to worry, that they'd been given the wrong cards for that flight. They were written in German, the flight attendant said. Root found this even more curious. Then Root felt the plane turn around. They were going back to Gatwick airport in London. There was a "security concern" about U.S. airspace, Root was told.

"A little bit further on," Root recalls, "we were told that there were attacks in New York and in Washington, but nothing about Shanksville. So there was a brief period of time when I thought it was some kind of nuclear attack, and I thought everything I knew was gone." Root had a son who worked in Manhattan and who, from his office window, had seen the second plane hit the World Trade Center. Root and his wife didn't get home for almost a week.

At about the same time that Ed Root's plane was turning back to Great Britain, United Airlines Flight 93, apparently headed for the U.S. Capitol, crashed in a field outside Shanksville, Pennsylvania. Passengers aboard the plane had apparently engaged the hijackers in a desperate struggle for control of the aircraft. One of the people killed in the crash was a flight attendant named Lorraine Bay. She was Ed Root's cousin. In her memory, Root got involved with the effort to build a memorial to the passengers and crew of Flight 93 in the field where the plane went down.

In conjunction with the National Park Service, several groups, including a task force made up of members of the families of the victims of Flight 93, winnowed through more than a thousand responses from architects bidding to build the memorial. They settled on five finalists, whose designs were on display for several months. Ed Root, who by then had become the president of the Board of Families of Flight 93, was a member of the jury that settled on a proposal by Paul Murdoch, a Los Angeles–based architect whose previous work had included the Bruggemeyer Library in Monterey Park, California, and Hawaii's Malama Learning Center.

Root was happy with Murdoch's plan, a gently curved structure that would comprise the names of the forty passengers and crew of Flight 93 engraved in white marble, a line of trees leading into the memorial itself, and the Tower of Voices, a structure containing forty wind chimes. However, Root saw that one local man had noted on a comment card that the memorial seemed to be in the shape of a crescent, and that the man thought this constituted a surreptitious attempt by the architect to memorialize not only the passengers and crew but the hijackers as well.

Root thought little of it. The events of September 11 had become fertile ground for conspiracy theories. There were people who believed that the towers had been rigged to fall, that a missile had hit the Pentagon, that Flight 93 itself had been shot down by a mysterious white jet. This was just another wacky idea, Root thought. Either by accident or because it was purposely brought to his ears, a blogger named Alec Rawls heard about it and ran with it.

Rawls, a son of the eminent liberal philosopher John Rawls, was so sure that the memorial's design was a subliminal tribute to radical Islam that he actually wrote a book, *Crescent of Be-*

trayal, that someone actually published. Rawls argued that the plot was clearly indicated by the memorial's crescent shape, that it was oriented to face Mecca, and that the Tower of Voices was positioned so that it would function as a sundial that would point Muslims to the east for their daily prayers. Rawls also claimed that the design would include forty-four glass blocks along the plane's flight path, one for each passenger and crew member as well as one for each of the four terrorists. There were no glass blocks in Murdoch's design at all.

To believe Rawls, one has to believe that the National Park Service, working in concert with an architect and the families of the forty murdered people, developed a memorial that honors the murderers. In an earlier time, this idea might have been mocked into silence long before it got within a mile of a publishing house. But Rawls made noise, and the noise drew the media, and the noise was enough.

Rawls's theories were picked up throughout the blogosphere—the conservative blogger Michelle Malkin was one of his earliest champions—and spread widely enough that a congressman from Colorado, Tom Tancredo, wrote a letter to the NPS championing them. Rawls also managed to convince at least one member of the jury in Pennsylvania that his claims were worthy of examination. "Alec Rawls should be listened to," Thomas Burnett, Sr., told the *Pittsburgh Tribune-Review* in 2007. "If it turns out he's all wet, OK. It's hard for me to believe that this was all by accident." Burnett's son died on Flight 93, and Burnett requested that his son's name not appear on the memorial.

The memorial commission spent hours consulting with religious experts who concluded that Rawls's theory was so much conspiratorial moonshine. It paid for and issued a white paper refuting his claims. Murdoch changed the name of his design from "Crescent of Embrace" to "Arc of Embrace." He even adapted the design so that it looked less like a crescent and more like a semicircle. Rawls's ideas kept circulating. Resentment and ill-feeling suffused the project and ran through the region like a low-grade fever. Rawls kept showing up at the meetings in Pennsylvania. Ed Root refused to shake his hand.

Debate over the building of memorials is not uncommon. Indeed, Kenneth Foote, of the University of Colorado, argues that wide-ranging debate is a necessary part of the process, particularly in situations regarding memorials of traumatic events such as the September 11 attacks. "Debate," Foote writes, "is an essential part of honoring victims and preserving memory. . . . Debate over what, why, when and where to build is best considered part of the grieving process." However, Foote further argues, such debate is productive only if it leads to a consensus over the eventual memorial. Persistent hecklers, no matter how well amplified, do not contribute to that process at all.

"Initially," Root explains, wearily, "it didn't have any legs. The only legs it had originally was in the blogosphere-type thing. Very few of the mainstream media picked up on it, originally. . . . Over time, there's been different benchmarks in the process [of building the memorial] and, every time one of these benchmarks happened, Rawls would come out of the woodwork. He'd raise his head, and the blogs and everything would start to come all over again.

"I mean, it's a free country and he's got a right to say what he wants to say, and I think there are people out there for whatever reason who are susceptible to conspiracies in this type of thing. And I honestly don't know that I'm qualified to judge those people as to why they believe what they believe, but I think those people have a tendency to make noise in greater numbers.

"It becomes more than a distraction. The park service, by

definition, they have to respond to citizen complaints, and my belief is that the park service has bent over backwards to accommodate this person—more so than any one person deserves who came up with a theory that's been debunked by every mainstream person that I can think of.

"On a personal level, that anybody would think that I would be in favor of anything that honors the people that attacked our country and murdered a member of my family, well, it's pretty much of a reach, I'd say."

Under the Third Great Premise, respect for the effort required to develop and promulgate nonsense somehow bleeds into a respect that validates the nonsense itself. Religion is the place where this problem becomes the most acute, where the noble tradition of the American crank is most clearly spoiled by respectability and by the validation bestowed by the modern media. Push religion into other spheres—like, say, politics and science—and the process intensifies. "Respect" for religion suddenly covers respect for any secular idea, no matter how crackpot, that can be draped in the Gospels.

Thanks to the First Amendment and the godless Constitution to which it is happily attached, mainstream churches flourished in the United States. The country even made peace with Catholics and Jews, after a while. Meanwhile, a thousand-odd flowers bloomed: American Baptists and Southern Baptists, splitting over slavery, and First Baptists, the grandchildren of the slaves themselves. Anabaptists and Amish. Quakers and Shakers. Splinters of all of them, forming and re-forming. A main characteristic of many of these religions was that they withdrew from the culture at large. They did not seek validation for their ideas. They didn't care whether they were respected. They preferred to be left alone. The desire to be left alone sent the Mormons to Utah and explains why the Amish still drive their buggies through the hills of southern Pennsylvania. Some sects, for example the Shakers, took it so seriously that they died out almost entirely. Even American fundamentalism, shaken by the consequences of having won the Scopes trial in 1922, withdrew from secular politics entirely before coming back with a vengeance in the 1970s. Neither the country nor the faith was better for their return.

Susan Jacoby cites a writer named Carson Holloway who, in a 2006 article in the conservative *National Review,* called the British evolutionary biologist and outspoken atheist Richard Dawkins a "poor public intellectual" essentially because Dawkins's scathing critiques of all religions failed to take into account the feelings of their adherents. "It is hard to imagine," Jacoby writes, "exactly how anyone might function as a public intellectual while taking care to avoid all issues that might trigger a spiritual, emotional, or intellectual crisis among his or her readers."

Having freed up religion to grow in its own sphere, the founders went back to being inveterate tinkerers and arguers. These were fundamentally curious men. (Before dispatching Lewis and Clark into the Louisiana Territory, Thomas Jefferson ordered the pair to categorize as many new plant and animal species as they found. Considering they were also mapping all the terrain from Missouri to Oregon, this must have been a considerable pain in the canoe.) Further, the founders assumed that they had established a polity that guaranteed their posterity would be curious as well. In 1815, appealing to Congress to fund a national university, James Madison called for the development of "a nursery of enlightened preceptors."

It's a long way from that speech to the morning of February 18, 2004, when sixty-two scientists, including a clutch of Nobel laureates, released a report accusing the Bush administration of manipulating science for political ends. It is an even longer way from Franklin's kite to George W. Bush, in an interview in 2005, suggesting that intelligent design be taught alongside the theory of evolution in the nation's science classrooms. "Both sides ought to be properly taught," the president said, "so people can understand what the debate is about."

The "debate," of course, is nothing of the sort, because two sides are required for a debate. The very notion of a debate on evolution's validity is a measure of how scientific discourse, and the way the country educates itself, have slipped, through lassitude and inattention, across the border into Idiot America. Intelligent design is religion disguised as science, and it defends itself as science by relying largely on the "respect" that we must give to all religious doctrine. Fact is merely what enough people believe, and truth lies only in how fervently they believe it.

If we have abdicated our birthright to scientific progress, we have done so by moving empirical debate into the realms of political, cultural, and religious argument, where we all feel more comfortable, because there the Gut truly holds sway. By the rules governing those realms, any scientific theory is a mere opinion, and everyone's entitled to those. Scientific fact is as mutable as a polling sample.

The rest of the world looks on in wide-eyed wonder. The America of Franklin and Edison, of Fulton and Ford, of the Manhattan Project and the Apollo program, the America of which Einstein so wanted to be a part that he moved here, seems to have enveloped itself in a fog behind which it's tying itself in knots over evolution, for pity's sake, and over the relative humanness of blastocysts and the victims of Parkinson's disease.

Kit Hodges is a scientist who studies the geology of the Himalayas, when he is not dodging the local Maoist guerrillas. Suffice it to say that Hodges's data do not correspond to the six-thousand-year-old earth of the Creation Museum, whereupon dinosaurs and naked people do gambol together.

"Even in the developing world, where I spend a lot of time

doing my work, if you tell them you're from MIT and you tell them that you do science, it's a big deal. If I go to India, and I tell them I'm from MIT, it's a big deal. If I go to Thailand, it's a big deal. In Iowa, they could give a rat's ass. And that's a weird thing, that we're moving that way as a nation.

"Scientists are always portrayed as being above the fray, and I guess to a certain extent that's our fault, because scientists don't do a good enough job communicating with people who are nonscientists that it's not a matter of brainiacs doing one thing and nonbrainiacs doing another. The reason, for example, that the creationists have been so effective is that they've put a premium on communications skills. It matters to them that they can talk to the guy in the bar, and it's important to them, and they are hugely effective at it."

Bush was not talking about science—not in any real sense, anyway. Intelligent design is a theological construct—ostensibly without God, but with a Designer that looks enough like him to be his smarter brother—and an attempt to gussy creationism up in a lab coat. Its fundamental tenets cannot be experimentally verified—or, more important, falsified. That it enjoys a certain cachet ought to be irrelevant. A higher percentage of Americans believes that a government conspiracy killed John F. Kennedy than believes in intelligent design, but there's no great push to "teach the debate" about what happened in Dallas in the nation's history classes. Bush wasn't talking about science. He was talking about the political utility of putting saddles on the dinosaurs and how many votes there were in breaking Ganesh's theological monopoly over the elephant paddock.

＊ ＊ ＊

THERE is still hope for any country that remains as easy to love as this one, in no small part because this is still the best country ever in which to be a public crank. The United States is an easy country to love because you can take it on faith that, at some point in every waking hour of the day, there is among your fellow citizens a vast exaltation of opinions that test the outer boundaries of the Crazoid.

Americans can awaken on a fine and sparkling spring morning happy in the knowledge that hundreds—nay, thousands—of their fellow citizens believe that space aliens landed in New Mexico, that Lyndon Johnson had John Kennedy killed from ambush, that the Knights Templar meet for coffee twice a month in the basement of the United Nations building, and that the Bavarian Illuminati control everything from the price of oil to the outcome of the fourth race at Louisiana Downs. Let us be clear. This is still the best country ever in which to peddle complete public lunacy.

"A silly reason from a wise man," Mr. Madison once wrote to his friend Richard Rush, "is never the true one."

We will have to sort ourselves out again here in America. We will have to put things back on the right shelves. We will have to remember where our cranks belong in our national life, so that they can resume their proper roles as lonely guardians of the frontiers of the national imagination, prodding and pushing, getting us to think about things in new ways, but also knowing that their place is of necessity a lonely and humble one. There is nothing wrong with a country that has people who put saddles on their dinosaurs. It's a wonderful show and we should watch them and applaud. We have no obligation to climb aboard and ride.

CHAPTER THREE

Beyond Atlantis

In 1789, President Madison told Congress: "Gentlemen will recollect that some of the most important discoveries, both in arts and sciences, have come forward under very unpromising and suspicious appearances." Once tested and found wanting, a new idea should be mined for whatever merits it might have, and the rest abandoned. All he hoped was that the people in that society could educate themselves sufficiently to distinguish between the good ideas and the transparently crazy ones, and engage with one another well enough to use the best parts of the latter to improve the former. They needed us to celebrate our cranks by keeping them in their proper place, from where they can help the rest of us live our lives. Madison is an imperfect guide, but he is as good a guide as any other.

* * *

THE success of *Atlantis* flabbergasted Donnelly, but it also deeply reinforced the feeling he'd always had, and which had been exacerbated by his political setbacks and the financial collapse of his Nininger project, that he was a genius for whom the world was not yet ready, and against whom the dunces had entered into confederacy. "We have fallen upon an age when the bedbugs are treated like gentlemen and the gentlemen like bedbugs," he wrote in his diary one day in 1882. "My book has helped me very much because my prestige before it was below zero. . . . A succession of political defeats and an empty pocket would destroy the prestige of Julius Caesar or Benjamin Disraeli."

The book's success also encouraged Donnelly to move even further out in his scientific speculations. That same year, he followed up *Atlantis* with *Ragnarok: Age of Fire and Gravel.* Finished in a mere two months, *Ragnarok* is even more densely argued than *Atlantis.* "Reader," Donnelly begins, "let us reason together," and he then leads said reader hopelessly into the weeds.

Ragnarok postulates that the earth's land masses were formed by what Donnelly called the Drift, and that the Drift was caused, not by the movement of glacial ice sheets, as conventional science would have it, but by an ancient collision with a passing comet. Mankind existed in a kind of golden age before the Drift and then, when the comet arrived, fell back into a darkness out of which it continues to struggle. (The comet turns out to have been the same one that did in Atlantis.) In support of his theory, Donnelly again called on ancient legends. He noted that prehistoric societies from the Aztecs to the Druids all included in their mythology the story of a cataclysmic event that involved the darkening of the sky.

Donnelly concluded that a collision with a comet was the source of all of these stories, and that the sky turned black due to the dust and gravel thrown into the atmosphere by the impact. ("Ragnarok" was the Scandinavian myth of "the twilight of the gods." Donnelly wrote that hundreds of scholars had mistranslated the word from the Icelandic, and that it actually meant "rain of dust.") He notes that both Milton and Shakespeare used comets as harbingers of doom, drawing on an ancient, visceral terror of them. "They are erratic, unusual, anarchical, monstrous," Donnelly writes, "something let loose, like a tiger in the heavens, athwart a peaceful and harmonious world." That this was a curious string of adjectives for anyone like Ignatius Donnelly to sling at an innocent comet apparently eluded the author.

Ragnarok is such almost perfect pseudoscience that Donnelly can be said to have helped invent the form. It so gleams with the author's erudition that you don't notice at first that none of it makes any sense. In addition, Donnelly was a master cherry picker. He seized on data that support one conclusion only to discard the same data when it seems to undermine another. For example, some people theorized that the continents were formed by the actions of the waves. Other people attributed their formation to the forces of the continental ice shelves. Donnelly dismisses the first theory using evidence developed in favor of the latter. He then dismisses the ice-shelf hypothesis by saying the whole notion is impossible. This leaves him with his comet theory, which he admits is complex, but then, Donnelly argues, so are all the others, so why shouldn't his be as true as they are, especially with the Druids on his side. "I believe I am right," Donnelly wrote in his diary, "and, if not right, plausible."

Ragnarok bombed. Notwithstanding the success they'd had with *Atlantis,* Harpers refused to publish it. Scribners passed, too. The reviews were scathing. The reception convinced Donnelly that his genius was as threatening to the scientific community as his political ideas had been in the Congress.

The sheer preposterousness of *Ragnarok* seems to have overwhelmed even Donnelly. At the end, it seemed to dawn on him that he'd written not a work of science but an allegorical narrative of the fall of man. "And from such a world," he writes in the book's final sentence, "God will fend off the comets with his great right arm and angels will exult over heaven." It's as though Donnelly went to bed one night as Darwin and awoke the next morning as Milton.

There are echoes of *Ragnarok* in the modern "scientific" case for intelligent design, and there's not a great distance between the codes that Donnelly found in Shakespeare's plays and the impulse that today sends people prowling the Louvre looking for the clues that a popular novel has told them are encoded in the paintings of Leonardo da Vinci. When Dan Brown got to the end of his treasure hunt, Ignatius Donnelly was there, waiting for him. It's wrong to believe that our abiding appetite for counterhistory simply makes us a nation of suckers who will fall for anything. Sometimes, that appetite makes us a harder people to fool. It's meant to operate parallel with the actual country and to influence it, but subtly, the way a planet, say, might influence the orbit of a comet. It's meant to subvert, but not to rule.

* * *

IN 2003, the state of Texas determined that it would build itself something called the Trans-Texas Corridor (TTC). This was a transportation megasystem involving highways, railbeds, and freight corridors that would stretch over four thousand miles and price out at nearly $200 billion. According to a report by Christopher Hayes in *The Nation,* the TTC would pave over almost a half a million acres of the state. The first leg would be a massive toll road, built and operated by a Spanish company.

From the start, there was a great deal of resistance to the plan. Local landowners hated it because of the amount of Texas that would disappear beneath it. The process was insufficiently transparent, which was hardly a surprise, given that Texas has operated largely as an oligarchy since they sank the first oil well there. There aren't many toll roads in Texas, and the ones that exist are not popular, especially not among the long-distance commuters of the state's several sprawling metroplexes. What ensued was a classic political knife fight, with local opposition arrayed against powerful special interests and at one point, as Hayes reported, Republican governor Rick Perry arrayed against his own state party's platform, which opposed the TTC. The battle engaged many of the issues of the day regarding the globalized economy, but it was not particularly remarkable.

And then the road took an even wilder turn, disappearing into the mists where Ignatius Donnelly once looked for cosmic gravel.

Through the magic of modern mass communication, most particularly through the Internet, the TTC has been transmogrified into an ominous behemoth called the NAFTA Superhighway, which will run up the gut of the North American continent, four hundred yards wide. It will be more than just a massive conveyor belt bringing cheap goods from cheap labor to every market from El Paso to Saskatoon. It also will represent the spine of the forthcoming North American Union, which will supplant forever the sovereignty of the United States of America in favor of some corporate megastate called Mexicanica or something.

If it actually existed, we all would have to agree, this would be some kind of road.

In fact, the NAFTA Superhighway is a phantasm, concocted out of very real fears of economic dislocation resulting from the global economy, and cobbled together from the TTC proposal and a business coalition called North America's SuperCorridor Coalition, or NASCO, which was formed to study improvements in the country's transportation infrastructure as it related to international trade. At one unfortunate point, the coalition put together a map of how it hoped trade one day would flow across America's existing highway system. That was all it took. The map became a blueprint for the highway that would devour America, starting with that toll road in Texas.

Suddenly, letters to the editor began popping up. Political candidates got questions about where they stood on a project that didn't exist. The legislatures of eighteen states passed resolutions condemning the NAFTA Superhighway, and a bill to that effect in the U.S. House of Representatives somehow garnered twenty-seven cosponsors. Jerome Corsi, one of the masterminds behind the fanciful attacks on Senator John Kerry's military service during the 2004 presidential campaign, found that it was possible to sail his Swift Boat up the NAFTA Superhighway, and has written extensively about the dire consequences of the nonexistent road. CNN's Lou Dobbs dedicated a portion of his nightly show on the topic, calling the road "as straightforward an attack on national sovereignty as there could be outside of a war." There is no evidence that anyone at CNN ever pointed out to Dobbs that covering the "issue" of the NAFTA Superhighway made approximately as much sense as dedicating a segment to the threat posed to American jobs by cheap labor from the moons of Neptune.

However, as Hayes pointed out in his definitive study of the phenomenon in *The Nation,* there were advantages in attacking a road that didn't exist, and these advantages crossed ideological and party lines. No less a labor lion than James Hoffa, Jr., excoriated the Bush administration for its plans to build the road. And in Kansas, a Democrat named Nancy Boyda defeated incumbent Republican congressman Jim Ryun at least in part because she staunchly opposed the highway that nobody is planning to build. The issue, Boyda told Hayes, "really touched a nerve." Which was all that mattered, it appears.

There were real-world consequences. As Hayes reported, a proposal to turn Kansas City into an all-purpose "smart port" was sucked into the furor when it was learned that a Mexican customs inspector might be stationed there to oversee goods headed to that country. And, more to the point, the conspiracy theory, lively and attractive on so many levels, subsumed the genuine questions regarding the consequences of North American free trade, including legitimate matters of national sovereignty. "The biggest problem with the conspiracy theorists," an international trade specialist told Hayes, "is that they're having an effect on the entire debate."

There is nothing fundamentally wrong in believing in the NAFTA Superhighway. Indeed, there's something essentially American in doing so. The NAFTA Superhighway includes almost every element of traditional American conspiracy theory. There are the secret moneymen, plotting to steal the country's economic future. There is the nativist fear of foreign hordes. There's the feeling that a cabal of experts is working against good old common sense. And there's the overall threat to American identity.

Unfortunately, thanks to the media of instant communication, the matter of the road that doesn't exist bled so swiftly into the mainstream that nobody was able to break it down into its component parts, keeping those that were helpful and jettisoning those that were not. It couldn't function as a starting point for healthy democratic skepticism about the issues of trade and national sovereignty in the globalized economy. It had to be accepted whole, and it was.

Though it exists only in the mind, the NAFTA Superhighway leads through Idiot America via the Third Great Premise. The road exists because enough people believe it does, and because they believe it fervently enough to act on their belief. They write letters. They quiz candidates. They cheer on Lou Dobbs. They act as though the NAFTA Superhighway is real, and things go out of place again. When that happens, even conspiracy theories lose their value, which always has been considerable in a country built on imagination.

CHAPTER FOUR

The Templars in Town

Between **1798** and 1799, Mr. Madison spent much of his time wondering about the wheels within wheels. Both Great Britain and France had been playing cleverly behind the scenes, seeking to influence the new American republic. Conspiracy theories abounded, not all of them fanciful. President John Adams, distrustful of the revolution in France, beset at home by noisy political opponents and impertinent newspaper editors, and seeing hidden hands in every fresh outburst against him, had signed the Alien and Sedition Acts. Thomas Jefferson referred to the period as the "reign of witches," and he and Madison worked surreptitiously in Virginia and Kentucky to pass resolutions arguing that the states had the right to nullify acts of the federal government they deemed unconstitutional.

(This theory of republican government would have unfortunate consequences when southern politicians revived it with a vengeance in 1861. Indeed, in his later years, Mr. Madison saw clearly where the doctrine was headed. Between 1828 and 1833, fearful of the civil war he knew was coming, he supported Presi-

dent Andrew Jackson in the nullification crisis against South
Carolina, and he spent years attempting to erase from history
his involvement in the Virginia and Kentucky Resolutions. Even
for him, there were wheels within wheels.)

Madison saw the inherent value of inflamed public opinion as a spur to political action, but he was also wary of the
demagogic threat to reason if public opinion was not kept in
its proper place. He'd helped create channels in which public
enthusiasms could be made to work for the common good, like
a wild river run through a mill. He did that because he believed
that the republican spirit was present in all human endeavors,
from politics to popular culture to the fashions of the day. He
saw that the dangers unreason presented to that spirit were as
prevalent in the shops as they were in the Congress.

In 1792, he had taken up the cause of some twenty thousand
British buckle manufacturers thrown out of work because the
fashion of the day had changed and shoes were now being made
with laces, or as slippers, with no fasteners at all. "Can any
despotism be more cruel than a situation in which the existence
of thousands depends on one will," Mr. Madison wrote, "and
that will on the most slight and fickle of motives, a mere whim
of the imagination?" Nothing, he believed, was as dangerous to
reason as fashion was.

* * *

IN 1887, Ignatius Donnelly attempted to demolish Shakespeare.
Say what you will about him, he didn't aim small.

Donnelly was a Baconian, one of those people who assert
that Francis Bacon was the real author of the plays attributed
to that semiliterate hayseed from Stratford. It was a snob's argument, and it ran counter to the populist principles that still
animated Donnelly's politics. But he adopted it with a ferocity

that surpassed even his enthusiasm for prehistoric comets. He published *The Great Cryptogram,* a massive doorstop in which he attempted to prove not only that Bacon had written the plays, but that he'd encoded clues to his authorship within them. Donnelly claimed to have discovered in the First Folio edition a "cipher" involving dots and dashes, and the spaces between words. He then applied this cipher to certain words that he called "constants," and, mirabile dictu, he discovered exactly the messages he expected to find and those messages proved exactly the case he'd wanted to make.

The book was as big a flop financially as *Ragnarok* had been, and as poorly reviewed, but it wasn't ignored. Donnelly was shredded by the critics this time. A certain Joseph Gilpin Pyle wrote *The Little Cryptogram,* in which Pyle used Donnelly's method to find in *Hamlet* the message "The Sage [of Nininger] is a daysie."

Undaunted, Donnelly went to England and defended his work at the Oxford Union. It became the great cause of the rest of his life. He wrote a couple of bizarre works of speculative fiction, but he came back to Bacon and Shakespeare in 1899, with *The Cipher in the Plays, and on the Tombstone.* By now, Donnelly was arguing that Bacon had written not only Shakespeare's plays but those of Christopher Marlowe, and the novels of Miguel de Cervantes.

Donnelly fell into obscurity, burying himself in the splintering rural Populist movements at the turn of the century. His wife died and, in 1898, he married again, to a woman forty years younger, which caused no little scandal among the society set in St. Paul. On New Year's Day, 1901, at the house of his new father-in-law, the Sage of Nininger died. He was sixty-nine years old. It was the first day of the twentieth century.

He was himself alone. He joined science to the popular culture in such a way that his work remains the ur-text for almost all treatments of Atlantis to this day. In 1969, the folksinger Donovan had a hit single called "Atlantis" in which he relates, almost by rote, the story of Atlantis as it's told in Donnelly's book, although Donnelly didn't go so far as to croon, as Donovan does over an endless coda, "my ante-di-looov-i-ahn bay-beeee!" The refinements Donnelly wrought in the art of pseudoscience were advances as profound as were Darwin's refinements of actual science. In many ways, Ignatius Donnelly helped create the modern counterhistory that America was born to have.

Donnelly was the perfect American crank. When *Ragnarok* failed, he didn't write three more books trying to get it to succeed. He moved along to debunking Shakespeare. He didn't care what the accepted wisdom was, nor did he insist that his work be included in it. He seemed to realize that the struggle to be respectable renders a crank worthless to the culture. The crank must always live where the wild imagination exists. The crank pushes and prods but does not insist that his ideas be judged by standards that do not apply. The crank lives in a place of undomesticated ideas, where the dinosaurs do not wear saddles.

It's always been there, in the oldest folk songs, in the whispered politics of the colonial tavern, in the angry speeches at the grange hall, in the constant rise of fringe religions, and in the persistence of theories about who's really in charge and what they're doing. There are gray spaces in the promises of freedom that made inevitable the rise of a country of the mind wilder and freer than the actual republic, what the critic Greil Marcus calls "the old, weird America." That country has its own music, its own language, its own politics, and its own popular culture. It has its own laws of reality. Ignatius Donnelly didn't discover Atlantis off the coast of the Azores. He discovered Atlantis in this country of the mind, in the willingness of Americans to believe.

What Donnelly did was to keep this counterhistory in its

proper place as a subtext, as grace notes, as the niggling little doubts that are as firmly in the democratic tradition as any campaign speech is. After all, sometimes there *are* wheels within wheels. Sometimes people are keeping real secrets, and sometimes those secrets involve actual events that are as cosmically lunatic as anything Ignatius Donnelly ever dreamed up. We should always listen to our inner Donnellys. But we shouldn't always take their advice.

* * *

A brief word, then, about politics.

It will appear to most readers that the politics in this book concerns the various activities of the modern American right. This would seem to make the work something of a piece with Richard Hofstadter's in the 1960s. However, we are emerging from a period of unprecedented monopoly by modern American conservatism—what some people call "movement conservatism"—over the institutions of government.

The long, slow march from the debacle of the Goldwater campaign in 1964 through the triumph of Ronald Reagan and, ultimately, the consolidation of power under George W. Bush from 2000 to 2008 depended in everything on how tightly the movement fastened itself to popular irrationality from economics to fringe religion. The movement swallowed whole the quack doctrine of supply-side economics, adopting it with almost comically ferocious zeal.

The movement lapped up Reagan's otherworldly tales, such as the famous one about how he had helped liberate Nazi death camps, even though he'd spent most of World War II defending the bar at the Brown Derby. It was thereby prepared to buy whole hog the notion of George W. Bush, the brush-clearing cowboy who was afraid of horses. It attached itself to the wildest of religious extremes, sometimes cynically and sometimes not. On one memorable occasion in 2005, just as the controversy over intelligent design was heating up generally in the media, *The New Republic* polled some of the country's most prominent conservative intellectuals concerning the theory of evolution. The paleoconservative pundit Pat Buchanan stated, flatly, that he didn't believe in Darwinian evolution, but a number of others confessed a thoroughgoing fondness for it. Jonah Goldberg, for one, despite his heavily footnoted distrust for priestly experts who use science to discredit traditional notions of faith, was notably lucid on the subject. But once intelligent design—with its "scientific" implication of a deity—was thrown into the discussion, an exhibition of tap dancing erupted the likes of which hadn't been seen since Gene Kelly in *On the Town*.

Norman Podhoretz, the godfather of neoconservatism, told the reporter that the question of whether he personally believed in evolution was "impossible to answer with a simple yes or no." And Tucker Carlson, the MSNBC host, seemed to be chasing his opinion all around Olduvai Gorge. Asked whether God had created man in his present form, Carlson replied, "I don't know if he created man in his present form. . . . I don't discount it at all. I don't know the answer. I would put it this way: The one thing I feel confident saying I'm certain of is that God created everything there is." In June 2007, a Gallup poll found that 68 percent of the Republicans surveyed said that they did not believe in evolution at all. And this was the ascendant political power of the time.

Movement conservatism was so successful that it drove its own media, particularly talk radio, and conservative media fed back the enthusiasm into the movement, energizing it further. The movement's gift for confrontation was ideally suited to media in which controversy drove ratings, which then drove the controversy, and so forth. The more traditional media joined in, attracted, as they always are, by power and success. The more the movement succeeded politically, the tighter it was bound to the extremes that helped power it. The September 11 attacks functioned as what the people on the arson squad would call an accelerant. Even popular culture went along for the ride. The vague, leftish conspiracies of *The X-Files* gave way to the torture porn of 24.

It was a loop, growing stronger and stronger, until a White House aide (rumored to be Karl Rove himself) opened up to the journalist Ron Suskind in 2004 and gave him the money quote for the whole era. Suskind, and those like him, the aide said, "represent the reality-based community," which is to say, the kind of people who believe "that solutions emerge from judicious study of discernable reality. . . . That's not the way the world works anymore." If this book seems to concentrate on the doings of the modern American right, that's because it was the modern American right that consciously adopted irrationality as a tactic, and succeeded very well.

Which brings us, for the moment, to the two U.S. senators from the great state of Oklahoma, a pair of the most entertaining primates ever to sit in the world's greatest deliberative body. Once, they might have been beloved local cranks, amusing their neighbors, scandalizing their friends, and enlivening the meetings of the local town council with their explanations of how everything went to hell once the Illuminati took us off the gold standard. Now, though, they are members of the U.S. Senate. And, even given the proud history of that great deliberative body, which includes everything from the fulminations of Theodore Bilbo to Everett Dirksen's campaign to make the marigold the national flower, the Oklahoma delegation is a measure of how far we have come.

Usually, states will elect one boring senator and one entertaining one. For example, until 2006, Pennsylvania was represented by Arlen Specter and Rick Santorum. The former was aging and bland, but the latter was the funniest thing about Christianity since the Singing Nun fell off the charts in 1964. Massachusetts has as its senators Edward Kennedy and John Kerry, which is like being represented simultaneously by Falstaff and Ned Flanders. However, Oklahoma has demonstrated almost unprecedented generosity in sharing with the nation its more eccentric political fauna.

The senior senator is James Inhofe, who once chaired the Senate's Committee on Environment and Public Works. In that capacity, he once informed the nation that global warming "might be the second-largest hoax ever played on the American people, after the separation of church and state."

With all due respect to Senator Inhofe, he doesn't know his great American hoaxes. Global warming isn't much of one, what with all that pesky scientific data, all those pesky collapsing ice shelves, all those pesky tropical diseases, and all that other troublesome reality. And Inhofe has the same problem with that church-and-state business. The founders wrote an awful lot about it and it's hard to believe that they all died without writing down the punch line. These are great American hoaxes? What about the spiders in the beehive hairdo, and the prom-night hitchhiker, the thumb in the bucket of fried chicken, the maniac on the other phone in the house? What about the hook on the handle of the car door? Whatever happened to the classics?

This is the country where the Cardiff Giant, the Ponzi scheme, and the Monkees were concocted. Aimee Semple McPherson worked this room, and so did P. T. Barnum. Inhofe's hoaxes don't deserve to stand in the proud tradition of American bunkum—not least because they're, well, true. Unfortunately for

Inhofe, his sad misreading of the history of American sucker-dom was surpassed almost immediately by his junior colleague Tom Coburn, a doctor elected in 2006.

Coburn showed promise during the campaign, when he happened to mention that he'd been talking to a campaign worker from the tiny town of Coalgate in central Oklahoma. This person, Coburn said, told him that, down around Coalgate, lesbianism was "so rampant in some of the schools . . . that they'll only let one girl go to the bathroom."

Presumably, Coburn meant one girl *at a time*. Otherwise, some young lady had been accorded a rather dubious honor on behalf of her classmates. She'd probably have preferred to be elected prom queen. Speaking of which, one can only imagine what dark conspiracies must have occurred to young Tom Coburn at his prom, when all five girls at his table excused themselves at once.

On the other hand, Coburn likely could teach Inhofe a little something about great American hoaxes. According to the most recent figures, there are only 234 students at Coalgate High School, and fewer than half of them are girls. It's doubtful that much of anything can be said to be "rampant" in that small a sample, except, perhaps, gossip about something being "rampant." (Yeah, right. Whatever. As if.) Coburn probably should check to see if there's a cannibal murderer listening on his upstairs phone.

Encouraged by the infrastructure of movement conservatism, and insulated by its success from any carping that might arise from outside a mainstream political establishment that respects success and power more than it does logic, these two paid no political price for saying things in their official capacity that would have cleared out their end of the bar in any respectable saloon. It wasn't always this way. Once, aggressively promulgating crazy ideas could cost you dearly. Global warming a hoax? Rampant lesbianism on the Oklahoma prairie? You might as well believe in Atlantis or something.

* * *

IT is October 13, 2007. Exactly seven hundred years ago, King Philip IV of France undertook to round up all the members of the crusading order of the Poor Fellow-Soldiers of Christ and of the Temple of Solomon, commonly known as the Knights Templar. The Templars had amassed great wealth; supposedly, they found their seed money while excavating the site of Solomon's Temple in Jerusalem. They also accrued considerable influence as a protected prefecture of the Vatican, so much so that they scared Pope Clement V as well, and he signed off on the dragnet personally. (This is a dreadfully ungrateful way to treat people who invented, among other things, the traveler's check.) Philip picked up many of the French Templars, including most of the leadership. He tortured them horribly and killed them even more horribly. But most of the order got away—probably on a fleet of ships that the Templars kept, as the Wizard of Oz says about his balloon, "against the advent of a quick getaway"— and reportedly the majority wound up in Scotland where, legend has it, they came riding out of the mists at Bannockburn to help Robert the Bruce kick the English king back across the border where he belonged. And that was pretty much it for the Templars—unless, of course, they've been controlling the world ever since.

Perhaps they're doing so from deep in a place like this one, on Walnut Street, in Newtonville, Massachusetts, a tall, handsome brick building across the street from a massive old Congregational church that most recently has done service as an office complex and a Chinese restaurant. The brick building has one round corner, a series of spires on its roof, and carefully wrought carvings on its façade. At street level, it houses a book-store and a defunct Christian Science reading room. The people who may be controlling the world are upstairs, on the second and third floors. They're having an open house today.

The Dalhousie Lodge of the Freemasons was founded in Newton in 1861, in the upper story of a Methodist church. An earlier anti-Masonic fever in Massachusetts had largely sub-sided, and Masonry was beginning to revive again. Not only the Dalhousie Lodge, but various Masonic subgroups, such as the Royal Arch Masons and the Gethsemane Commandery of Knights Templar, were flourishing in town, and they all needed a larger place for their meetings. In 1895, they bought the prop-erty on Walnut Street, laying the cornerstone of their temple in September 1896 in a ceremony that shared the front pages of all three Newton newspapers with news of local men involved in that fall's heated presidential campaign. "The craze for political secret societies, advertising, and slangy buttons is particularly widespread now," one of the papers noted. The combined mem-bership of the three lodges helped put up the building. It was dedicated on December 6, 1907. The Masons expected to rent the ground and second floors out to local businesses and to use the third and fourth floors for their functions.

The upper floors of the old building are awash in dusty au-tumn sunlight, the corridors sweet with the smell of old wood and varnish. In the past, the building has hosted reunion meet-ings of the Grand Army of the Republic; one wall displays the autographs of Generals Grant, Sherman, and McClellan. The club room features the mounted heads of big game killed by Masons past. On one wall is an impressive old print of the Temple of Solomon in Jerusalem, where the Templars supposedly found the treasure—or the Holy Grail, or some valuable, if theologically inconvenient, evidence regarding the early Christian church—that supplied the basis for their wealth and power and influence. The connection between the Templars and the Masons seems to have been made first by those Templars who escaped to Scotland, most notably in the construction of the famously symbol-laden Rosslyn Chapel.

In truth, nobody knows exactly what the Templars found in Jerusalem, if they found anything at all. But the order's secretive nature and the elaborate plot under which they suddenly were hunted down have made them central to almost every conspiracy theory that arose in Europe after their fall from grace. Meanwhile, the Masons prospered in Europe, particularly through their role in building the great cathedrals. They were particularly careful to keep the secrets of their trade away from ambitious competitors. They became adept at codes and various other forms of sub-rosa communication. Many of their vaunted symbols were little more than rudimentary copyright emblems carved into the stone by individual craftsmen—what Philip Ball calls "medieval bar-codes."

"There seems to be no indication of any 'esoteric' content in Freemasonry until the lodges began to admit 'non-operative' members in the seventeenth century," writes Ball in *Universe of Stone,* his history of the building of the great cathedral at Chartres. "Gradually, these non-operatives, who did not work in stone but instead had antiquarian interests in the masonic tradition, came to dominate the organization, transforming it from a trade guild into the 'speculative' fraternity that still exists today." The Masons' role in American history centers largely on the actions—alleged and real—of these "non-operatives." George Washington was famously a Mason, but nobody would ever have hired him to build a wall.

The Masons, then, right here on Walnut Street, renting space to the Christian Scientists and having their open house on a fine fall day in an American suburb, have long been assumed by the fertile American conspiratorial mind to be either the heirs to the Templars, or their ideological stepchildren. And, the unfortunate historical resonance of the day aside, it's a good time to be a Mason. Or a Templar.

The Masons are having an open house because the national organization is in the middle of a thoroughly modern membership drive. There are television commercials featuring an actor portraying Benjamin Franklin, a Mason himself, talking about the benefits of membership. Their official recruitment pitch has been helped immeasurably by the explosion of interest in the Templars prompted by Dan Brown's speculative literary supernova, *The Da Vinci Code*, which postulates that the Templars discovered the bones of Mary Magdalene, who was actually the wife of Jesus Christ. In Brown's book, Mary flees Jerusalem after the crucifixion and takes up residence in France, where she gives birth to little Sarah Magdalene-Christ, their daughter.

For the benefit of the eleven human beings who have neither read the book nor seen the movie: The Templars dedicate themselves to guarding Mary Magdalene's bones, blackmailing the Vatican with what they know until Clement V gets fed up and sets Philip on them. Some of them escape with the bones, set up an absurdly complex system of perpetual guardianship that inevitably breaks down, and protect their secret down through the years against a network of shadowy clerical operatives, including a self-flagellating albino monk. The book ends with the discovery that the gamine French detective who has been helping the hero is actually the long-lost Magdalene-Christ heir. To his credit, Brown wrote an intriguing thriller. It's hardly his fault that people read it and integrated it into their personal views of the hidden world. The Masons, for example, play a tangential role in the book, but by all accounts, the novel's success spurred a great burst of interest in Masonry worldwide.

In fact, *The Da Vinci Code* touched off a Templar frenzy in the popular culture. The hit movie *National Treasure* has Nicolas Cage running down the Templars' treasure—which, in this case, actually is a treasure, and not a desiccated figure from the Gospels—by following a map that the various Masons who signed the Declaration of Independence secretly drew on the back of the original parchment. This map can only be read by someone wearing complex multifocal glasses invented by that future Masonic television pitchman Ben Franklin. (The movie posits that the treasure was whisked off to the New World on that famous Templar fleet.) The History Channel ran so many programs about the Masons, the Templars, and the Holy Grail that the subject actually threatened the long-standing primacy of World War II on that outlet.

Soon, everybody had climbed aboard. On the very day when the Masons were holding open houses all over the country, and on the seven-hundredth anniversary of the Templars' last roundup, the Vatican announced that it would release copies of the minutes of the Templars' trials.

The document—"Processus Contra Templarios"—had been unearthed in 2001 from deep in the Vatican archives. Now, the Vatican planned to publish a handsome, limited-edition, leather-bound collector's edition of the documents, including expert commentary and reproductions of the seals used by the various inquisitors. And at only $8,333 a copy, too. The Vatican always was a little more open about its treasure-hunting than the Templars were.

"We were talking in the other room about the Vatican releasing this today," says Larry Bethune, the Grand Master of the

Dalhousie Lodge. "Is it a coincidence that they release these documents on the seven-hundredth anniversary? This is how conspiracy, or conspiracy theories, get started."

Bethune is the vice president for student affairs and dean of students of the Berklee College of Music in Boston, and he got into Masonry through the De Molay Society, which he joined as a teenager in New Jersey. He cheerfully admits that his organization has benefited from the renewed interest in the various conspiracy theories involving the Masons. It's not that dissimilar to the *Da Vinci Code* tours offered in Europe, which take devotees of the book around to the spots where the big moments in the novel take place, so that they can pester elderly museum guards with questions about exactly what secrets the elderly museum guards are being paid to conceal.

"It's made a big difference," Bethune explains. "We have to be careful now because there are a lot of people who come to us now because they're taken by the mystery of it, and that's not the point of the organization. The people who come thinking that, it's very hard to argue with them because a lot of it is just hypothesis, even within the organization.

"They'll come in here thinking it's Indiana Jones and all that Knights Templar stuff and they'll be sort of disappointed."

Bethune himself is interested in the connection between the flight of the Templars and the rise of Masonry. In his ancestral home on the islands west of Scotland, he's seen Templar graves, the monuments flat on the ground and depicting the knight interred there. "I happen to believe it's true," he says, "but it's still just hypothesis. When Philip rounded them up, he hardly got any of them. A whole bunch of them were gone. They did disappear and the story is that they went to Scotland. And that part of Scotland where my family comes from had a lot of Masonic lodges. A connection between the Templars and the Masonic lodges, so far as I know, has never been proved.

"There are probably four or five million Masons, so there's probably some group that's doing something. I always say to potential candidates that they should come to one of our annual dinners first. Watch us plan that dinner and see if you think we're capable of pulling off some major conspiracy. We can barely get that dinner done."

Of course, that's what they would say.

Hmmmmm.

* * *

EVEN though the action in his novel takes place in Europe—the bones of the late Ms. Magdalene-Christ eventually are discovered to be resting beneath the Louvre—Dan Brown could not have tossed his novel more directly into the American wheelhouse. For good or ill, there's nothing more fundamentally American than conspiracies or, more precisely, conspiracy theories. There is always secret knowledge, somewhere, being kept from us somehow, by someone. It's just not the secret knowledge everybody presumes is there.

For example, Brown published his novel concerning a secret cabal within the Roman Catholic church in 2003. At the time, the church in the United States was reeling from almost daily revelations about how its institutional structure had been used for decades as, at best, a conspiracy to obstruct justice. The newspapers that published the exposés ran into storms of criticism and disbelief. It seemed that people were more willing to suspend disbelief in the case of fictional murderous monks than they were concerning the elaborate lengths to which the church had actually gone to cover up its complicity in the sexual abuse of children.

Secret knowledge—at least, temporarily secret knowledge—was essential to the founding of the nation. In 1787, when the delegates to the Federal Convention in Philadelphia agreed to debate and write the new Constitution in complete secrecy, they had a number of reasons to do so—most notably, the desire of some to maintain their political viability if the whole enterprise crashed and burned later.

Not everyone approved. (Lobbing his objections from Paris, Thomas Jefferson made it clear that he hated the idea of a secret convention.) When the Constitution finally did emerge, it was greeted by some people as though it were a collection of magic spells, written in mystic runes and decipherable only to a handful of initiates. According to political polemicist Mercy Otis Warren of Massachusetts, the convention was nothing less than a cluster of "dark, secret, and profound intrigues" aimed at creating, at best, an American oligarchy. In reply, the people defending the convention, and the Constitution that it produced, argued that they were afflicted on all sides by dark cabals. Some time passed before the Constitution was debated primarily on its merits. At first, everyone chose up sides to defend themselves and their position against the black designs of the conspirators arrayed against them.

Not much has changed. In November 2007, a Scripps Howard poll revealed that nearly 65 percent of Americans surveyed believed that the federal government ignored specific warnings prior to the September 11 attacks, and that fully a third believed in a whole host of other conspiracies, including a plot to assassinate John F. Kennedy and a government effort to conceal the truth about UFOs.

Conspiracy theories are basic to most American popular culture as well. The rise of black American music—blues, jazz, rock and roll, hip-hop—to a position of dominance within the culture is richly attended in history by a dynamic of Us versus Them. Aficionados enjoyed an undeniable frisson of underground excitement that was sharpened and hardened by a demonstrable organized reaction from the predominant culture of the times. The endless, nearly incomprehensible "culture wars" are a manifestation of one side's oppositional identity to the cabal meeting across the faculty lounge. There is a misapprehension about conspiracy theories that ought not to make us lose sight of their true value. In fact, it can be argued that a conspiracy theory—airy and vague and not entirely moored to empirical fact—can be more important than is the revelation of an actual conspiracy itself.

Conspiracy theories do engage the imagination. In their own way, they are fragments of lost American innocence in that they presume that the "government" is essentially good, but populated at some deep level by evil people. At the heart of some of them, at least, is a glimmering of the notion of self-government. They tumble into Idiot America when they are locked solely into the Three Great Premises, when they're used merely to move units, and when they're limited to those people who believe them fervently enough to say them loudly on television. To look at how that can work, you have to spend some time in Dealey Plaza.

❋ ❋ ❋

I do not shrink from this responsibility. I welcome it.
—JOHN F. KENNEDY, *Washington, D.C., January 20, 1961*

My God, they are going to kill us all.
—JOHN CONNALLY, *Dallas, Texas, November 22, 1963*

There is an X in the middle of Elm Street, just down the little hill that runs away from the Book Depository and toward the grassy hill with the fence behind it. The sun in Dealey Plaza is merciless on a summer's day. People squint and shade their eyes. They toss a couple of bucks to the freelance experts who work the plaza every day, with their diagrams and their newsletters. They wander up the knoll, through the blessed shade, and behind the fence—not the original fence, long ago lost to souvenir hunters, but a newer one, rebuilt there because the fence is important to people who wander into the plaza and never find their way out. Even this fence is weatherbeaten now. On one board, almost in a line with the X in the roadway, there once was a line of graffiti.

"Thanks for Chicago and West Virginia," it said. "Sincerely, Sam Giancana."

In his study of the Kennedy presidency, the political writer Richard Reeves quotes Kennedy describing himself as the center of a spoked wheel and, in doing so, inadvertently posing an insoluble riddle to what would become, after his murder, a nation of his biographers. By the time he touched down in Dallas, Kennedy had grown comfortable living in the plural.

"It was instinctive," Kennedy said. "I had different identities, and this was a useful way of expressing each without compromising the other." Consider what we have come to know about him in the decades since he was killed: that he was an icon of vigor—vigah!—who was deathly ill and gobbling steroids and shooting speed just to function daily; that he was the golden child of a golden family with a sex life that can properly be called baroque; that he was a public intellectual whose books were ghostwritten; that he bought West Virginia in 1960, probably with the mob's money, in a deal brokered by his good friend Frank Sinatra.

After all, every frontier is a New Frontier, landscape and dreamscape at once, a horizon but also an architecture of belief.

But frontiers are also wild and uncivilized places where people struggle to survive, where people die over private grudges, and where people, a lot of them, carry guns. John Kennedy needed every identity he'd crafted for himself to survive on the New Frontier he proclaimed. In 1960, he got up in Los Angeles and promised to make all things new. In his murder, three years later, he managed to do it for the ages.

Consider Dallas, the nexus of distrust that became the template for modern political paranoia, and consider that, while Kennedy was president, the executive branch was a writhing ball of snakes. A memo has survived in which the Joint Chiefs of Staff seriously suggest blowing up John Glenn on the launchpad in order to concoct a casus belli for invading Cuba again. Consider that this lunacy made it all the way up the chain of command to the secretary of defense before someone finally turned it off. Consider Dallas when you consider how quickly theories sprang up about who might have known what before the airplanes were flown into the buildings in Washington and New York.

It turns out there were actual conspiracies going on throughout the brief history of the Kennedy administration. It was a fertile time for conspiracy, since so many things seemed to be changing all at once. The issue of civil rights had moved swiftly past the hope of easy compromise; there were murderous plots planned under the Spanish moss in Mississippi, and the people involved in them believed they were arming themselves against a conspiracy from the North that dated back to Lincoln. Elsewhere, there were off-the-books efforts to kill Fidel Castro in Cuba, and covert wranglings in (among other places) Iraq, where a young officer named Saddam Hussein backed the right side in a CIA-sponsored coup. A rat's nest was growing in Southeast Asia that already seemed beyond untangling.

The Joint Chiefs were barely under civilian control; Fletcher Knebel did not pluck the plot for *Seven Days in May* out of the air. Knebel was a veteran Washington journalist who knew what he heard around town. The intelligence services vanished into the dark blue evening distance of the frontier in which John Kennedy had declared could be found the nation's best new hope. These were actual conspiracies, many of which have come to light in the years since the assassination, just as the conspiracy theories about the president's murder have hit high tide, but they have had less historical resonance in that context than the notion, completely unsubstantiated by anything resembling a fact, that Kennedy was shot from a storm drain beneath the street in the plaza.

Back in 1991, shrewd old Daniel Patrick Moynihan saw clearly what would happen. In an essay prompted by the release of Oliver Stone's film *JFK*, Moynihan argued that the Warren Commission's capital mistake from the start was the failure to recognize that Americans were not predisposed to believe it.

"I was convinced that the American people would sooner or later come to believe that there had been [a conspiracy]," Moynihan wrote, "unless we investigated the event with exactly that presumption in mind."

By the time Moynihan published his essay, a solid 70 percent of the American people did not believe the conclusion of the Warren Commission that, acting alone and from ambush, Lee Harvey Oswald killed John F. Kennedy. This percentage has not changed substantially since the day in 1964 when the commission first published its findings, even though both the journalist Gerald Posner and the former prosecutor Vincent Bugliosi have published lengthy and detailed defenses of the Warren Commission's conclusions. To this day, the official U.S. government report into the public murder in broad daylight of the president of the United States has rather less credibility with the American people than does the *Epic of Gilgamesh.*

No matter what the polls indicate, the reality is that we have kept the Kennedy assassination as a conspiracy theory, rather than accepting it as an actual conspiracy. Once we believe in the latter, it becomes a deadening weight on the conscience. It loses its charm. Accepting it as a reality means we probably are obligated to do something about it, and that we have chosen, en masse, not to.

The revelation of an actual conspiracy—the Iran-Contra matter, say—has come to have a rather deadening effect on American politics and culture. It runs through stages. There is disbelief. Then the whole thing dies in banality. It's too hard to understand, and it's Just One More Damn Thing that proves not that something called "government" is controlled by a secret conspiracy, but that "government" itself is the conspiracy. This is commonplace and boring, and it leads to distrust and to apathy, and not, as it is supposed to do, to public outrage and reform. There is no "Us." There is only a "Them." There's no game if there's only the other team playing.

In fact, Iran-Contra was a remarkable piece of extraconstitutional theater, far beyond anything the Watergate burglars could've dreamed up. Arming terrorist states? Using the money to fund a vicious war of dubious legality elsewhere in the world? Government officials flying off to Teheran with a Bible and a cake in the shape of a key? A president whose main defenses against the charge of complicity were neglect and incipient Alzheimer's disease? Who could make this up? Iran-Contra was a great criminal saga, even up to the fact that it was first revealed not by the lions of the elite American press, but by a tiny newspaper in Beirut.

Iran-Contra should have immunized the American public

forever against wishful fact-free adventurism in the Middle East. It would have, too, if the country had been able to bring to this actual conspiracy the fervor that it readily brings to conspiracy theories. As has become sadly plain over the past seven years, the Iran-Contra affair had no immunizing effect. (Remarkably, several of its architects even returned from think-tank limbo in 2001, eager to reassert their fantastical visions.) People pronounced themselves baffled by the plot, and the production closed out of town. It is little more than a footnote in history. It sells no books. It moves no units. Mark Hertsgaard, in his study of how the press functioned during the Reagan administration, describes in detail how interest dried up. "Editors were convinced that, after months of heavy play, readers and viewers were tired of Iran-Contra."

Consider Dallas when you consider Watergate and Iran-Contra, in which we learned that the Nixon and Reagan White Houses were not the Kennedy White House primarily because we found out about the covert wiretapping and the crackpot foreign policy moves. Consider Dallas when you consider the Monica Lewinsky affair, through which we learned that the Clinton White House was not the Kennedy White House primarily because we found out about the sex. Consider Dallas when you consider poor Vincent Foster, dead by his own hand, and the speculation hovering over his body almost before the cops were. Consider Dallas when you consider a White House set up almost as a living diorama of the Kennedy White House, one beset by real political enemies acting in secret concert, a White House in which the nickname of presidential aide Sidney Blumenthal closed the circle for good: "Grassy Knoll."

A country that so readily rejects the official story about how its president was killed should not have taken almost three years to fully believe the truth about Watergate. It shouldn't have taken the White House tapes—on the most damning of which, it should be recalled, President Richard Nixon tells his aide H. R. Haldeman to have the CIA turn off an FBI investigation into the break-in with a cover story about how this will open up "that whole Bay of Pigs thing"—to seal the deal. A country that readily puts shooters almost everywhere in Dealey Plaza should not have found Iran-Contra to be so "complicated" that the criminals got away simply because the country got too bored to pursue them.

Logic dictates that a people who believe that their president was gunned down in broad daylight as the result of a conspiracy made up in part of dark forces within their own government would become aggressively skeptical, rather than passively cynical. They would be more difficult to govern, in the sense that they would become harder to fool. For example, you wouldn't think of trying to scare them by floating stories that a tinpot tyrant in the Middle East could launch a fleet of drone aircraft, and that these puppet airplanes, having eluded a multibillion-dollar air-defense system, would then blithely cruise up and down the East Coast, spraying anthrax as they go. We entertain ourselves with skepticism or, at worst, cynicism. But we govern ourselves with apathy or, at worst, credulity.

The JFK conspiracy sells, so it remains nothing more than mass entertainment. Dealey Plaza functions as a performance venue. Considering Dallas means accepting that, for more than forty years, we have believed the unthinkable and gone right on with our lives. Because John Kennedy led plural lives, Dealey Plaza freezes us in the plural. If you make that bafflingly tight turn from Houston onto down-sloping Elm, a turn that still doesn't make any sense if you're trying to protect a president riding in an open car, hair in the breeze, if you enter in the first-person plural—"we lost our innocence"—then you must leave in the third:

They killed him.

But it ends there, in Dealey Plaza, where there is an X on the roadway and where German tourists cool themselves in the shade of the trees atop the grassy knoll. It wasn't always so. The country once managed to make actual conspiracies, and the theories that attend them, work in concert in such a way that our appetite for the grotesque was satisfied, our appetite for hidden knowledge sated, and, most important of all, our appetite for freedom was sharpened. And, yes, the Masons were behind it all. Or so some people believed.

* * *

ON an October day in 1827, people in the small town of Lewiston in western New York state, hard by Lake Ontario, fished a body out of Oak Orchard Creek. The body was badly decomposed. Townsfolk, however, were sure they knew who it was. It was a man who had been snatched from the jail in Canandaigua a year earlier—kidnapped and murdered, the townsfolk believed, because of what he knew. This unpleasant-looking lump of recent fish food, they said, was William Morgan, and it was the Masons who killed him.

Morgan had come to New York from Virginia, a tramp bricklayer and stonemason, and a full-time pain in the ass. He joined one Masonic lodge, moved, and was denied admission to another, upscale lodge, probably because its membership looked upon Morgan as something of a bum. In retaliation, Morgan wrote and distributed a pamphlet describing in lurid detail Masonic rituals and ancient legends. The local Masons fought back, repeatedly having Morgan tossed into various local hoosegows as a habitual debtor and, eventually, even trying to burn down the shop of the fellow who'd printed up the pamphlet. The second time Morgan was incarcerated, two mysterious men showed up at the jail, paid his debt, and took him away. Nobody ever saw him again, unless it actually was William Morgan who was pulled out of the creek.

(Morgan's wife and his dentist both said the body was his. It was disinterred several times and, amid charges that someone had tampered with the corpse to make it look like Morgan, the local coroner just gave up entirely, declining to identify the corpse. The historian Sean Wilentz writes that a positive identification eventually became unnecessary: a local anti-Masonic leader admitted that the corpse was "a good enough Morgan" for the purposes of local political agitation.)

Western New York exploded with the controversy. Local Masons were hauled before grand juries. The jailer in Canandaigua, who was a Mason and who had released Morgan to his two abductors, was indicted. When some Masons were brought to trial, other Masons refused to testify against them. Charges often were swiftly dismissed—because, people said, of Masonic influences on the judges and the juries.

The Masons had been central to early American conspiracy theories, most of which connected them not to the Templars but to the Bavarian Illuminati, an obscure group founded in 1776 by a wandering academic named Adam Weishaupt and suppressed by the elector of Saxony eight years later. As Sean Wilentz points out, anti-Masonry had its beginnings in America not as a populist revolt against a mysterious, monied elite, but as the reaction of high-toned Protestant preachers in Federalist New England, who saw the hidden hand of Weishaupt's group behind everything they considered politically inconvenient.

The Illuminati were a constant, stubborn presence in the emerging underground American counternarrative. By 1789, in addition to being blamed for the Jacobin excesses in France, and accused of attempting to import those excesses, the group also had been linked to the hidden secrets of the Templars and, therefore, to the Masons. At one point, they were charged by the Catholic Church with engineering a Masonic plot to overthrow the papacy while, simultaneously being accused elsewhere of being central to a conspiracy between the Masons and the Jesuits to take over the world. The Illuminati were enormously useful.

(Theories about the Illuminati have never really gone away. They were blamed for the Russian Revolution. In the 1950s, the John Birch Society saw the hand of the group behind a movement toward one-world government based in the United Nations. A writer named Jim Marrs, whose book *Crossfire* was one of the primary texts Oliver Stone used to concoct the plot of *JFK,* puts the Illuminati not only in those places, but in Dealey Plaza as well, and also in prehistory. Marrs makes them the keepers of the knowledge that came to earth with our alien ancestors, a group of space wanderers called the Annunaki. And, before hitting it big with *The Da Vinci Code,* Dan Brown used the Illuminati as the villains in *Angels and Demons,* the novel in which he introduced the Harvard symbologist Robert Langdon. The plot is kicked off when a priest is found murdered in a church with "Illuminati" carved backward into his chest.)

Even in 1827, then, there was a history on which the anti-Masonic movement in New York State could build. However, the fervor was fueled by rising political and social tension between the local farmers and rural landowners, and the expanding commercial class that had grown up in the area since the opening of the Erie Canal.

Class tensions were exacerbated when justice seemed thwarted in every venue that attempted to parcel out guilt in the murder of the person believed to be William Morgan. Less moneyed citizens saw the rise of Masonry as the rise of an unaccountable elite—an idea that still had fearsome power only fifty years after the revolution. For all the conspiratorial filigree attending the movement, and for all the lurid speculation about what went on behind the doors of Masonic temples, there was a powerful class-based political opportunity here, and there also were people more than ready to grab it.

At the time, national politics was locked in a struggle between President John Quincy Adams, the son of a president himself, and the populist enthusiasm for General Andrew Jackson of Tennessee—who was, it should be noted, a Mason. In 1824, when the tangled and messy four-way presidential election was thrown into the House of Representatives, Adams managed to defeat Jackson, partly because he cut a deal with Representative Henry Clay—who was, it should be noted, a Mason—that made Clay secretary of state in exchange for throwing his support to Adams.

The "corrupt bargain"—a boiling stewpot of conspiracies and conspiracy theories in its own right—set off a raging brawl in national politics. Jackson never accepted his defeat. By the time somebody who might have been William Morgan was fished out of Oak Orchard Creek, it was clear that the old general had become an even more formidable political power. Those lining up behind President John Quincy Adams needed something just as formidable to match Jackson.

In Rochester, New York, not far from the hot zone of anti-Masonic fervor, a publisher named Thurlow Weed bought a local newspaper. When the Masons refused to produce Morgan's murderers, Weed put his publication behind the anti-Masonic cause. However, he did so in such a purely pragmatic way that the anti-Masons soon became a legitimate political force. Gradually, talk of secret rituals gave way. In its place, Weed—and his eventual ally William Seward—brilliantly exploited legitimate grievances of class, and the inevitable issues that were arising from the growth of the country.

Neither Weed nor Seward had any use for Jackson, and both

men did believe in a Masonic elite that endangered democratic institutions; Wilentz points out that they called for a "Second Independence" from the elite. But they grafted anti-Masonry onto their National Republicanism by tempering the more ou-tré elements of the conspiracy theory, and by channeling the emotions raised by that theory into pragmatic, even liberalizing, politics. By 1832, Weed and Seward had helped build a political party so big that it held the first national nominating convention in U.S. history. The anti-Masons now held the balance of power in the political opposition to Andrew Jackson, and the party's most surprising convert was a retired politician from Massachusetts named John Quincy Adams.

Stewing in Massachusetts, the aristocratic Adams had soured on politics generally and on political parties in particular. He was not overfond of his countrymen, either, and at first he considered the conspiratorial basis for anti-Masonic politics to be an unpleasant inflammation of distant hayshakers. However, Adams found in the evolving movement a new constituency. It was rougher than he might have liked it to be, but its enthusiasm revived the old man. In 1830, he was elected to a seat in the House of Representatives.

By then, as Wilentz writes, anti-Masonry was spent as an independent political movement, but it had played a critical role in transforming the National Republicans into what would become known as the Whig party. Among Whigs, it was the politicians whose careers had begun in anti-Masonry who often were ahead of the party, particularly on the issue of slavery, which was gathering a fearsome power within the country's politics. In 1835, William Henry Seward bolted the anti-Masonic party that he'd done so much to promote and joined the Whigs.

For the next fifteen years, Seward and Weed and the other anti-Masons worked within the Whig party to close the ideological gap. They didn't talk much about the Masons anymore, but the anti-elitist energy that had fueled the anti-Masonic movement in upstate New York was easily translated into a dislike of southern plantation society when the slavery issue became inflamed. The abolitionist movement pressed on the Whigs from the outside while Seward and the rest of them pushed from the inside, until the party could bend no further. Gradually, as their conspiracy theorizing fell away, and their visions of a dark Masonic cabal went up in smoke, the democratizing part of the anti-Masonic movement stayed, and it helped to defeat the slave power in America, which actually *was* the conspiracy that was running the country.

The Whigs imploded. Seward and his fellow renegades left, founding the Republican party and, eventually, nominating Abraham Lincoln. Seward would serve Lincoln as secretary of state until he was nearly killed in his home on the same night Lincoln was shot in Ford's Theatre. It was a confederacy of drunks and idiot children that attacked Lincoln and Seward, not the Masons. That would have been crazy. And still, nobody was sure who they'd pulled out of Oak Orchard Creek all those years before, although some people continued to have their suspicions.

* * *

NOT far from where the Masons gathered in Newtonville, and not long after the Masons held their open house, the Royal Order of Hibernians opened their hall to a convention of UFO enthusiasts and some fellow travelers: there was some interest on display in Bigfoot, and in lost civilizations. The Hibernians had already decorated for their annual Halloween party. The walls were adorned with old movie posters—*King Kong* and

The Bride of Frankenstein. Black and orange balloons bobbed to the ceiling in every corner of the hall.

Browsing through the literature, it was easy to see the lasting impact that Ignatius Donnelly's work had had on the national historical counternarrative. Even those volumes arguing that Atlantis had an alien origin conformed to Donnelly's notions as to where the place was and what had happened to it. And clearly, Dan Brown's labors had done as much for the Illuminati-Templar-Masonic publishing industry as it had for the membership of the Masons themselves.

But the main focus of the conference was lights in the sky—or, in several cases, lights under water. There was about the whole evening a sense of faintly acknowledged bunkum mixed with a charming desire for a kind of personal revelation, for acquiring hidden knowledge. There was nothing theoretical about what these people knew. The conspiracy or conspiracies were almost beside the point. It was the hidden knowledge that was important, a Gnosticism for the media age, with action figures for sale.

"There's a little P. T. Barnum and a little Don King to it, I guess," said Jack Horrigan, who organized the conference. "There's some substance to it, and then there are the guys from the Planet Beltar, and this is a photo of their alien spaceship. Pass it on."

The essential Americanness of the whole thing was hard to deny. The isolation of conspiracy theories as mere commercial commodities, tightly circumscribed within the Three Great Premises, has not been a good thing. It has forced upon conspiracy theories the role of history's great patent-medicine show. The creative imagination at work in them never crosses over into what's glibly described as the real world. How different would American politics look if people generally applied to it what every poll says they believe about what happened in

Dealey Plaza? The people looking into Iran-Contra could have used a little of the attitude Ignatius Donnelly brought to the works of Shakespeare. Not that Donnelly was right, but that he allowed himself to believe there was knowledge hidden somewhere to which he had a right; in pursuit of it, he summoned all his creative powers, which, as we've seen, were considerable. To demand to know is the obligation of every American. That it occasionally leads people down blind alleys, or off to Atlantis, is to be celebrated, not scorned.

In 2007, Jonathan Chait published *The Big Con,* a mordantly funny examination of how conservatives in general, and the Republican party in particular, came to believe so deeply and fervently in the crackpot notion of supply-side economics. Chait is a fanatically moderate liberal, a bright and wonkish soul, and a positive sobersides on almost every issue. And yet, on the very first page of his book, he's already calling supply-side enthusiasts "a tiny coterie of right-wing extremists, some of them ideological zealots, others merely greedy, a few of them possibly insane." And, well, boy howdy, it gets rougher from there. By page 21, we learn that "American economic policy has been taken over by sheer loons."

However, Chait seems just a bit troubled by this. "I have this problem," he writes. "Whenever I try to explain what's happening in American politics—I mean, what's really happening—I wind up sounding like an unhinged conspiracy theorist. But honestly, I'm not." This disclaimer is utterly unnecessary. If there weren't something of the conspiracy theorist in him, he wouldn't have been able, clearly and hilariously, to depict the lunatic economic nonsense that the country's dominant political party so rigidly adopted. He should be proud of sounding that way. We all need to unleash our inner Donnellys from time to time.

Modern conservatism, of which supply-side economics is the beating heart, did more than anything else to devalue traditional

American conspiracy theories. People who held to the old conspiracies did so because they knew something important was
at stake. They considered the government something of value.
That's why the anti-Masons were so hell-bent on exposing the
Masons who were running government.

But to the supply-siders, and to the movement behind them,
government is not worth the trouble. For all their faults, the old
iron American conservatives did believe in the essential importance of the American government, which was why they were
so afraid of what the Bavarian Illuminati might be doing with
it. On the other hand, movement conservatism is a style, not a
philosophy, and the government is merely a performance space.
Thus, conservative conspiracies have lost their essential lunatic
tanginess. If you've made yourself rich and powerful deriding
the government, what do you care if some shadowy cabal is
running it, as long as it's not also running the corporations who
fund your research?

Every election cycle or so, we still get some tub-thumping
about the shadowy liberals who are running things, but now the
dark forces are the Dixie Chicks, not the Rothschilds. Where's
the threat, except perhaps to the memory of Patsy Cline?

Chait needn't have worried. The people he's writing about
don't care whether he sounds unhinged or not. They don't even
care if he's right. (He is.) Their theory is valid because it has
made them money and sold itself successfully. The facts are
what they believe, and the truth depends on how fervently they
believe it. All Chait has done is to show them for what they
are—charlatans, but not cranks. Cranks are much too important. They are part of the other America—Greil Marcus's old,
weird America. A charlatan is a crank with a book deal and a
radio program and a suit in federal court. A charlatan succeeds
only in Idiot America. A charlatan is a crank who succeeds too
well. A charlatan is a crank who's sold out.

Part II

✳

TRUTH

CHAPTER FIVE

Radio Nowhere

For an unobtrusive little bookworm, Mr. Madison understood the Gut and what it could do better than most of his peers did. He saw it for what it was—a moron, to be sure, but more than that, too. The Gut is democratic. It is the repository of fears so dark and ancient and general that we reflexively dress up the Gut as good ol' common sense, which we define as "whatever the Gut tells us." The Gut inevitably tells so many different people so many different things at so many different times that it causes them to choose up sides. Good ol' common sense is almost never common and it often fails to make sense. Because of this, Madison was wary of the Gut from the start, and he tried to devise a system within which the Gut could be channeled and controlled, as by the locks in a canal. "So strong is this propensity of mankind to fall into mutual animosities," he wrote in *Federalist* 10, "that when no substantial occasion presents itself, the most frivolous and fanciful distinctions have been sufficient to kindle their unfriendly passions."

Political debate channeled itself into political parties. Madison made peace with their inevitability, and he even helped Thomas Jefferson start one, but he never really trusted them, either. In retirement, he wrote to James Monroe that "there seems to be a propensity in free governments which will always find or make subjects on which human opinions and passions may be thrown into conflict. The most perhaps that can be counted on is that . . . party conflicts in such a country or government as ours will be either so light or so transient as not to threaten any permanent or dangerous consequences to the character or prosperity of the republic."

Here, of course, he calamitously misjudged his fellow Americans. Following the Gut as though it were not the moron it is, Americans do have a positive genius for choosing up sides. Madison wanted conflicts to be so ephemeral as to not endanger anything important. He did not reckon with the fact that, one day, the country would become so good at choosing up sides that it brought the same unthinking dynamic to questions of life and death, war and peace, and the future of the planet that it does to arguments about center fielders or alternative country bands.

We choose up sides in everything we do. In 2006, for example, writing in the conservative *National Review,* a man named John J. Miller listed the "50 Greatest Conservative Rock Songs." Now, to be fair, Miller was a little bit out of his comfort zone. He'd emerged from the halls of the Heritage Foundation, an institution that never has been confused with the Fillmore West. Nevertheless, he soldiered bravely on, never noticing the absurdity that was piling up around his knees. For example, among the addled Tolkienisms with which Robert Plant larded Led Zeppelin's "The Battle of Evermore," the essential conservatism appears in a single lyric:

"The tyrant's face is red."

Miller somehow failed to move on to a study of those noted communist propagandists the Cyrkle, whose 1966 hit contained the following summons to revolution:

"The morning sun is shining like a red rubber ball."

A bubblegum "Internationale," that one.

Miller dug deep. In what may have been an attempt to send Bono into seclusion, he cited U2's "Gloria" because it's about faith and has a verse in Latin. (Miller fails to pay similar homage to the "Rex tremendae majestatis" lyric in the Association's "Requiem for the Masses.") Two songs wholly or partly about the difficulty of scoring really good dope made Miller's list: "Der Kommissar," as a commentary on the repression in East Germany, where only Olympic swimmers ever got really good dope, and "You Can't Always Get What You Want," as a lesson that "there's no such thing as a perfect society." Not even Keith Richards has ever been stoned enough to interpret that song that way.

Miller lists some antigovernment punk songs without noting that the government in question was run by that longtime *National Review* pinup Maggie Thatcher. The Sex Pistols as an anti-abortion band? The notion of the Clash as spokesfolk for adventurism in the Middle East might have been enough to bring Joe Strummer back from the dead. To his credit, Miller was sharp enough to immunize himself against any family-values tut-tutting from his side of the aisle by admitting that a number of the songs on his list were recorded by "outspoken liberals" or "notorious libertines."

Led Zeppelin? Notorious libertines? Who knew?

Thanks to that disclaimer, Miller could write, with a straight face, that the Beach Boys' "Wouldn't It Be Nice?" is pro-abstinence and pro-marriage, although it was recorded at a moment when Brian Wilson was hoovering up the Chinese heroin. Possibly Miller saw Wilson as following a trail through moral consistency already blazed by Newt ("Got a cold, dear? I want a divorce") Gingrich, Rush ("Why wasn't I born an East German swimmer?") Limbaugh, and Bill ("Where the hell's 'Tumblin' Dice'?") Bennett. In any event, he can listen to the Kinks while being completely deaf to Ray Davies's sense of irony, which is roughly akin to listening to the "1812 Overture" and failing to hear the cannons.

This is disorder. There are so many things in the wrong place here—entertainment standing in for identity, identity standing in for politics—that any actual appreciation of the art is impossible to find. It's on the wrong shelf. Or it's slipped down off the windowsill and behind the radiator where nobody will find it. Mr. Madison was right to be worried. Americans do nothing better than we choose up sides and, once we do that, we find it damn easy to determine that someone—the Masons! the refs! liberals! dead white males!—is conspiring against us. And sometimes, they are. Or so the Gut whispers. The Gut is, if nothing else, a team player.

* * *

THE New Media Conference begins with an old joke.

"I go back to the days when the Dead Sea was just sick," says Joe Franklin, a man who has been broadcasting from New York since shortly after Peter Minuit blew town. His audience takes just a moment to laugh, possibly because the joke does not translate well from the original Sumerian.

The conference is being held in a hotel in lower Manhattan, about three blocks from Ground Zero and two blocks from the Hudson River. "New Media" is a little misleading, since by now it's a general term for everything that isn't CBS or the *New York Times*. The new media include blogs and webcasts and podcasts. The New Media Conference, however, is a talk show convention.

There is a great homogeneity to the gathering. Golf shirts and khakis are the uniform of the day. The conventioneers do morning drive in Omaha and evening drive in Nashville. As a matter of fact, the conference isn't even a "talk show" convention per se. One of talk radio's most successful and profitable genres, sports talk, isn't represented at all. There are very few people here who dispense home improvement advice on Saturday morning, or run the Sunday afternoon gardening show. Rather, this is a convention for people who do "issue-oriented" talk radio. It is sponsored by *Talkers* magazine, the bible of the industry, and its majordomo is Michael Harrison, an Ichabod Crane–ish character who bustles about the lobby, snapping photos of talk radio stars like Laura Ingraham and G. Gordon Liddy, and saying "Wow!" a lot.

Liddy's very presence says a great deal not only about the conference but about the industry it's celebrating. Not to put too fine a point upon it, Gordon Liddy is an authentically dangerous man. Back in the 1970s, he was the Nixon campaign operative who proposed firebombing the Brookings Institution, murdering the news columnist Jack Anderson, and hiring yachts as floating brothels for the purposes of blackmailing delegates to the Democratic National Convention. And he did all this from inside the executive branch of the government. Even Nixon's felonious attorney general, John Mitchell, thought Liddy was a lunatic, and Mitchell was no field of buttercups himself.

Liddy crashed and burned when burglars he'd organized got caught in the Watergate offices of the Democratic National Committee, touching off Nixon's prolonged Götterdämmerung.

Liddy went to prison, having named no names, but not before he offered to present himself on any street corner in case anyone from the White House wanted to silence him. Alas for that plan, the only person working for Nixon crazy enough to shoot Gordon Liddy in public was Gordon Liddy.

So off to the federal sneezer he went for a while, and then he came out again and gradually, improbably, made a celebrity out of himself. He toured college campuses with the LSD guru Timothy Leary, whom he had busted years ago as a local prosecutor in upstate New York. This is not so bad. Everybody has to earn a living. It was clear, though, that no country serious about its national dialogue on any subject would allow Gordon Liddy near a microphone, for the same reason that we would keep Charlie Manson away from the cutlery. There was a time in this country when Gordon Liddy could have moved along to a notable, if unprofitable, career as a public crank.

However, in "issues-oriented" talk radio, threatening to poison a journalist is a shining gold star on the résumé. Westwood One, a huge radio syndicator, gave Liddy a national platform, and Liddy did with it pretty much what you might expect. On one memorable occasion, he gave his radio audience pointers on how to kill a federal agent. ("Head shots," he advised.) The comment caused no little outrage, particularly among federal agents with heads. President Bill Clinton mooed earnestly about the corruption of our national dialogue. This sent the talk radio universe into such collective hysterics that the New Media Conference in 1995 gave Gordon Liddy its coveted "Freedom of Speech" award for boldly speaking truth to power. Which is why Gordon Liddy is here today, and why Michael Harrison is taking his picture and saying "Wow!" a lot. Harrison will help the conference hand out this year's "Freedom of Speech" award, a subject on which he waxes particularly messianic.

"There's always a big battle around this award," he says in his opening speech to the conference, "and a lot of it goes back to when G. Gordon Liddy got it. That was a defining experience for so many people with this award. The press likes to take things out of context and blow them up for their own political agenda."

Harrison is glowing with pride now over how his organization handed its most important award to a guy who, inside the government and out, has counseled murder. "People who don't understand this don't understand the First Amendment. Even people who claim to defend the First Amendment don't understand it," Harrison continues. "This is an ongoing battle because if we don't understand the First Amendment, we don't understand America. The process of America is very different than the flag or the president or the government. Presidents or governments are very dangerous whether they are American or Soviet or whatever. Names don't mean anything. Processes mean things. The spirit in which something is done means something."

Everybody in the room sits up a little straighter. Heads nod. Chests puff out a bit. It's hard to know how many of those present actually buy the bafflegab that Harrison is slinging them— that Gordon Liddy was what Mr. Madison had in mind, and that they are information warriors of free expression, keeping the Enlightenment values of the founders alive between jokes about Hillary Clinton's hindquarters and the 5:15 traffic report. Some of them may in fact believe that Harrison is correct in his lemonade libertarianism about the great beast Government, that there is no true difference between the authoritarian ambitions of, say, Bill Clinton and those of Leonid Brezhnev. It's impossible to gauge the effect of all that blather at the end about America being a "process" and about "the spirit of things," probably because it sounds like de Tocqueville filtered through Tony Robbins.

One hungers at this point for someone—anyone!—to come out and make the simple point that talk radio exists because it makes money. "The trick is to be what your bosses also call revenue," confides a consultant named Holland Cooke. This comes like a cool breeze, cutting through the stagnant self-congratulation of Harrison's quasi-profound rambling. "If you are good at this, you could be bulletproof."

Talk radio is a very big fish in a very small barrel. It has a longer history than is usually believed. It probably dates back in its essential form to the likes of Father Charles Coughlin, the radio priest from Michigan, whose career cratered when he abandoned his support for the New Deal in favor of nativism and (ultimately) anti-Semitism. As it has evolved, talk radio is a conversation between Coughlins.

Many markets took up talk radio in the 1950s and 1960s, when it coexisted with AM Top 40 radio. As the music moved over to the FM dial, talk filled the void on AM. But the format did not truly explode until 1987, when, in the deregulatory fever of the Reagan years, the Federal Communications Commission revoked the Fairness Doctrine. This rule, adopted in 1949, had required licensed broadcasters to air all sides of the debate on controversial issues.

Some very farsighted young conservative leaders saw the demise of the Fairness Doctrine as a way to develop a counterweight to what they perceived as the overwhelming liberal bias of the rest of the mass media. Even some liberal groups joined in, attacking the regulation on First Amendment grounds. (Ironically, some older conservatives argued for the retention of the Fairness Doctrine, which they had used for years in order to be heard.) After a favorable ruling in a federal court, and after Reagan vetoed a revival, the Fairness Doctrine was dead. Talk radio exploded on the right. As more and more stations became the property of fewer and fewer companies—the repeal was only a small part of the general deregulation of the public airwaves—the medium's ideology hardened like a diamond. These days, the conservatives' dominance of AM radio is overwhelming.

According to a 2007 joint study by the Free Press and the Center for American Progress, on the 257 stations owned by the five largest owners of commercial stations, 91 percent of weekday talk programming is conservative. On an average weekday, the study found, 2,570 hours and 15 minutes of conservative talk is broadcast, but just 254 hours of what the study called "progressive" talk. Ordinary demographics wither in the face of this juggernaut. A 2002 study focusing on Eugene, Oregon, the crunchy-liberal home of the University of Oregon, found that the local stations pumped out 4,000 hours of conservative talk per year, *none* on the other side. This is nothing short of a triumph in how we choose up sides in our national life.

(Today, the Fairness Doctrine is what conservative talk radio hosts use to scare their children at bedtime. The conference was alive with terror that the newly elected Democratic Congress might bring the beast back to life. Almost every speaker warned ominously of that possibility, even though Harry Reid, the leader of the Democratic majority in the Senate, already had rejected it out of hand.)

Since right-wing populism has at its heart an "anti-elitist" distrust of expertise, talk radio offers the purest example of the Three Great Premises at work. A host is not judged a success by his command of the issues, but purely by whether what he says moves the ratings needle. (First Great Premise: Any theory is valid if it moves units.) If the needle moves enough, then the host is adjudged an expert (Second Great Premise: Anything can be true if someone says it loudly enough) and, if the host seems to argue passionately enough, then what he is saying is judged to be true simply because of how many people are listening to him say it (Third Great Premise: Fact is that which enough people believe. Truth is measured by how fervently they believe it). Gordon Liddy is no longer a gun-toting crackpot. He has an audience. He must know something.

Talk radio was the driving force in changing American debate into American argument. It moved discussion southward from the brain to the Gut. Debate no longer consists of thesis and antithesis, moving forward to synthesis; it is now a matter of choosing up sides, finding someone on your team to sally forth, and then laying the wood to each other in between commercials for male-enhancement products.

Talk radio provides a template for the clamorous rise of pundit television and for the even swifter interactivity on the Internet. And, because the field of play has moved from the brain to the Gut, talk radio has helped shove the way we talk to each other about even the most important topics almost entirely into the field of entertainment. In doing so, it has created a demand for inexpertise—or, more accurately, anexpertise—whereby the host is deemed more of an authority the less he is demonstrably polluted by actual knowledge.

After an extensive study of talk radio, and of the television argument shows that talk radio helped spawn, Professor Andrew Cline of Washington University in St. Louis came up with a set of rules for modern American pundits:

1. Never be dull.
2. Embrace willfully ignorant simplicity.
3. The American public is stupid; treat them that way.
4. Always ignore the facts and the public record when it is convenient to do so.

"Television is an emotional medium," Cline explains. "It doesn't do reason well. This is entertainment, not analysis or reasoned discourse. Never employ a tightly reasoned argument where a flaming sound bite will do. The argument of the academic is sort of dull, but a good pissing match is fun to watch. To admit anything more complicated is to invite the suggestion that you may be wrong, and that can never be. Nuance is almost a pejorative term—as if nuance means we're trying to obfuscate."

There is some merit in being skeptical of experts. It is one of the most American of impulses. It drove almost all of the great cranks in our history. However, there is something amiss in the notion that someone is an expert because of his success in another field as far from the subject under discussion as botany is from auto mechanics. If everyone is an expert, then nobody is. For example, Rush Limbaugh's expertise as regards, say, embryonic stem cell research is measured precisely by his ratings book, but his views on the subject are better known than those of someone doing the actual research, who, alas, likely is not as gifted a broadcaster as he is. Consequently, Limbaugh's opinion is as well respected. Often, the television news networks—CNN is particularly fond of this—will bring on an assortment of talk show hosts to discuss issues even though, on the merits of the issues, most of them are fathoms out of their depth. But they all are good enough at what they do to stay on the air, so enough people must agree with them to make what they say true.

"Human beings," says Cline, "are storytelling creatures. We structure reality in terms of narratives. In other words, we start at Point A and get to Point B, and everything in between is called hope. If you're a human, you're a storyteller, a story believer, and that's just the way it is."

By adopting the ethos of talk radio, television has allowed Idiot America to run riot within all forms of public discourse.

It's not that there is less information on television than there once was. (Whether there is less actual news is another question entirely.) In fact, there is so much information that "fact" is now defined as something that so many people believe that television notices it. A 2006 *Wall Street Journal* story quoted a producer for *Hardball,* the exercise in empty bombast hosted by Chris Matthews that precedes Keith Olbermann's show on MSNBC, who said that she heard from more than a hundred people a day who aspired to be television pundits. "We call them street meat," she said.

"There is an entire network [the Fox News Channel] that bills itself as news that is devoted to reinforcing people's fears and saying to them, 'This is what you should be scared of, and here's whose fault it is,' and that's what they get—two or three million frustrated paranoids who sit in front of the TV and go, 'Damn right. It's those liberals' fault," says Olbermann. "Or, it's those—what's the word for it?—*college graduates'* fault. Somewhere along the line, we stopped rewarding intelligence with success and stopped equating intelligence with success."

However, following the pattern laid down by talk radio, Fox has managed to break off a larger segment of a smidgen of a piece of the audience than MSNBC has.

The conference itself is something of a giveaway. Twenty-two percent of those responding to a 2003 Gallup poll considered talk radio their primary source of news, and here was the cream of the industry, all together, three blocks away from Ground Zero. The country was at war. The climate was in disarray. The economy was tanking. What promised to be a sprawling presidential election was just gearing up. Over the course of the weekend, there are dozens of small workshop sessions, all of them about running a better talk show, about building your brand, about the latest breakthroughs in technology. "Programming a News Talk Station in Interesting Times" dealt with the damage to the brand done when cranky old Don Imus called the Rutgers women's basketball team "nappy-headed ho's" and was forced to absent himself (briefly) from the airwaves.

"We have a liner card in the studio that says, 'As edgy as you can get with the kids in the car,' " explains Heather Cohen, the director of programming for GreenStone Media. Jack Swanson, of KGO in San Francisco, said he'd have fired Imus and then resigned, too, "for allowing it to happen." David Bernstein, the programming chief of the progressive Air America network, disagreed with his fellow panelists.

"The dude got fucked," Bernstein explains.

This is a trade show, nothing more. You can learn a great deal about how to talk on the radio, but very little about anything you might be talking about. Wandering the halls over the course of the weekend, Todd Bowers, a veteran of Afghanistan and Iraq, is reduced to buttonholing whomever he could find just to talk about the wars, and the issues confronting his fellow soldiers, topics that most assuredly will come up on the call screener back at the station.

"Most of them thanked me for my service," he says.

"Talk radio is the biggest con to be perpetrated ever," explains a host named Lionel—né Michael Lebron—who works for the perpetually struggling Air America network. "We create the veneer that we know what we're talking about, a veneer of expertise. We pontificate on TV. This TV guy called me and asked, 'What do your listeners think?' I don't know. We talk to people who have nothing better to do than listen to us." This cri de coeur was not well received by those in attendance, many of whom, one suspects, saw in their mind's eye a naked emperor walking off toward Battery Park.

It becomes obvious that there are no workshops on the issues because there really isn't a need for them. Most of the people present know exactly what they believe, because what they believe is fundamentally defined by their niche. They have chosen up sides, and what is most important is that what you say is what your side believes. A good talk radio host is playing a role; he knows what the team expects of him—he "skates his wing," as hockey coaches say. That said wing is usually the right one is a function of the fact that modern conservatism recognized early on the importance of vicarious politics in America—understood that everything is entertainment now, and what matters is not how much you know, but how well you can entertain your portion of the audience. This depends on how convincingly you can portray the character you play on the radio.

Rush Limbaugh brilliantly created the template. He constructed an entire universe with himself at its center, and he sold memberships to it, every day for four hours, on the radio. With his listeners self-identified as "dittoheads," Limbaugh created a place with its own politics (where Hillary Clinton may have had Vince Foster snuffed), its own science (where tobacco has no connection to lung cancer), and its own physical reality (Rush is a roué who makes Errol Flynn look like a Benedictine monk). He created a space for vicarious reality at its highest level, and lesser hosts have been scrambling to keep up ever since. And he sold it like the radio pitchman he once was.

(In fact, the track record indicates that when the world he's created comes into contact with reality, Rush fares rather less well. His TV show was a debacle. A guest shot hosting Pat Sajak's late-night show ended with him nearly booed into the Pacific and sweating like a whore at high mass. And he had a brief stint as an NFL analyst on ESPN that foundered when he divined a liberal conspiracy to promote the career of Philadelphia Eagles quarterback Donovan McNabb. You see, McNabb was black and all the baby John Reeds in press boxes throughout the NFL were pushing him out of some devotion to affirmative action. This wasn't any more loopy than most of what Limbaugh said about the Clintons, but football analysts are a harder sell than most political editors, and Limbaugh was laughed off the air. He has since largely eschewed events not of his own devising.)

When Limbaugh got caught sending his maid out to score his dope, one of the most pathetic drug busts since Joe Friday was running down the hopheads on the old *Dragnet* TV show, his hold on his audience remained unbroken. This was largely because listeners didn't choose to associate Rush Limbaugh, the character on the radio, with Rush Limbaugh, the actual person who gobbled OxyContin like M&M's, even though the radio character regularly inveighed against people just like himself. The great thing about living vicariously is that you only take on yourself the admirable aspects of the person through whom you are living vicariously. Their flaws don't exist in you; therefore, their flaws don't exist at all. Thus can Limbaugh pop pills, Bill Bennett gamble with both fists and a steam shovel, Newt Gingrich chase tail all over Capitol Hill, and Bill O'Reilly engage in creepy phone-stalking that would have embarrassed Caligula, while all four make a comfortable living talking to America about the crisis in the nation's values. More than anything else, the "culture war" is a masterpiece of niche marketing. Buy Us, not Them.

In 2003, the psychologist Paul Ginnetty examined this dynamic in *Newsday,* focusing on Limbaugh's show but analyzing the appeal of the entire genre, what he called "the potent narcotic of reassuring simplicity."

"Many of [the callers] probably also derive a sense of inclusion and pseudo-intimacy via this electronic fraternity of kindred spirits," Ginnetty wrote. "They get a chance to feel smart when the master seems to agree with them, failing to see that it is actually they who are agreeing with him."

(It's possible that Limbaugh will finally be done in by getting old. In the vicarious life, nobody's getting old, and a talk show host who reminds his audience that they're doing just that, usually because he's aged out of the valuable twenty-five-to-fifty-four demographic, as Limbaugh has, is not long for the airwaves. This would certainly account for Limbaugh's serial marriages, his detention for illicit possession of Viagra in the Dominican Republic, and his endless bloviating about his studliness and his golf game—as though those two pastimes weren't self-evidently oxymoronic. The end is near.)

The issues do come up, mostly in the plenary sessions held in a vast movie theater within the hotel complex. The Great Talk Show Rumble is a desultory affair. There are eight panelists, four on either ideological side. (That the organizers managed to find four liberals in the place would be the biggest upset in New York that weekend outside of Rags to Riches' winning the Belmont.) Onstage, smiling like a guy you'd change cars on the subway to avoid, is Gordon Liddy, so the panel actually comprises seven panelists and one felon. A good-hearted soul named Jack Rice is alleged to be the moderator, but he rather loses control early on when a guy named Jerry Doyle says of Hillary Clinton, "She's just so full of shit." And we're off.

Things get little better. As the discussion turns to the war in Iraq, one of the liberals on the panel, a lovable goofball named Stephanie Miller—the daughter of Barry Goldwater's 1964 running mate, William Miller—achieves a certain level of bipartisan amity when she announces that, in not forcing a quick end to the conflict, "The Democrats are pussies."

"I agree," chimes in Lars Larson from the right end of the table. "Democrats are pussies."

Nothing moves. Nothing progresses. It's all Kabuki bullshit, and the audience begins to stir with a certain level of boredom broken only when Liddy interrupts a discussion about tossing illegal immigrants into the clink in California by saying, "I am the only person here who's actually done time in the LA County jail." He had them there.

Sean Hannity also talks about the issues, in his keynote address. Hannity occasionally seems to make an earnest attempt at avuncularity. He looks like the bouncer at an Irish bar in Southampton, the big lug in the golf shirt who throws you out for singing "The Rising of the Moon" atop the bar but, as he does so, presses a couple of drink tickets into your hand with a wink and tells you to come back next week.

His academic background is sketchy. He had a brief, unsuccessful encounter with higher education at New York University. Claiming to have become politically energized by the proudly accessorial behavior of Oliver North during the Iran-Contra investigations, Hannity ground his way to the top. His one setback came when a California station canned him for a blatantly homophobic segment on his show. Seeking more fertile pastures for such things, he moved south, finally ending up in Atlanta, where he honed his craft and hitched his wagon to the rising star of Newt Gingrich. In 1996, the fledgling Fox operation brought him to New York, where they put Hannity on a prime-time show with putative liberal Alan Colmes.

Once in New York, Hannity was also hired by WABC to replace Bob Grant, whose bigotry had gotten so far out of control that even talk radio couldn't contain it. Hannity's show was an instant success. Fueled in part by his nightly television visibility, it quickly went into national syndication and now is said to reach thirteen million listeners a day. He has risen to prominence by the seemingly limitless means of being sure of everything about which you actually know very little. You pitch it to the Gut, is what you do.

Hannity's show is a superlative example of how much better conservatives have become at taking advantage of how Americans choose up sides, and how gifted they are at the new forms of vicarious politics that were created when the media's balance shifted from information to entertainment. Callers regularly tell Sean that he is a "great American." He replies that they are, too. Having established these simple proletarian bona fides, the $4-million-a-year host works the niche with exactly what his audience expects to hear.

Hannity has been wrong about almost everything, from the vicious police assault on Abner Louima in New York City (Hannity attributed Louima's injuries to a "gay sex act") to the conflict in Kosovo (President Bill Clinton didn't have "the moral authority or ability to fight this war correctly"), to the war in Iraq (Hannity was one of the last people to cling to the notion that, rather than use them, you know, to defend himself against an imminent invasion, Saddam Hussein shipped his weapons of mass destruction to Syria). In any other job in the communications industry, such (and let us be kind) bungling would end a career. In his chosen field, it has made Hannity a multimedia force.

He's in a terrific mood this morning, discussing the rise of talk radio, whose success he links to the rise of the conservative movement. Two of the first milestones he cites are the election of Ronald Reagan in 1980 and the Gingrich-led sweep of the congressional elections in 1994. He's not wrong, especially not about the latter. He gracefully acknowledges the deregulatory regime that made Limbaugh and him possible.

"We are living through a moment today that we have not seen since the end of the Fairness Doctrine and the emergence of Rush Limbaugh," he says. "The second wave is going to be as growth oriented as the first wave was."

Hannity sees the talk format moving gradually into FM radio, dominating that dial as thoroughly as it took over AM. "Just as music on AM was in trouble in the late 1980s," he says, "music on FM is in trouble today. What kid today doesn't have an iPod? Every car sold in 2009 is going to have a connection for an iPod. Why would anyone who loves music listen to a station programmed by a strange PD [program director] when they can listen to their own music?"

This would be an ironic twist. FM music radio rose in opposition to the Top 40, when the album replaced the single as the primary musical format. Top 40 died, and talk radio took its place. Now, with the iPod and the MP3 changing everything, it may very well be that FM music will die out and be replaced by talk radio, cheaply produced cheese with a guaranteed market. FM used to be the place where people fled to avoid Bobby Goldsboro. Then it became the place where people fled to avoid Sean Hannity. Soon, there may be no escape at all.

The speech gets a little iffier when Hannity starts talking about how important talk radio was in the aftermath of the September 11 attacks. "We are one major event away," he says, "from being the most relevant format again."

This is where talk radio abandons its honorable history as a platform for cranks and passes over the border into Idiot America. If it defined itself as entertainment—along the lines of professional wrestling, say—it would be a perfectly respectable enterprise. Indeed, whenever a talk radio host is criticized for remarks that seem beyond the pale of civil discourse, the almost reflexive reply is that talk radio is entertainment and that its critics should lighten up. (Limbaugh is particularly fond of proferring this excuse for himself.) But the whole conference is based on the notion that talk radio is something more—a vehicle of national unity, a town meeting of the air, and so on.

Talk radio pleads entertainment as an alibi for its most grotesque excesses while at the same time insisting on a serious place in the national discourse. It seeks camouflage against the not unreasonable notion that it's mainly a very noisy freak show. It justifies both claims by the simple fact that it moves the ratings needle. This confers upon a talk show advertising revenue, but it does not confer upon its host any real level of expertise. It does that through the Three Great Premises.

Hannity's remark about talk radio and the September 11 attacks was remarkably ahistorical. In the first place, after the initial shock of the attacks wore off, no medium was more instrumental than talk radio in the destruction of the unity forged by those attacks. And it did what it did because it is primarily entertainment. As soon as it sank back into its niche again, talk radio quickly leaped to blame those same people whom it would be blaming for all the other ills of the world anyway. One of the great canards thrown around after September 11 was the fact that we would become a more serious, united nation again. Settling right back into the old tropes, energized by the emotions that were running high at the time, talk radio and the opinion entertainment industry did more than anything else to demonstrate what a lie that was.

In November 2001, for example, former president Bill Clinton gave a speech at Georgetown University in which, addressing the question of how long-standing historical debts can be, he made the unremarkable observation that the United States was still "paying a price" for slavery to this day. A reporter for the *Washington Times* wrote a meretricious story claiming that Clinton had attributed the September 11 attacks to a debt the country owed, that he was somehow saying that the United States had brought the attacks on itself. Glad to have Clinton to chew on again, talk radio hosts made a dinner of the story for several days. TV pundits adopted the comfortable role of the Professionally Obtuse. To be fair, some of the people who ran with the story walked their own criticism back once they read the original article. However, Sean Hannity, to name only one person, liked it so much that he included it in one of his best-selling books, long after the episode had been roundly debunked.

Now, though, as Hannity speaks about the vital role that talk radio will play when the next attack comes, it's hard not to hear a distressing glee in the prospect. After all, this is someone who wrote a best seller called *Deliver Us from Evil: Defeating Terrorism, Despotism, and Liberalism.* Another attack would put these people on top again. Gordon Liddy, it turns out, is a piker. It's mass murder that's the true ratings bonanza. The best is yet to come.

AM radio wasn't always like this. Once, in a sunburnt brick building in Nashville, Tennessee, radio was a truly revolutionary thing, carving out its own niche without the help of gargantuan syndicators, media megaliths, and marketing strategies meant to divide before conquering. It forced the country to look at itself in different ways. It didn't rely on what people already felt. It didn't encourage them. It challenged them. Listen to this, it said, and see if you feel the same way about things. It changed people's hearts before it changed their minds. Here was where the true revolutionaries were, some of them. Here was where they changed the country.

* * *

HEY, John R. Whatcha gonna do?
C'mon, John R., play me some rhythm and blues.
—*Radio introduction, WLAC Radio, Nashville, Tennessee*

In 1951, radio station WLAC in Nashville was celebrating its silver anniversary, so it put out a souvenir program recounting the highlights of its twenty-five years on the air. There was an unmistakable midcentury Babbitry about some of them. Bettie Warner of Chattanooga, a sophomore, had won the "Voice of Democracy" contest for high school students. James G. Stahlman, the publisher of the *Nashville Banner,* had a regular spot, "Stahlman Speaks Out for Freedom," in which he harrumphed that "every day, right here in America, these freedoms are in constant jeopardy. . . . Once they're gone, only your life or that of your children, or theirs, will be the price of their return."

A young congressman named Albert Gore, Sr., of Tennessee's Fourth Congressional District, took to the airwaves to deliver a talk entitled "The Iron Curtain vs. Freedom," and Richard D. Hurley, the chairman of the U.S. Chamber of Commerce, came to town to appeal for moral leadership. "Who," asked Hurley, "is going to bail America out if we follow Britain down the economic skid row of socialism?" It was not all grim business at WLAC, though. The listeners also were treated to entertainment by Audrey Holmes ("The Lady of the House") and Charlie Roberts ("Let's Go Fishing") as well as the gardening advice of Tom Williams, the Old Dirt Dobber, whose "The Garden Gate" came courtesy of the Ferry-Morris Seed Company. Things were different, though, when the sun went down.

WLAC had started out in 1926 as just another radio station, operating at 1510 on the AM dial, and broadcasting from fairly opulent studios in the building owned by the Life and Casualty Company, from which the station took its call letters. Its most formidable competition in town was WSM, the radio home of the Grand Ole Opry, which brought the likes of Ernest Tubb and Hank Snow to homes throughout the South. WLAC played some country, too, even hosting live musical acts in its studio. The problem was that the station sold so little advertising that everyone there, including the musical acts, often found themselves moonlighting at other jobs around the station. F. C. Sowell was hired in 1930 to sell advertising and as an on-air announcer. In an interview recorded as part of Columbia University's "Radio Pioneers" oral history project, Sowell explained that the station "was owned by the insurance company and they didn't push it very much."

WLAC puttered along until 1945, when the station hired a man named Gene Nobles to work as an announcer.

Nobles was a disaster. "He didn't develop according to our wishes," recalled F. C. Sowell. "He wasn't good at handling straight copy. We'd had a great deal of trouble with our late recorded show, a disc jockey show. None of our announcers that we had tried seemed to take an interest in it, so he came in and requested permission to try out.

"We let him try it and we found out within a couple of weeks that we had something that was a rather unusual approach to kidding the public along. . . . The mail started pouring in."

Gene Nobles had found his calling. He specialized in snappy DJ patter. (The girls in his audience were "fillies.") Soon, he'd partnered up with Randy Wood of Randy's Record Shop, a mail-order house in Gallatin, Tennessee. Randy would sponsor the show. Nobles would plug the records. They broke the mold with what they began pitching: records of what was then called "race music," the work of black R&B artists. Race music had heretofore been largely restricted to black audiences throughout the South. Now, WLAC was putting fifty thousand watts behind records by artists like Amos Milburn and T-Bone Walker. (Walker's "Stormy Monday" was one of Wood's biggest-selling singles.) It seems safe to say that not many of the people who tuned in to hear the Old Dirt Dobber also tuned in to hear the anarchy that was breaking out on WLAC after dark. The station programmed a solid block of the music all night long. Nobles, and later Herman Grizzard and Hoss Allen, became stars. In 1942, a former New York radio soap-opera star named John Richbourg took over the one A.M.–to–three A.M. shift.

Richbourg was born in the small town of Davis Station, in South Carolina. He worked in radio in New York and auditioned for a job at WLAC during a vacation back home. After a brief stint in the Navy, he came back to the station and stayed for thirty-one years. "John R.," he called himself; his deep voice and command of the slang led a great portion of his listeners to believe that John R. was black, and not the very straight-looking gent who would go home after work to narrate the Christmas pageant at the Harper Heights Baptist Church. Black artists who came to the station to be interviewed, Richbourg remembered, "well, their mouths would fall open."

He committed himself from the start not only to playing black music, but also to creating a national audience for himself and the music. "I·suppose it had something to do with the war coming on," he told an interviewer in 1974. "Otherwise, there may have been more resistance. I did get a few phone calls from your dyed-in-the-wool so-called rednecks who would call up and say, 'Who do you think you are?' I just said, 'Well, that's fine, so why don't you just listen to another radio station, then?'

"See, we had already decided that our night programming at the station would not be for Nashville. We were interested in directing our night programming to the rural areas, the areas that were not being serviced at all. Many areas, in every state, particularly [where] black people [lived], had no service at all."

In many ways, WLAC was still an underdog station. The atmosphere in the studio was wild and uninhibited. People reading radio copy would find that someone had set the paper on fire. The station once broadcast a phony report announcing the end of World War II. The DJs played poker and drank whiskey during their shifts; Nobles legendarily passed out once, producing a moment of dead air before he regained consciousness and flawlessly cued up another record. The station's commercials sold Royal Crown Hair Dressing and White Rose Petroleum Jelly. They even sold baby chicks. And they sold the music. Randy's mail-order business went from $20,000 to $300,000 over three years.

There was no sales plan. No marketing scheme. Nobody knew this music, except the black audiences, and they were isolated by law, by culture, and by three hundred years of ugly history. John R. scoured the record shops for sides by Little Richard and Ruth Brown and Big Mama Thornton. Every night after midnight, his show sponsored by Ernie's Record Shop, John R. threw this music out over WLAC's huge signal. It was said that you could drive from New York to Los Angeles and never miss his show. The clear air was his syndication.

He got letters from thirty states and from Iceland and Greenland and Australia. In Canada, Robbie Robertson heard the show long before he became the guitarist for the Band. Young Johnny Winter listened in Texas, and Bob Seger tuned in from Detroit. A songwriter named Bob McDill recalled listening to the show and wrote "Good Old Boys Like Me," a country hit for the singer Don Williams that placed it in a long list of essential experiences for a southern boy of that time:

> John R. and the Wolfman kept me company.
> By the light of the radio by my bed,
> with Thomas Wolfe whispering in my head.

John R. also promoted and produced new artists. It was he who got a hot young guitar player named James Stephens to call himself Guitar Slim. In 1967, Jim Stewart, cofounder of Stax

Records in Memphis, signed over his share of the publishing rights to a single called "These Arms of Mine," by an unknown soul belter named Otis Redding. Richbourg "must have played that record for six months literally, every night, over and over, and finally broke it," Stewart later recalled. With the Grand Ole Opry two blocks away, he helped turn Nashville into a center for R&B.

"One city in particular that tends to be associated with a single genre of music is Nashville, Tennessee," wrote David Sanjek, in a study of African-American entrepreneurship after World War II. ". . . Nashville has been a thriving center for the playing of a wide range of African American musical forms over the public airwaves—principally through the disc jockeys Gene Nobles and John Richbourg (John R.) of . . . WLAC."

Gradually, John R. and WLAC were integrating the country, even if the country pretended not to notice. They recognized no rules, so they abided by none. They introduced the country to a soul it didn't know it had, one so vast and indomitable that it was able to overcome—in the three minutes it took to play a 45 record—even the artificial barriers of race and class and region. John R. carved a niche big enough for everyone, and he helped develop the next generation of artists, who would break down the barriers entirely. WLAC was deeply and truly subversive, and you could buy baby chicks from its advertisers if you wanted.

It couldn't last, although John R. hung on for three decades. Top 40, ironically, did him in. WLAC went to a tightly programmed musical format, and John R. hated it. He did his last shift on June 28, 1973. He kept his hand in, producing some records and teaching broadcasting. In 1985, his health went bad. Phil Walden of Capricorn Records put together an all-star tribute to him in Nashville. Walden was one of the thousands of southern kids who'd fallen asleep by the light of the radio. "I am a better person just for knowing you," Walden wrote to him in a letter not long before the show. Rufus and Carla Thomas played. So did B. B. King and James Brown. John R. died a year later, at seventy-five. Ella Washington sang "Amazing Grace" at his funeral.

WLAC moved out of the old insurance building. It's now in an office on a hill not far from the gleaming towers that have housed Music Row since the record companies moved up and out and the Opry moved out of the Ryman Auditorium. WLAC is now owned by Clear Channel, the massive media conglomerate, and you can see from the signs by the door how radio has resegregated itself, not by race, but by niche. There's WUBT ("The Beat") and WNRQ ("The Rock"), and WRVW ("The River"). And there's WLAC, 1510 AM, now Nashville's "News-Talk Leader." Except for Steve Gill, who does a local show in the afternoon, WLAC relies on nationally syndicated talk shows for its basic programming.

The station is the state of the art. It is a quiet place. Nobody bustles from room to room. Phones ring softly in small cubicles. There is a low buzz of quiet conversation, but there's no sense that anyone is really working here. Even the sales department is placid. You can no more imagine a whiskey-soaked poker game breaking out than you can imagine an elephant stampede in the hallway. The inside of the building is of a piece with the sign on the wall outside. It is a place made of niches, each one carefully cut and shaped to fit a specific audience, each making its quotas, the space between them dull and impermeable.

The national shows all come in by satellite. "Every commercial break, every news break, has a tone that we receive, so we know they're coming," says Patrick Blankenship, a young man who's engineering the programming at WLAC the afternoon of my visit. He's heard the history of the station, and he thinks it might have been fun to work here "when they were doing R&B, and there was that kind of frenzy."

Every day from three P.M. to six P.M., Sean Hannity's show goes sailing out over the 50,000 watts of WLAC, saying exactly the same thing that he's saying to thirteen million people on five hundred other stations, talking to this particular part of a country full of people grown bored with talking to themselves. Once, WLAC did something remarkable—it developed and sustained a subversive unity that would help undermine the divisions that held America together. Now, though, far away, one computer talks to a satellite, and the satellite talks to another computer down in Nashville in an office filled with the low and melancholy hum of remorseless corporate efficiency. Nobody sells baby chicks here anymore.

* * *

"I've heard the stories," said Steve Gill, whose show precedes Sean Hannity's on WLAC. Gill's a big, friendly bear of a guy with a down-home accent that stands out at the New Media Conference. "One time, Jesse Jackson was in Nashville," Gill recalled, "and he came on the station and talked about how he used to listen to WLAC when he was coming up in North Carolina.

"When I started there, Hoss Allen [another legendary WLAC DJ, whose show followed John R.'s back in the old days] used to still be around, and he used to talk about how surprised people always used to be back in his day to find out he was white. I mean, everybody thought he was black."

Gill stood talking outside the movie theater in which the conference was about to give its coveted Freedom of Speech Award to a nationally syndicated talk host named Michael Savage. It is not a major exaggeration to say that Savage makes Gordon Liddy sound like Bertrand Russell. Not to put too fine a point upon it, Michael Savage, whose work this conference is preparing to drape in ermine, is a raving public nutcase.

Born Michael Weiner, he studied anthropology and ethnobiology, picking up two master's degrees at the University of Hawaii and a Ph.D. from the University of California. In the latter field, he briefly came into the public eye in the 1980s, when he took an obscure research paper concerning the high incidence of Alzheimer's disease in Canadian bauxite miners and turned it into something of an international brouhaha in which aluminum came to be blamed for the disease. People threw out aluminum cookware. Glass bottlers ran TV commercials meant to scare the people who still drank their beer out of cans. The frenzy didn't truly abate until the genetic markers for AD began to be discovered.

But Weiner didn't go off the rails until he'd changed his name and become a talk show host. Based in San Francisco—on KGO, the station run by the same Jack Swanson who would have fired Don Imus and then himself—Savage quickly went national. An estimated six million listeners on three hundred stations were treated to rambling, barely coherent babble about "Turd World" immigrants, gay people, treasonous liberals ("They'll kill you because they're deranged!"), castrating feminists ("human wreckage in high heels"), self-hating Jews, and other denizens of the menagerie that Savage apparently has running around between his ears. The Million Mom March was "the Million Dyke March." Speaking of high school students who were spending time feeding the homeless, Savage suggested that, "There's always the thrill and possibility that they'll be raped in a Dumpster while giving out a turkey sandwich."

And he'd said all of this before MSNBC decided to put him on television.

Savage, said Erik Sorensen, the alleged adult who hired him, was "brash, passionate, and smart." Thus Sorensen pretended, in vain, that he wasn't just trying to bring in those six million listeners attracted by someone who celebrates Yom Kippur by running tapes of Adolf Hitler's speeches.

Mercifully, the TV show proved short-lived, Savage celebrated the Fourth of July by stuffing sausages into his mouth while telling a gay caller to "get AIDS and die, you pig," thus burying himself beneath a half ton of Freudian irony. This might have been enough to sink most careers but, once carved, a niche is forever. Now a victim of the dreaded censorious liberal media—and not, as reality would have it, of a rare spasm of common decency in the world of pundit television—Savage found his talk radio career flourishing even more, until we all gathered in New York to honor him. Less than a year later, Savage would pass along the shocking news that childhood autism was "a fraud and a racket. . . . I'll tell you what autism is. In ninety-nine percent of the cases, it's a brat who hasn't been told to cut the act out. That's what autism is. What do you mean they scream and they're silent. They don't have a father around to tell them, 'Stop acting like a moron. You'll get nowhere in life. Stop acting like a putz. Straighten up. Act like a man. Don't sit there screaming and crying, idiot.' "

The autism community exploded in rage. Savage lost some sponsors, and some stations even canceled his show. Mark Masters, whose Talk Radio Network brings Michael Savage to the nation, summoned up all the spine of a ficus to complain: "Unfortunately, by condensing his multifaceted concerns into 84 seconds of commentary, the . . . context for his remarks was not apparent."

Savage's remarks could not have come as any shock to anyone who'd been in the theater on the afternoon of the Free Speech presentation. Michael Savage got this award because people were willing to pay him to say exactly the kind of thing he said.

The award was preceded by a speech by Alan Colmes, a tall, passive-looking man who once played the role of Sean Hannity's heavy-bag every night on Fox television. Colmes took the pseudo-Lockean high road previously trod by Michael Harrison: "As much as I find much of what Michael Savage says despicable," he intoned, "I am reminded that there are many people who find what I say despicable. I don't want to live in a country where Michael Savage can't say the things he says, because I'm next, or any one of us could be next."

Colmes declined to mention how many times he's speculated on his show how lucky it would be for, say, comely freshmen at Bob Jones University to experience the "thrill" of being raped behind an athletic dorm. He also failed to explain exactly how Michael Savage has been imperiled by anyone save the voices in his own head. But, good liberal that he was, he did mention that Savage had been "the first conservative to speak out against this so-called conservative administration."

Of course, Savage did so because the administration had declined to fulfill his fondest wish, which was to clap in irons everyone who looked like an illegal immigrant and drop them into San Francisco Bay. Savage was operating well within his niche, selling the product he was paid to sell. To do anything else would be to throw on the table a new intellectual commodity, for which his market might not pay. What Colmes praised as an act of intellectual courage really was little more than Savage's reluctance to try to sell New Coke to his established audience. "Who gets to decide?" Colmes meeped. The answer, apparently, was nobody. We are all ennobled by the blessings of a country in which someone can make a fortune talking about "dog-grilling" Koreans on the radio.

One tires of this easily. Colmes's attempt to graft an intellectual conscience onto an industry based on profitable ignorance was exhausting. It was like watching someone try to explain that his hippo could conjugate verbs. Fortunately, Mark Masters came along with precisely the right corrective. "When I heard Michael Savage," he said, "I thought this was the spark that might give life to independent syndication. Everyone thought I was crazy, and we didn't get paid for two years. But, eventually, Savage proved we could do it, and I'm grateful for that. If it hadn't been for Michael Savage, I couldn't have relaunched Talk Radio Network."

Savage didn't come to New York to pick up his award. Unexplained "personal reasons" kept him home in the city he calls "San Fran Sicko." Instead, he sent a DVD of his acceptance speech. The house lights dimmed. Savage appeared on screen, mysteriously walking down a dock by the ocean. He looked like someone who'd gotten drunk at the yacht club cotillion and spent the next four days sleeping in the boat basin. The video mysteriously kept jump-cutting between Savage on the dock and Savage standing in front of what appeared to be a clam shack. It was an altogether remarkable film. It looked like a hostage tape.

Savage veered wildly between truckling gratitude for the recognition, and paranoid ramblings about the people who have set about to destroy him, and thus, presumably, all of us. These included adherents of the "environmental faith" who "want to make it a crime to deny global warming." The identity of these Tofu Torquemadas remains a mystery.

There is some stirring in the theater. This display is not what many of those present had in mind. This is the acknowledged leader of their profession, and he's acting like a guy you'd run away from on the sidewalk. He waves his arms. He shouts at the sky. If there were a moon out, he'd be howling at it.

"Freedom of speech has never been in such a perilous state as it is today," Savage bellowed, as a few people in the distant rows begin to filter toward the back doors of the theater. "That is because in Venezuela, the dictator Hugo Chavez just shut down a TV network. That can't happen here, you say? Oh, it can't?

"As I speak, Congressman [Maurice] Hinchey of New York . . . and others are circulating a bill in Congress to return the so-called Fairness Doctrine. Which means that people like Michael Savage will not be able to speak freely. Is that any different than Chavez shutting down a TV network? Is that not dictatorship?"

Well, no, of course it's not dictatorship, even if it were going to happen, which it isn't. Nobody's going to put Michael Savage in jail. Nobody's even going to take him off the radio, even though he's plainly tetched. By this standard, the United States was a dictatorship in its public discourse from 1939 until 1987, and at least some of the people in the hall are old enough to remember some robust debates over things like civil rights and Vietnam that occurred while the airwaves were bound by the iron shackles of the Fairness Doctrine—which, even if it came back, which it won't, would require only that, if a station wanted to broadcast Michael Savage, it also would have to find a mushy nonentity like Alan Colmes to achieve "balance."

The lights come up and there's some low murmuring as the crowd files out. The First Amendment, God love it, lives to fight another day in a country that's grown bored with talking to itself. America's always been a great place to be crazy. It just used to be harder to make a living that way.

CHAPTER SIX

God and Judge Jones

In November 1784, the Virginia legislature was in an uproar. A proposal had come before it to support "teachers of the Christian religion" through a new general tax. No less a figure than Patrick Henry lent his voice to the proposal. His arguments will sound somewhat familiar: Henry maintained that this tax was needed because of the "moral decay" that had set in since Virginia disestablished the Anglican church in 1777 by adopting its own Bill of Rights. "Many influential men," writes Ralph Ketchum, ". . . retained the hallowed ideas that religion was essential to the well-being of society and that the well-being of religion required state support."

Nevertheless, since Virginia had relieved itself of an established church, the spiritual life of the Commonwealth had exploded. There were Baptists and Methodists flourishing, especially in the western parts of the state. The Presbyterians had gained in strength and numbers. All of these denominations howled in outrage at the notion that tax monies should be sluiced off into the Episcopal Church. The issue so roiled the politics of the state that many of the people who'd supported the law lost their seats in a subsequent election. In June 1785, Mr. Madison took up his pen in opposition to the proposal.

His "Memorial and Remonstrance Against Religious Assessments" is the most closely reasoned argument for a separation of church and state ever written. As Ketchum puts it, it is "a defense of freedom for the human mind worthy of Milton, Jefferson or Mill. The Remonstrance argued that government suffered when religion was established, and that religion suffered the closer it got to government, and that human liberty suffered in either case. Its phrases were clear and unequivocal."

"It is proper to take alarm at the first experiment on our liberties," Madison wrote. ". . . Who does not see that the same authority which can establish Christianity, in exclusion of all other Religions, may establish with the same ease any particular sect of Christians, in exclusion of all other Sects? that the same authority which can force a citizen to contribute three pence only of his property for the support of only one establishment, may force him to conform to any other establishment in all cases whatsoever?"

Citizens had a right to follow any religion they wanted, Madison wrote. They had a right to follow no religion at all. The primacy of the individual conscience was paramount. His language was unsparing. Religion established by the state is of necessity corrupted. Madison "argues that religion will best support morality if it is free and pure, working up from its independent and spontaneous roots," observes the historian Garry Wills. Moreover, Madison contends, the commingling of religion and government is inevitably a recipe for civic discord.

"Torrents of blood," Madison wrote, "have been spilt in the old world, by vain attempts of the secular arm, to extinguish

Religious discord, by proscribing all difference in Religious opinion." He notes that simply proposing the bill has led to great disharmony. "What mischiefs may not be dreaded, should this enemy of public quiet be armed with the force of a law?"

As in all things, Madison had done his homework. He rooted his arguments in one of the oldest precedents in Christendom: the adoption by the Emperor Constantine of Christianity as the official religion of what had become a fractious Roman empire. Constantine had brought in Christianity not as a moral code, but as a tool to enforce political unity.

"He attempted to use Christianity as a means of bringing order to society," writes the historian Charles Freeman. ". . . In many of his other laws, he maintained a traditional Roman brutality. . . . If a free woman had a sexual relationship with a male slave, both were to die, the slave by being burnt alive. Slaves who were found to be an accessory to the seduction of a young girl were to have molten metal poured down their throats. Christians played very little part in Constantine's administration and the army remained pagan."

This, Madison believed, was not a promising start for the notion of an established religion. "Madison agreed with [Joseph] Priestley and other Enlightenment figures that the purity of Christian belief and practice was corrupted when Constantine made it a state religion," writes Garry Wills. "All the abuses of power through the Middle Ages reflected the entanglement of the spiritual with the worldly." What nobody anticipated fully was that both politics and religion would adopt the characteristics of the modern marketplace, that this would bring them into contact with each other, to the detriment of both, and that they would meet inevitably in the heart of Idiot America.

Today, with the rise of the megachurch faithful and the interminable meddling in secular politics by various mall rat

Ezekiels whose theological credibility is calculated by the number of vacant parking spaces they have on a Sunday, we have a market-deformed politics influenced by a market-diluted religion. Niches are created and products tailored to fill the niches. While modern evangelical Christianity has undeniable historical roots, its explosion over the past thirty years is a triumph of the Gospel According to Wal-Mart.

* * *

"MY contention," writes George Barna, a "church consultant," in 1988, "is that the major problem plaguing the church is its failure to embrace a marketing orientation in what has become a market-driven environment." This situation did not last long.

Today, suppliers of "Christian" products, up to and including the various churches themselves, have created a self-contained and profitable universe in which almost everything that was worthwhile about Christianity's contact with the secular world has been cheapened and fashioned into tawdry souvenirs for the suckers. Sacred music has traded Gregorian chant, Beethoven's Missa Solemnis, Thomas Dorsey, and Mahalia Jackson for "worship anthems" sung by stubby white guys who look like they flunked the audition for Counting Crows. A literature that once produced C. S. Lewis and G. K. Chesterton now sells millions of copies of the "Left Behind" series, written by Jerry Jenkins and the noisome political preacher Tim LaHaye, in which the end times occur and the Antichrist arrives in the person of one Nicolae Carpathia, so named, perhaps, because the authors didn't think of calling him "Evil J. Transylvania." Carpathia comes to power preaching a one-world government based in the United Nations, which, at least, proves that Jenkins and La-Haye have rooted their profitable Apocalypse in the American conspiratorial tradition. As far as can be determined, however, Mr. Carpathia is not a Mason.

Anyway, he has a good run of it until Jesus comes back to earth and does a lot of bloody slaying and dismembering in and around the village of Megiddo, which has had enough trouble. (Jesus, it seems, has developed a talent for disemboweling people in the years since he left town.) The plot is preposterous. The characters all speak as though they learned English from the Ostrogoths. And the series is a genuine publishing phenomenon, selling tens of millions of copies.

It has sold so well and so widely that *Time* put the authors on the cover, and the article inside the magazine did not find it at all necessary to point out that (a) Jenkins and LaHaye are peddling a fringe interpretation of Scripture rejected by most scholars; and (b) the whole scenario is absurd, no matter how many people believe it. Thousands of people ascending bodily to heaven? Antichrists from the UN with names like James Bond villains? Jesus chopping folks up in the sand? To call this medieval is to insult Thomas Aquinas; this is the kind of thing dreamed up by religious lunatics, dying of thirst in a cave in the Sinai.

Yes, the old Roman Catholics once sold off their saints piecemeal, and sometimes the saint's finger you bought turned out to be a pig's knuckle, but the vendors of holy relics were absolute pikers compared with those who traffic in the notion of an embattled elect surrounded by a scornful world. Because nothing sells in the modern Christian marketplace like the notion that Christians are beset on all sides by powerful forces desperately in need of a good disemboweling, it was inevitable that religious marketing would flow into the country's politics. And religion has been sold there solely as a product.

Mr. Madison saw this coming. Political religion always has

been a sucker's game for marks and prayerful mama's boys, an ever vain search for a nonexistent pea hidden beneath the swindler's overturned chalices. It exchanges the loaves and fish for the rigged wheel and the marked deck. It speaks not in tongues but in euphemisms. A politician discussing his religion now refers to himself as a "person of faith," which tells you more about the politician's balls than it does about his soul. He doesn't have enough of the former to call himself "religious," because that leads to the question of which religion and why he chooses to follow it and not one of the dozens of others, or none of them at all.

Such questions cause actual thought to break out, something that all modern politicians endeavor to avoid. So a politician becomes a "person of faith," and good for him. So is the fan in the bleachers who roots for the Red Sox and so is the guy in Oregon who's looking for Sasquatch. Torquemada was a person of faith. So were Marx and Lenin. So is almost any atheist. In its essential cowardice, the phrase means nothing. It's a slogan. A sales pitch.

Consider the sad case of David Kuo, born-twice victim of his own sanctified bunco game. In his memoir, *Tempting Faith,* Kuo vividly describes his career as the last of the suckers. Kuo came to Washington to work for the second Bush administration on "faith-based" initiatives. The government would divert public money to religious charities, which were presumed to do a better job of confronting the nation's social problems. An Office of Faith-Based and Community Initiatives would even be established within the executive branch, Mr. Madison thereby having been told exactly where he could stick his Remonstrance.

Kuo was sincere. At least on the surface, this was a God-drunk administration. There was regular Bible study. The staff came from evangelical diploma mills, and like hired like. (According to a questionnaire obtained by the *Washington Post,* applicants to the Department of Justice were routinely asked whether they believed in God.) Kuo assumed his bosses were sincere as well, at least until it became plain to him that the program had a lot more of Boss Tweed than Beatitude to it. Kuo writes:

> Every other White House office was up and running. The faith-based initiative still operated out of the nearly vacant transition offices. Three days later, a Tuesday, Karl Rove summoned [Don] Willett [a former Bush aide who initially shepherded the program] to his office to announce that the entire faith-based initiative would be rolled out the following Monday. Willett asked just how—without a director, office, or plan—the president could do that. Rove looked at him, took a deep breath, and said, 'I don't know. Just get me a fucking faith-based thing. Got it?' "

A fucking faith-based thing.

And why not? "Faith-based" is another dishonest term for a dishonest time. It's a word for people too cowardly to call themselves religious and it is beloved by politicians too cowardly to debate something as substantial as faith. It was eagerly adopted by Idiot America, which is too lazy to do either one, because it conforms to the Three Great Premises. It's a cheap salesman's term of art, something you'd use to pitch a television program or a breakfast cereal. It even sounds like an additive—"faith-based"—an artificial flavoring to make crude biases taste of bread and wine. It's camouflage under which religion is sold like smuggled goods in places where it doesn't belong.

To call something "faith-based" for the purposes of hiding the clearly sectarian character of what you're actually talking about is to admit that there really is no difference between what went on at Lourdes and what went on at Roswell. In truth, the United States of America can be said to be "faith-based," and one of the primary articles of that faith is that religion—in all its forms—should be kept out of the country's secular institutions, both for religion's own good and for the good of the institutions in question. Mr. Madison knew it in his bones. To invite religion into government is to invite discord and to establish the tyranny of the righteous. Now, today, in Idiot America, where everything is a marketplace, to sell religion through government is to invite discord and to establish the tyranny of fraud. The transaction becomes just another fucking faith-based thing.

* * *

ON the steps of courthouses, people speak in low tones, head down. They cling to what they're saying as though all of it is secret. Every word. Every syllable. Every diphthong. Every letter. The people on the steps hold all of them close because, once they get inside, everything will come out. Every secret will be revealed. The top step of the courthouse staircase is the last place where anything is private anymore. Inside the courtroom, everything belongs to the world—even, and most dangerously, the truth.

It's a warm day running toward spring in Williamsport, Pennsylvania. Lawyers and their clients mill around on the sidewalk, in the shade of ancient trees. There are not many people this morning, not enough of them to get in anybody's way. It's a slow Monday at the federal district court. Upstairs, the windows are open in the judge's chambers and there's hardly any noise from the street below. In many ways, the judge is grateful for the quiet.

"I'm an optimist," Judge John E. Jones III explains. "I really am. I think the system ultimately works the way it's supposed to work. What's the old adage? If it doesn't kill you, it makes you stronger. I really believe that. And although this is a very imperfect system in many ways, at the end of the day, I think it works pretty well."

He's a peppery, open man, as far from the stereotypically monkish and imperial federal judge as can be imagined. (*The New Yorker* was to describe him as looking like a cross between Robert Mitchum and William Holden, which is a bit much. Gig Young, maybe.) His grandfather came to Pennsylvania from Wales at the age of eight, taking a job as a "breaker boy," picking the useless rock out of bins of anthracite in the coal mines of northeastern Pennsylvania. Farsighted and ambitious, he worked his way out of the mines and became a civil engineer, investing his salary back into the coal industry and becoming wealthy enough to buy up some contiguous farm property in and around Orwigsburg, in Schuylkill County.

In the 1940s and 1950s, the anthracite business collapsed, and the Jones family business changed radically. They turned their farm property into a series of five public golf courses. They caught a market on the rise. Golf was being liberated from the restricted country clubs of the privileged and thrown open to the postwar suburban masses, in no small part thanks to the arrival on the national scene of Latrobe, Pennsylvania's own Arnold Palmer. The golf courses, not the coal, helped put John Jones through Dickinson College and law school.

His father died at forty-nine, of heart disease. ("He got some bad genes," Jones says.) Jones's first job in the law was as a clerk in the Schuylkill County courthouse. "In the first six months," he recalls, "I had this germ of an idea. I thought, 'Gee, I'd like to do this.' That's not unusual. A lot of lawyers want to become judges. So, I held that thought."

He built a successful law practice, but he also developed a taste for politics. A lifelong Republican, Jones ran unsuccessfully for a congressional seat in the 1990s and ultimately took a job in the administration of Governor Tom Ridge, a rising star in national Republican circles. "At that point, I sort of tucked that whole thing about being a judge away," Jones says.

However, in the aftermath of September 11, 2001, Bush appointed Ridge the first director of the Department of Homeland Security. Ridge recommended Jones, who was then working as a public defender, for a federal judgeship that had opened up in the Middle District of Pennsylvania. His confirmation sailed through. For three years, Jones sat on cases large and small. In 2004, he began to take note of a controversy in the small town of Dover, in the southern part of the state.

It is an area of rolling hills with valleys like deep green bowls between them, planted thick with wheat, apples, and odd religion. The Amish still drive their buggies here, trying to live their lives while avoiding the relentless attempts by tourists to turn those simple lives into a horse-drawn diorama. (The movie *Witness,* in which Harrison Ford plays a detective who hides from crooked cops in an Amish community, was filmed nearby.) The Ephrata Cloister, a splinter group of the German Baptist Brethren, ascetic and strictly segregated by sex, established itself near Lancaster under the leadership of Conrad Beissel. (Beissel was an authentic religious crank. There were rumors that he trafficked with the Rosicrucians and, yes, the Masons.) Ephrata developed its own liturgy and sacred music. The community nursed the wounded of both sides after the battle of Gettysburg. When Beissel died, the Cloister began to die as well. While the Amish try to hold to their faith and avoid becoming a living museum, a museum is all that's left of the Ephrata Cloister.

Both the Amish and the people of Ephrata espoused religions that were in the secular world but not of it. Religion has always been in the air of the place. In October 2004, a firestorm erupted that engulfed Dover and, eventually, the courtroom of Judge John E. Jones III. The Amish and the inhabitants of Ephrata might have had the right idea all along.

That month, the Dover school board proposed to change the biology textbook used in the town's high school. The town itself was undergoing great changes: there had been an influx of new people into the area, and there also had been an explosion in the number of evangelical Protestant churches. A volatile demographic mix was brewing.

This made Dover no different in its local politics from thousands of other small towns that were being devoured by urban sprawl. There were fights over taxes and land use that pitted the older residents of the community against the newly arrived suburbanites. In 2001, three new conservative members were elected to the school board, having run on their opposition to an expensive proposal to renovate the town's old high school building. Once on the board, however, the new members began to lard their remarks with a conspicuous religiosity that unnerved the others. There was talk about the morality of Dover's students. There was talk of bringing back classroom prayer and, eventually, of teaching creationism in biology classes. The conservatives also seemed to have their own idea of how to best renovate the high school.

"As somebody who used to be involved in politics," Judge Jones muses, "I tell everyone there's an overarching lesson here and that's that you can't take your eyes off the ball. I can't imagine that these guys and gals campaigned on a strictly religious platform. I don't think they did."

School board dissension got uglier in 2003, when a maintenance man took down a mural painted by a former student that depicted the evolutionary process leading from hominids to humans. It had been hanging in the high school for five years. The groundskeeper took the painting home and burned it because, he said, it had offended his faith. Besides, his granddaughter was about to enter high school and he didn't want her exposed to, well, the exposed. The humans in the mural had been naked, after all.

His punishment by the reconstituted school board was mild, if he was punished at all, which to this day seems unclear. Bertha Spahr was a science teacher at the high school. She told Gordy Slack, the author of *The Battle Over the Meaning of Everything,* an examination of the controversy, that a board member confessed to her that he'd watched the painting burn. Something was running amok on the Dover school board. Then, a year after the mural was destroyed, everything came together in what would become one extremely noisy, extremely prolonged—and, ultimately, extremely expensive—event.

Over the summer of 2004, it became clear that the board was preparing to change the biology curriculum. The previous textbook would be abandoned because, as one board member put it, it had been "laced with Darwinism." The school board was laying the groundwork to teach creationism in its public schools. Controversy flared. The ACLU threatened to bring a lawsuit. Rather than back off, as the summer ground along, the members of the school board pushing creationism changed tactics. They replaced "creationism" with "intelligent design." They stopped proposing that the previous textbook be abandoned. Rather, they said, they would agree to purchase the new edition of the standard text as long as they could also purchase a book called *Of Pandas and People: The Central Question of Biological Origins,* which argued for intelligent design. On this, they were adamant.

They lost one vote, but wrangled a compromise in which *Of Pandas and People* would be available for "reference" in the classrooms. Then, in October 2004, the board passed a resolution mandating that intelligent design be mentioned in the classroom. Two members of the board quit. A month later, the board announced that science teachers would be required to read a statement promoting ID and criticizing the theory of evolution to all incoming biology students. The statement read, in part:

> Because Darwin's Theory is a theory, it continues to be tested as new evidence is discovered. The Theory is not a fact. . . . Intelligent Design is an explanation of the origin of life that differs from Darwin's view. The reference book, *Of Pandas and People,* is available for students who might be interested in gaining an understanding of what Intelligent Design actually involves.

The science teachers, led by Bertha Spahr, went up the wall. Even the Discovery Institute, a Seattle-based idea mill dedicated to the promotion of faith-based science, thought the Dover school board had pushed too far.

The town split down the middle. School board meetings degenerated into dockside hooleys. Two more board members gave up and quit. "The town," writes Gordy Slack, "had divided into warring camps." Which was not surprising at all. The whole controversy had left religion, if it ever truly was religious at all, and entered the realm of politics, which meant it had entered the marketplace. Once that happened, the Three Great Premises of Idiot America were engaged.

They were engaged because intelligent design is not science, but a sales technique, developed to respond to a specific need in the political marketplace. (In this, intelligent design is to creationism what "faith-based" is to "religious.") This is of a piece with everything that has gone on since creationism won the battle but lost the war in the Scopes trial. Ever since creationism fell into public ridicule and scientific obsolescence, there have been efforts to rebrand it, gussying it up with scientific filigree to sneak it past the gimlet eye built into the First Amendment and the finely calibrated bullshit detectors of the federal courts.

In the 1980s, there was an attempt to sell the notion of "creation science" as an alternative to evolution. In 1982, creation science suffered a blow in the case of *McLean v. Arkansas*; five years later, the state of Louisiana tried it again and got slapped down, hard, by the U.S. Supreme Court. In *Edwards v. Aguillard*, the court determined that "creation science" was religion in sheep's clothing and, hence, violated the establishment clause of the First Amendment. The decision was based partly on what had come to be known as the *"Lemon* test."

In 1971, in the case of *Lemon v. Kurtzman*, the Supreme Court fashioned a three-part test to determine whether governmental funding of private-school programs violated the First Amendment. The program had to have a legitimate secular purpose. It could not have "the primary effect of advancing or inhibiting religion." And it could not entangle the government excessively with religion. Any program that fails any part of the test is unconstitutional. The *Aguillard* decision made teaching creationism—or, more specifically, "creation science"—in the public schools illegal. This put a considerable crimp in Christian right's marketing strategy and, almost immediately, another attempt at rebranding was under way. *Aguillard* forced, Gordy Slack writes, with no little irony, creation science's "evolution into a new species." The new brand name was "intelligent design."

The rebranding was brilliant. On the surface, intelligent design accepts science, even praises it. It simply posits that, at the end of the day—or, more accurately, at the beginning of the day—there was a guiding intelligence behind creation, an intelligence that ID proponents even decline to label "God." Proponents cite various lacunae in Darwin's work as evidence. They speak in the language of democratic inquiry; having created the "controversy," they then ask "only" that schools be granted the right to "teach the controversy." Their papers and books are mild, couched in the language of science, if not in its most basic principles. How, after all, can anyone develop an experiment to falsify the existence of a guiding intelligence?

And ID even has a historical pedigree, going back even before Darwin climbed aboard H.M.S. *Beagle*. One of the books Darwin read as a student was William Paley's *Natural Theology*. "The basic premise . . . was that the glories and complexities of living nature were to be seen as prima facie evidence of God's creative hand," writes Keith Thomson, an Oxford philosopher and historian. "Natural science and theology were not at odds, therefore, but complementary." Paley's work lives on in ID most directly in his analogy of the universe as a watch, whose existence must needs imply a watchmaker. In 1996, Thomson points out, the analogy was cited in defense of ID by Michael Behe, a biochemist and prominent ID proponent who one day would be reduced to stammering incoherence in a Pennsylvania courtroom.

In fact, ID sells itself so reasonably that hard-core creationists disdain it as so much materialist backsliding. (In his museum outside Cincinnati, where the humans and dinosaurs romp together, Ken Ham is more withering in his criticism of ID than Bertha Spahr ever was.) However, in its origins and goals, ID is creation science with a thicker scientific gloss.

It comes out of the work of the Discovery Institute, founded in 1990 to promote new ideas in fields like bioethics, ideas that nonetheless would conform to hard-line conservative ideals. As Gordy Slack points out, the institute floundered for a while, whipsawing between enthusiasm for scientific progress and the rigid demands of a biblical worldview. It was brought to the light, finally, by one Philip E. Johnson, who immersed himself in the study of how to counteract what he saw as the self-destructive "materialism" of modern American culture. Based in the institute's Center for the Renewal of Science and Culture, institute scholars, few of whom have actually worked in the physical sciences, laid siege to their targets. These included almost all of modern America, but especially the secular world of the sciences.

Slack quotes extensively from what he calls the "Wedge document," a Discovery Institute fund-raising memo that leaked in 1999, and which pretty much gives the game away. The goal of the institute, it says, is to reestablish "the proposition that human beings are created in the image of God [which is] one of the bedrock principles on which Western civilization was built. . . . Yet a little over a century ago, this cardinal idea came under wholesale attack by intellectuals drawing on the discoveries of modern science." The document goes on to describe how the CSC—it had dropped the "Renewal" part of its name like a hot rock because of the word's religious connotations—would bring down Darwinism, first by publishing its own "research," then by selling that research through the broadcast media. This process would help build up "a popular base of support among our natural constituency, namely, Christians."

In short, ID, because it is a sales pitch, was relying on the Three Great Premises to carry the day. ID would be sold in such a way that people would speak loudly and authoritatively in its support; then, enough people would believe it to make it a fact, and they would believe it fervently enough to make it true. As Gordy Slack writes, "Whether they have paved the way for a scientific revolution or not, they have unquestionably brought about a revolution in public perception . . . they have made ID a household acronym, and have given an eccentric theory an aura, in some circles anyway, of intellectual and scientific credibility."

As deftly as it sold the new idea, the Discovery Institute treated it very delicately. The institute did not want ID measured by the *Lemon* test or judged against the standards of the *Aguillard* decision too soon. When the proponents of ID on the Dover school board announced their intention to defend a lawsuit brought against them by the ACLU, the Discovery Institute argued against the move. But Dover was too deeply enmeshed in the controversy to untangle itself. The fight over ID was a fight over schools, and morals, and income, and class, and over the primacy of political and cultural tribes. Like so much that happens in Idiot America, where everything is judged by how well it sells, it was a war between proxy armies. The Discovery Institute's one mistake was to believe the fight could be avoided. In his office in Harrisburg, Judge Jones still thought the case might never come to court. That hope lasted as long as the first meeting he had with both sides.

"I usually try to check the body languages of the attorneys and see whether I should ask them to come into chambers, to see if I can resolve it," he recalls. "You could tell everyone was polarized. There were a lot of lawyers there and their body language was such that I thought, 'Well, I'm not even going to try to settle this.'

"Through the summer of '05, though, I thought cooler heads might prevail and they'll find a way to work this out. Right up until the trial convened, I had some sense or hope that it might work out. But, it did not." On October 7, 2005, the case of

Kitzmiller v. Dover Area School Board opened. On the eve of the trial, a local pastor named Ray Mummert had drawn the best map of the battlefield. His summing-up was reported all over the country. The fight within the Dover school board went worldwide.

"We've been attacked," Mummert said, "by the intelligent, educated segment of our culture."

* * *

IT did not take long for Judge Jones to suspect that he was being asked by the Dover school board defendants to pass judgment on the efficacy of a marketing plan, and not on the constitutionality of their actions, let alone on empirical scientific truth. What was playing out in front of him had very little to do with the law and almost everything to do with local politics driven by anger that was in the fullest way "faith-based," in that the people pushing intelligent design went out of their way to deny, preposterously, that any of this had anything to do with religion.

Bill Buckingham, a member of the board's curriculum committee and a minister, denied in a pretrial deposition that anyone had ever mentioned creationism during the fight over the biology curriculum, only to be confronted during his testimony at trial with a videotape of himself using the word in an interview. Another revealing witness was the school board chairman, Alan Bonsell, whose answer regarding who donated money to purchase copies of *Of Pandas and People* for the high school completely contradicted what he had said in a deposition. Judge Jones stepped in and reduced the man to a blithering mess on the stand.

"It was a significant issue because they had passed the hat at a church to get those books," Jones explains. "And that goes through the *Lemon* test that we use that the books were being used for a religious purpose. They deliberately, in my view, lied.

"Your mind does wander during a trial, and there are different times when your curiosity is piqued. That is the moment when I listened for an extended period of time to Bonsell's testimony. He was, of course, the president of the school board. My mind didn't wander at all during his testimony. If Bonsell and Buckingham had answered truthfully in their depositions, I think there was a good possibility that counsel for the plaintiffs would have sought an injunction and shut down the policy before it even started. They did not answer truthfully."

In Jones's view, the members of the Dover school board had volunteered their town as a test market for those who wanted to sell ID nationwide. And while both sides in the case had brought formidable legal teams into his courtroom—"It was 'The Charge of the Light Brigade' in there," Jones laughs—he cast a particularly wary eye on the attorneys from the Thomas More Law Center, a right-wing legal foundation funded originally by Thomas Monaghan, the ultramontane Catholic founder of Domino's Pizza. The Thomas More lawyers, appearing on behalf of the defendants, were working for free and that may have blinded the people from Dover to the true cost of the action they had undertaken to defend. Under federal law, the loser in a civil rights action has to pay the costs of the litigation, which can run into millions of dollars.

"I was discouraged by the fact that this community of good people, you know, they pay their taxes and all, and they maintained a generally good school system, were going to end up paying I don't know what the legal fees were going to be," Jones says. "I thought, 'It's going to come to me to tag this school district with potentially a couple of million dollars in fees.'"

The More Center's interests in the case went far beyond a parochial scuffle over textbooks. The center wanted a case, any case, through which it could litigate intelligent design all the way up the system until it could get the issue before what the More Center believed was an increasingly sympathetic Supreme Court. Further, the center's strategists believed that they could use an ID case to relitigate a whole host of holdings involving the First Amendment's "Establishment" clause with which the center and its backers disagreed. Among those holdings were the *Lemon* test and the *Aguillard* decision. The latter, in shutting down creationism in Louisiana, had made necessary the invention of intelligent design. Styling itself the "Christian answer to the ACLU," the More Center thought it had found its dream vehicle in Dover. Jones thought they were playing the town for fools.

"When you're not paying your counsel, you think there's no price to be paid," Jones explains. "It's pretty clear now that then comes the Thomas More Law Center, and they jump in the cockpit and they say, 'We'll represent you through this litigation.'

"There was a disconnect that we didn't notice until the trial started. You could see what happened where the Discovery Institute said to the Thomas More Law Center, 'Don't do this. Don't litigate this case. You're going to get us killed here.' And they shoved the Discovery Institute out. The Thomas More Law Center was litigating this case for the Supreme Court of the United States, it is quite clear. Justice [Antonin] Scalia has had a number of dissents in Establishment clause cases. And the way they phrased their case, the way they structured their briefs, all of that went to Scalia's dissents.

"You could tell. I was fully familiar with all the cases. I think their strategy was, 'Look, if Jones dings us, we'll just take it up. We will go to the Supreme Court. Here's the case where we are going to eviscerate the endorsement test as it relates to the Establishment clause.' "

Almost nothing went right for the school board and its legal team. On cross-examination, the members of the board sounded like people asked to explain why they sold their public responsibility for a bag of magic beans. Far removed from the niche market of conservative religion in which it was sold, intelligent design and its proponents came off little better. Michael Behe, one of the most influential scientific voices in support of ID, spent several uncomfortable hours being demolished by a plaintiff's lawyer named Eric Rothschild.

Behe's major contribution to what is termed the scientific basis for ID is "irreducible complexity," the idea that, if you could discover a system from which you could not remove one element without demolishing the system, then that system could not have evolved through natural selection. (Darwin, it should be said, agreed.) Behe's favorite candidate for this was the flagellum. Flagella are the tiny filaments that allow bacteria to swim. Behe argued that the flagellum was made up of so many parts that the removal of any one of them would destroy its function. Being "irreducibly complex," the flagellum refutes Darwin and implies the existence of an intelligent designer, who may or may not be God; Behe wasn't saying.

The role of bacterial flagellum got a long workout in Jones's courtroom. Scientists explained at length how Behe was wrong about it. And under cross-examination, Behe stumbled badly, admitting at one point that a definition of science he had given during his pretrial deposition would fit astrology as well as it fit ID. It went downhill from there. But the worst damage done to the defendants' case centered around the textbook that had started it all, *Of Pandas and People,* not because it made the proponents of ID and their lawyers look like zealots, but because it made them look like clowns.

Barbara Forrest, a philosopher and vociferous critic of the Discovery Institute, had been following the evolution of the anti-evolution movement for years. She'd written scathingly about creationism, "scientific creationism," and ID. Based in Louisiana, Forrest was more than familiar with *Aguillard*. Just about the time that decision was being handed down, a new edition of *Of Pandas and People* was being prepared. (One of its authors, Dean Kenyon, had testified in *Aguillard* on the creationist side.) When the case threw out creationism, the authors of the book went to work adapting it. The Dover defendants based their entire case on the assertion that ID was science and not religion; Barbara Forrest blew the whistle.

She'd discovered that, in the aftermath of the *Aguillard* decision, *Of Pandas and People* had been run through a software program designed to replace specific creationist language with that of intelligent design. Gordy Slack points out that the process was as full of holes as the science it purported to explain: "Some careless editor or author must have tried to do a search-and-replace without taking sufficient care. They tried to replace 'creationists' with 'design proponents' and ended up creating an infertile hybrid: 'cdesign proponentsists.' "

Jones had come to believe that he was being asked to pass on the free-speech rights of con men. His job had turned into a matter of evaluating the efficacy of a sales pitch. He thought he was being asked to judge religion as science and science as politics. Whatever it was, it wasn't the law, and he was determined to judge this case under the law.

"I think 'mad' is an overstatement," he says. "I wanted to make a point. I think there were times during the trial that I felt a great deal of passion about the case and I wanted to reflect that in the opinion."

He did not believe that the pro-ID people had dealt with his court in good faith, and he did not believe their hired lawyers had the best interests of the town in mind. Over the summer of 2005, while the trial was proceeding, the citizens of Dover seemed to come to the same conclusion. In November, they voted out the entire school board but for the one member not up for reelection. An anti-ID majority rode a huge turnout to victory. Politically, if Jones ruled against intelligent design, the fight was over. This new board was not going to finance the appeal all the way through the federal court system.

By this time, Jones was bunkered with his staff, writing his decision in the case. One of his clerks, Adele Nyberg, pulled together the post-trial submissions from both sides and began to sketch out a rough draft from a preliminary outline Jones had prepared. Nyberg wrote some of the opinion and Jones wrote some of it. They swapped ideas back and forth. It was a long, grueling process.

"You just close the door and work on it," Jones recalls. "I can't tell you the number of drafts we went through." He kidded Nyberg that she should look at the drafting of the opinion as the vegetable she least liked to eat. "I kept finding edits and corrections I wanted to make," he says. "At the end, I couldn't look at the thing."

Every draft had one thing in common, though: Jones was angry, and it showed. He took one version home to show his wife, who told him it was too strident. He toned it down, a little. On December 20, 2005, he released the opinion to the world, and into the media maw that had gaped outside his office for going on two months.

If the earlier drafts were tougher, they must have been tied around a brick. The opinion ran 139 pages, and Jones determined that teaching ID was unconstitutional on the third page. Then he got going. His language was blunt and devastating. He found ID ludicrous as science and preposterous as law. He saw the attempts to foist it on high school students as the worst kind of bunco scheme, dealing harshly with the notion of "teaching the controversy"—a "canard," he wrote, designed merely as the next form of camouflage by which creationism hoped to insinuate itself into the public schools. ID, Jones concluded, was "a mere re-labelling of creationism." He saved his most memorable scorn for a passage in which he described the damage the fight over ID had done to the people of Dover.

"This case came to us as a result of the activism of an ill-informed faction on a school board," Jones wrote, "aided by a national public interest law firm eager to find a constitutional test case on ID, who in combination drove the board to adopt an imprudent and ultimately unconstitutional policy.

"The breathtaking inanity of the board's decision is evident when considered against the factual backdrop which has now been fully revealed through this trial. The students, parents, and teachers of the Dover Area School District deserved better than to be dragged into this legal maelstrom, with its resulting utter waste of monetary and personal resources."

That "breathtaking inanity" rang the loudest. (In fact, the phrase had survived from the earlier draft that Jones had revised at the suggestion of his wife.) For a federal judge, language like this was the equivalent of throwing a pie in someone's face. Commentators on both sides of the issue seized on the line. The opinion was released at 10:30 in the morning. By 10:45, people were yelling about it on CNN.

"I have these twenty-something clerks," Jones recalls, "and they kept looking at me and looking at the TV like, 'What in the hell have we done?' I was very satisfied that I'd got the decision out before the end of the year, so there's a sense of, Well, you cleared the deck. You did the heavy lifting." Channel surfing at home that night, Jones came upon Bill O'Reilly's nightly

show on the Fox News Channel. O'Reilly and his guest, a former judge named Andrew Napolitano, chewed on Jones for a
solid ten minutes. By the end of it, O'Reilly was calling him a
"fascist." Subsequently, the religious broadcaster Pat Robertson
called him "absurd." The next day, the death threats started
rolling in.

"They turned them in to the U.S. marshals, and the marshals
said, immediately, that they were going to put me under twenty-
four-hour protection," Jones says. The marshals set up a command post at his house. One of them went out with Jones's wife
when she walked their dog. "I figured if I ever got a threat, it
would be because I sentenced a crack dealer," Jones said.

Gradually, the furor died down. In January, however, the ul-
traconservative activist Phyllis Schlafly wrote a syndicated col-
umn in which she pointed out how vital evangelical voters had
been to the election of George W. Bush, and Bush had appointed
Jones, and Jones had stabbed the evangelical community in the
back. However, the notion that he owed his allegiance to some
political team got Jones angry enough to speak out. "I thought,
'Enough,'" he says. "I started to talk about exactly how judges
decide cases. I wanted to pivot off that and talk about my experiences, and the experiences of other judges, with cases like
this.

"In my view, the punditry—and to some extent, the mainstream press is responsible, too—has been responsible for dumb-
ing down people about how our political system works and, in
particular, in my case, how the judicial branch works.

"These are purely political creatures who don't understand
what Article Three of the Constitution says. If you poll the
United States today, you find that over forty percent, sometimes
over fifty percent, of the people in the United States believe in
creationism and not evolution. And they think that creationism

should be taught alongside, or even supplant, evolution in the public schools. So they don't understand why this federal judge in Pennsylvania, in my case, won't get with the program and bend to the popular will.

"Well, that's not the way the Framers designed the judiciary. We are supposed to be a bulwark against the popular will at a given time and responsible to the Constitution and to the law. But, boy, that's lost. People should get that."

Six months later, browsing in a bookstore, Jones came upon *Godless,* the most recent work by the right-wing polemicist Ann Coulter, whose gifts as an evolutionary biologist had been fairly well disguised heretofore. Coulter parroted much of the ID evidence that had been left in tatters during the trial; compared Jones to Joseph Wilson, the former ambassador whose criticism of the intelligence leading up to the Iraq War drew the ire of the Bush administration; and concluded that all you needed to know about Jones's intellect was that Tom Ridge had been his mentor. All of which made even less sense than the case for ID. "An 'activist judge.' That term is so misused," Jones says. "It's misused to the extent it's become useless. You know what it means? It means a judge that you disagree with. It doesn't mean anything else besides that. If I don't agree with a judge's decision, then he's an activist judge. It's ludicrous."

Like so much of the blasted landscape of Idiot America, the Dover trial was a war on expertise, and Judge Jones was the last expert standing. Pastor Mummert had laid out the shape of the battlefield early on, when he described Dover as besieged by its intelligent and educated elements. The people to be most distrusted were those who actually knew what they were talking about. This is how people get elected while claiming not to be politicians. This is how, through the new mass media technologies best exemplified by the successful know-nothingism of talk radio, everyone is an expert, if they can move units or budge the needle. Everyone is a historian, or a preacher, or a scientist, or a political sage. Why should anyone pay Sean Hannity, an NYU dropout, a dime to talk about stem-cell research?

Why not ask the guy who fixes your car?

Why not the guy on the next bar stool?

Why not you?

Of course, if everyone is an expert, then nobody is. The worst thing you can be in a society where everybody is an expert is, well, an actual expert.

It used to be that parents wanted their kids to be smarter than they were. It used to be that, when we had outbursts of primitive enthusiasms, as in the Scopes trial, we treated them as understandable interruptions in the relentless march of the American mind. It used to be that people scrapped and clawed their way up so that they could send their kids to Ivy League schools. Now so many of those children have emerged from the Ivy League as newly minted conservative friends of the soil, brimming with ersatz proletarian outrage and railing on behalf of the rubes in places like Dover against the kind of expertise produced in—wait for it—the Ivy League.

The founders wanted a nation of educated people: this, they believed, was essential to self-government. Some of the most heated arguments among them involved who would make up the educated elite. High Federalists like John Adams thought the elite should be exclusive and uncomfortably Anglophiliac in its attachment to the upper classes. The old democrats—most notably, Jefferson and Madison—suspected that the educated elite might just be everyone, although neither of these two plantation masters was completely convinced. What none of the founders believed was that the elite should be everyone and no one at the same time.

Three intermingled schools of idiocy are produced by this kind of society. All have proud histories as American phenomena, but all have been cheapened by their insistence on material success in their most unalloyed forms. (For example, intelligent design would have been perfectly unremarkable as a fringe religious theory. It became intolerable when it insisted on its commercial validity as actual science.) Political idiocy is best represented on the AM radio dial and on those evening cable television news programs, the booking philosophies of which seem to differ little from those once employed by soup kitchens on the Bowery. How much more interesting would Ann Coulter be if, instead of sprawling on the cover of *Time,* she was fighting to be heard in front of small, fervent audiences in rural Missouri? Coulter fumed for weeks after she was dismissed as a columnist by *USA Today.* If your biggest public gripe is that you got canned from that blob of mayonnaise, you have no right to stand in the company of Ignatius Donnelly. The Prince of Cranks was an American, dammit, and not an idiot. He never would've taken the job with *USA Today* in the first place. The man had his pride.

Commercial idiocy is the mechanism through which political idiocy (among other things) thrives, the mechanism through which the authentic revolution fostered by WLAC was diluted and homogenized into profitable syndicated outrage. Religious idiocy, formidable on its own, also functions as a baptismal font for political and commercial idiocy. Gussy up your extremist politics, or your bunco museum in which dinosaurs wear saddles, with the Gospels, and you can paint anyone who suggests that your goods are ridiculous a member of the intelligent, educated segment of the population, come to discomfit the faith-based folks.

Thus, it is considered impolite to point out, as Judge Jones did, that millions of Americans are paying millions of dollars to be willingly taken in by obvious hooey, such as books in which the loving Savior comes back to earth for his glorious premillennial encore as someone sprung full-blown from the mind of Stan Lee; or that the fringe interpretation of Scripture on which the books are based dates back only as far as the Taft administration.

American secular eccentrics once stood as proudly outside the world as any insular religious community did, rendering to God what is his, and rendering to Caesar not at all. Which made it all the more disappointing that the fight over intelligent design in Dover ever made it to the courthouse at all. And even more disappointing that it didn't end there. In the spring of 2008, a movie called *Expelled: No Intelligence Allowed* was released. Yet another defense of ID, this was a vanity project by Ben Stein, an economist who'd also been a speechwriter for Richard Nixon, a freelance pundit, a movie extra, a game-show host, and the spokesman for a popular brand of eye drops. Now that he had come to pitch intelligent design, Stein's career arc could safely be said to have gone from hogwash to eyewash and all the way back again.

The movie had two themes. It contended that scientists who believed in ID were being crushed by the academic establishment. (Stein's examples were fairly threadbare. It's easier to believe in ID than it is to believe that godless secularists have taken things over at places like Baylor and Iowa State.) However, the movie's second basic theme is startling and disturbing. Stein argues, seriously, that Darwinism led to the depredations of the Nazis. In a moment that seemed drawn from early Monty Python, Stein visits the place where the Nazis perfected their methods of genocide and then visits Darwin's house. The sequence ends with Stein staring balefully at a statue of Darwin. In an interview with a Christian radio network, Stein said: "When I saw that man . . . talking about how great science was, I was thinking to myself that the last time any of my relatives saw scientists telling them what to do, they were telling them to go to the showers and get gassed. . . . That was horrifying beyond words. . . . That's where science leads you.

"Love of God and compassion and empathy leads you to a truly glorious place and science leads you to killing people."

Science leads you to killing people.

Crazy history had been mustered to the defense of lunatic science. In the years since the end of World War II, none of Stein's relatives apparently ever rode a subway, or took a flu shot, or watched men walk on the moon. However, in an increasingly vicarious public discourse, if Jonah Goldberg can make money calling Woodrow Wilson a fascist, it was relatively simple for Ben Stein to drop the gangplank of H.M.S. *Beagle* at the gates of Auschwitz. This line—that science leads somewhat inevitably to inhumanity—was adopted sub rosa by conservative politicians who wanted to keep ID alive as a political weapon regardless of its transparent worthlessness as actual science. Stein did nothing less than confirm every word in Judge Jones's decision. He brought ID back to its creationist roots. He demonstrated that it is always and primarily a moral and religious concept.

After all, creationism and its spawn are hardly the only profitable alternative notions of how life on earth came to be. Ignatius Donnelly had his own ideas on the subject. The writer and historian Peter Bowler points out that both Immanuel Velikovsky and, later, Erich von Däniken proposed outré notions about life's origins so popular that they persist to this day. (The History Channel regularly runs programs based on von Däniken's ideas about the prehistoric influence of extraterrestrials on the development of human life. It should be noted here that, yes, sooner or later, these theories do bring you around to the Masons again.) Velikovsky and von Däniken shared as deep a distrust of conventional scientific expertise as exists among the creationists. However, their distrust was based on their eccentric interpretation of prehistory, and it was always purely secular.

But there is no ongoing fight in local school boards to "teach the controversy" about how space aliens built the pyramids. "Something more is at work here," writes Bowler, "and that something must be explained in terms of religious fundamentalism's offer of an alternative, not just to science, but to the whole direction of modern life. . . . Creationism works because so many people see their commitment to the Bible as both a source of salvation and a way of preserving traditional American values. This is why the biblical literalism of . . . creationism has become a dominant force in American society without undermining support for science as a practical activity linked to technology and medicine." That's how Ben Stein can make a buck or two selling eye care products without inevitably becoming Dr. Mengele. It's how he can rely on the scientific breakthrough of radio to make his case that all science leads to the gas chamber.

Not long after the Dover trial, Pastor Mummert spoke about what he'd said at its outset. He spoke softly and gently, but he did not back down an inch. "It seems to me," he said, "that it's the educated segment of society that reads the books and gets the new ideas, and that's the basis of the culture wars that we have going on now.

"I'm not anti-science, you know. I have one son who's a civil engineer."

Pastor Mummert came to preach in the southern part of Pennsylvania, where the Mennonites and the Amish came and settled, and where the people of the Ephrata Community slept on planks with blocks of wood for pillows. There, among the swelling hillsides and deep swales shivering with corn, these people came to escape in their own ways the perils of a sinful world. And they found a country that would welcome them, that had written its tolerance for their eccentricity into its founding documents, that was the best country ever devised to be a little off the beam. It might look askance at them, or turn them rather tastelessly into tourist attractions, but it would allow them the blessed freedom of their insularity. The Amish were not faith-based people. They were far too serious for that. They rendered to God and to Caesar in the proper measure. They kept things in the right places.

* * *

IN Derby Line in Vermont, they put their public library on the ground floor of the old opera house, cleanly melding public information and public entertainment. Curiously, though, down the middle of the library runs the border between the United States and Canada, indicated by a black line running across the library floor. (The line was drawn in the 1970s, after a fire, in order to demarcate the respective responsibilities of American and Canadian insurance companies.) If you want to borrow a book, you go to the stacks in Stanstead, Quebec, to find it, and then back to Derby Line, Vermont, to check it out.

For decades, it was a point of civic pride for the people in both towns that they lived right atop one of the friendliest stretches of one of the friendliest borders in the world. People wandered down the tiny, shady backstreets of the place, passing back and forth between the two countries without ever really noticing. By 2007, though, the Gut had come to rule in the United States. Borders were now dangerous places, shadowy and perilously permeable at any moment by international terrorists or illegal immigrant gardeners, or both. "They're proud of their history," an official of the Royal Canadian Mounted Police told the *New York Times*. "But because of what happened on September 11, 2001, we cannot do nothing. We have to react when there's a threat." The border authorities in both countries moved quickly to restrict access along the side streets in Stanstead and Derby Line. As part of the plan, it was proposed that anyone parking a car outside the library on the Canadian side might well have to pass through a port of entry before walking up the front steps, which are on the American side.

Of course, all of this brought the media, which fit Derby Line and Stanstead into the ongoing market-tested, focus-group national narrative of terror, adorned with ominous logos, laden with dark brooding music, and pitched for six years by relentless anchorpeople wearing their looks of geopolitical concern and their flag pins. "It was okay," says Mary Roy, a librarian in Derby Line, of the town's sudden celebrity. "But it was sort of like, 'Can't you guys get together and get it once, because you're all asking the same questions?'

"That one night we were on the seven o'clock news, NBC there, Brian Williams and, probably at seven fifteen, we got a telephone call from a gentleman calling from Pennsylvania, totally irate that the government was going to not be strong on [border security in the library], and what could he do. Wasn't there a blog, or a citizen's advocacy group he could join. This was the most ridiculous thing he'd ever heard."

It has not been an easy decade for libraries. A national network of libraries had been operated for decades by the U.S. Environmental Protection Agency; the Bush administration closed it, destroying a number of documents in the process. The USA Patriot Act, passed in the immediate aftermath of the September

11 attacks by a terrified and docile Congress, allowed the FBI virtually untrammeled power to rummage through the records of library patrons. Some librarians resisted by destroying their records before the Feds could get to them. One librarian in Massachusetts threw two FBI agents out of the library and told them to come back with a warrant. John Ashcroft, who was then the U.S. attorney general, pooh-poohed the privacy concerns of the librarians, claiming that the Feds never used their new powers, but neglecting to mention that the same law that allowed the FBI to come snooping in the libraries also forbade the librarians from disclosing their visits. Libraries are well-ordered places, and there were too many people profiting too greatly from a disordered age for libraries to go unscathed.

Libraries are still good places to visit while you consider what's gone wrong in the country. They're one of the few places left that are free and open and, at the same time, reliably well-ordered. Fiction is on one set of shelves. Nonfiction is on another. Books on theology lean on one another. Nobody puts them on the shelf with the scientific volumes. Aquinas and Mendel are in different places. Ignatius Donnelly's work does not abut that of Percival Lowell or Edwin Hubble. And, if libraries sometimes seem to be evolving into Internet cafés, still, once you step away from the computers, a library is a good and steady place, where the knowledge you're looking for is in the same place it's always been.

Idiot America is a strange, disordered place. Everything is on the wrong shelves. The truth of something is defined by how many people will attest to it, and facts are defined by those people's fervency. Fiction and nonfiction are defined by how well they sell. The best sellers are on one shelf, cheek by jowl, whether what's contained in them is true or not. People wander blindly, following the Gut into dark corners and aisles that lead nowhere, confusing possibilities with threats, jumping at shadows, stumbling around. They trip over piles of fiction left strewn around the floor of the nonfiction aisles. They fall down. They land on other people, and those other people can get hurt.

Part III

✻

CONSEQUENCES

CHAPTER SEVEN

A Woman Dies on Beech Street

In *The Politics of Heaven: America in Fearful Times,* Earl Shorris argues that fundamentalist Protestantism—and, indeed, American religion in general—has been changed, well, fundamentally by embroiling itself in the pursuit of secular political power. "It has changed from a congregation or a conference into a faction," Shorris writes.

Defenders of republican government all the way back to Aristotle have mistrusted factions. Mr. Madison went out of his way to wave red flags, most vigorously in *Federalist* 10, in which he cautions that "the latent causes of faction are [thus] sown in every man, and we see them everywhere brought into different degrees of activity, according to the different circumstances of civil society. A zeal for different opinions concerning religion, concerning government, and many other points . . . have in turn divided mankind into parties, inflamed them with mutual animosity, and rendered them much more disposed to vex and oppress each other than to co-operate for the common good."

It is not an accident that Mr. Madison listed religion first among the sources of dangerous faction. He looked on religious activity in the political sphere the way most people would look on a cobra in the sock drawer. While listing the faults of the government established by the Articles of Confederation, he went out of his way to note the failure of that government to restrain—or, at the very least, to manage—the "enthusiasms" of the people. "When indeed Religion is kindled into enthusiasm," he wrote, "its force like that of other passions is increased by the sympathy of a multitude."

* * *

THE neighborhood's not stylish enough for strip malls. It's an exhausted stretch of low-slung buildings of weatherbeaten cinder block and scraggly lots carpeted in dust and fire ants, a noisy, greasy place where they fix things that are made out of iron. Deep in the line of machine shops, something large and heavy and metallic hits the cement floor with a mighty clang, and someone curses almost as loudly, and the sounds ring through the heat of the high afternoon. Until they get to the fence along the property, and there the clamor seems to dissipate within the boughs of the pine trees just inside the fence, as though it's been swallowed up in a cool and private atmosphere through which discordant sounds cannot travel, through which not even the heat seems to be able to pass.

There's a brook running through the place. You hear it before you see it. There are silk prayer flags hanging in the pine trees, rippling and flowing on the breezes that stir the wind chimes into song. Gentle sounds merge into a kind of stillness. Even the birds seem muted here. There are stone paths to walk on, and stone benches to sit on. People walk the stone paths, lost in thought or abandoned to memory, noticing or not noticing the brook, watching or not watching the prayer ribbons, hearing or not hearing the wind chimes. They talk in low voices. They pray quiet prayers. They nod to other people who have come to walk the paths, and exchange a word, if they've come to know each other. Inside the low brick buildings behind them, their relatives are gently dying. That is why people come to the Woodside Hospice. They are looking for a good death, a peaceful death, a cool and private atmosphere where they can live, fully, until they cannot live anymore, and where their loved ones can come and be with them, and can be alone for a moment, if need be.

"There is a good ending," explains Annie Santa-Maria, the director of inpatient and residence care at the hospice. She's a dark-eyed, fierce woman, the daughter of Cuban émigrés. "Hospice people come to believe that there is such a thing as a good day and that there is such a thing as peaceful closure, that death is a reality," she says.

"All of us are going to die. We live in a culture that would rather give you Botox, have a bacteria rather than look old and face your death. Most of our culture doesn't accept death, but we all know we're going to die of something, so better to leave the world with a sense of completion and dignity, and have some support and compassion, and not just people diagnosing you, and shooting you up.

"After a particularly tough death, they'll come out here and take a walk. That's the staff, the other residents, the families, everybody."

The hospice grounds are designed for walking meditation, after the ancient English tradition of pilgrim prayer. The prayer flags reflect a Tibetan custom. You write a letter, or a prayer, to your loved one who has passed, and you hang it from the tree to stir in the breeze, and the thoughts and prayers find their way to whatever afterlife there may or may not be. In the center of the garden is a small chapel with stained-glass windows that face all four points of the compass so that, depending on the time of day and the angle of the sun, the chapel is flooded with different kinds of light. It is a sacred spot, but not a sectarian one. It could be Christian or Jewish, Muslim or Buddhist, Hindu or Wiccan. There's nothing here that suggests that there is a right answer to the biggest question of all. Just that the question is worthy of contemplation. "Depending on the time of day, the light changes in the chapel," Annie says. "There's a different kind of feeling in this place."

The main building of the hospice is divided by corridors off a main lobby, and the corridors are given street names. On March 31, 2005, in a room off Beech Street, a woman died after a long illness. A service was held for her in the little chapel along the stone path. The entire staff turned out. So did the woman's husband. Her parents did not come. Hers had not been a quiet death. The clamor had gotten through the fence, and nobody at Woodside ever was the same again.

"Over there," Annie Santa-Maria says, as an elderly couple pass along the stone path, "that's where the guy got over the fence, and the narcotics cops—we had off-duty narcotics cops patrolling the grounds at night—and over there's where they grabbed him."

She points past the pine trees and over the fence, toward one of the wide dusty lots across the street. That's where they all had been—the crowds with their bloody signs and their empty crosses, and their useless, vain cups of water; the cops and the crazy television monks. At the end was the field where the television trucks had parked, their tall transmitters spiraling toward the sky, the electronic Golgotha at the end of a vicarious Media Dolorosa that began outside her office where, early one evening,

two priests had nearly gotten into a fistfight. She'd have broken it up, she says, but there was a federal marshal standing in
her way.

"Your business," Annie Santa-Maria says to a curious visit-
ing journalist, her eyes flashing, and, for a moment, the quiet in
the little grove seems to have some heft behind it. "Let me tell
you about your business."

* * *

IN 1961, Rafael and Lillian Santa-Maria were trying to find
their way out from under Fidel Castro. Rafael was a neurosur-
geon, one of the few remaining in Havana, so he was watched
quite closely by government agents. He had trained in the
United States, and his family had roots there going back to the
antebellum South, where some of his ancestors had built a plantation that they had lost because they had insisted on giving
their slaves property of their own. Rafael and Lillian slipped
their children out of the country a few at a time, shipping them
off to live with uncles and aunts who'd already emigrated. The
last to leave were the two youngest, including Annie. "We were
divided," she recalls. "Myself and my brother, we stayed with
my dad so the government wouldn't know."

Finally, one day, Rafael was allowed to attend a medical conference in the United States. He was allowed to leave Cuba as
long as he brought along only $200 and a single suitcase. Lil-
lian left the door of their house open, knowing that they would
never be back. The family never learned what became of the rest
of their belongings.

The Santa-Marias settled in Ohio; Rafael took a job with the
Veterans Administration, which developed a dire need for neu-
rologists as the war in Vietnam ramped up. Eventually, he went

into private practice. Annie felt herself drifting into health care as well. She earned a degree from Miami University in Ohio. She hated the northern winters, though, so she moved in with her sister near Tampa and got a master's degree in social work from the University of South Florida.

It was the early 1980s, when the AIDS epidemic was beginning to reach flood tide. Much about the disease was still a mystery. AIDS put almost every hot-button issue into play all at once. It attacked gay men most conspicuously. It was a plague for the Gut, engaging unreasoning fear and apocalyptic religious fervor to feed off each other. "God is not mocked," the Reverend Jerry Falwell thundered at his television congregation, intimating that the disease was God's curse on a sinful population. Political calculation and religious judgmentalism became so thoroughly mixed that there were seventy thousand cases of AIDS in the United States before then-President Ronald Reagan said the name of the disease in public. In 1989, after Reagan had left office, Surgeon General C. Everett Koop, utterly fed up with theocratic sniping behind his back on this and other issues, simply quit in disgust. (At one point, Koop had been expressly forbidden from mentioning AIDS in public, an odd directive to hang on the nation's doctor.) "I am the nation's Surgeon General," Koop said after leaving his post. "I am not the nation's chaplain."

The reaction to AIDS was mindless and visceral. Annie watched as the unreasoning national hysteria broke out. Nursing homes rejected AIDS patients. Health-care providers refused to care for them, coroners refused to autopsy their bodies, and undertakers refused to bury them. This abandonment of the dead and dying gave new momentum to the hospice movement; AIDS patients had a 100 percent chance of dying from their disease. The community of the disease began to fend for itself, building a supportive infrastructure almost from scratch.

"In '81 and '82," Santa-Maria recalls, "we just knew of the gay men. It wasn't really until the mid- to late eighties where they started diagnosing Haitians and so on. So there were no services, so we were scrambling to put the services together,

"I was a volunteer at first, and we started at a local church, which has a large gay population. We started the services and then we started an AIDS coalition."

One of the coalition's biggest problems was to find places that would accept AIDS patients. Woodside was one of the few places that would take in AIDS patients. Annie went to the Centers for Disease Control in Atlanta to learn which dangers were real and which were imaginary. She came back armed with what she believed to be firm medical facts. It didn't matter. Even at Woodside, there were nurses whose husbands didn't want them working in a building with AIDS patients, let alone working with the patients themselves.

"That was the fear," she recalls. "I mean, if you're going to help people, help them. We had regular staff meetings for that."

The whole thing baffled Annie. Some of what she was hearing from the government and seeing in the media, and hearing from her friends and even from medical professionals, didn't seem to have anything to do with the reality of the disease with which she worked. Yet those things affected her work as surely as that reality did. The situation reminded her a little of the way things had worked in Cuba, where the government would tell you something that you knew from your own experience could not possibly be true, yet people seemed willing to believe that it was, and to act upon that belief, until the manufactured reality displaced the actual one. She felt she was working in parallel worlds. There was the world of the disease, and of the people who had it; and then there was another world, in which every-thing was a symbol and in which her patients stood for something. That second world orbited close by and caused the world of the disease always to wobble a little perilously in its orbit.

Eventually, in 1994, Annie went to work full-time at Woodside. She left briefly to work at another hospice but came back in a matter of months. Right about that time, a man named John Pecarek submitted a report to a Florida court. Pecarek had been appointed guardian ad litem to look after the interests of Terri Schiavo, a woman who'd suffered cardiac arrest on February 25, 1990, and who, having never regained consciousness, had been provided food and water ever since by means of a percutaneous endoscopic gastrostomy (PEG) tube.

Over the next three years, relations had deteriorated between Robert and Mary Schindler, the woman's parents, and Michael Schiavo, her husband, who had been appointed his wife's guardian three months after she was first hospitalized. In two separate malpractice suits, Terri Schiavo and her family had won well over $1 million. Shortly after the second of these awards, the relationship between Michael Schiavo and the Schindlers had broken down entirely. In 1994, the parents had tried to have Michael removed as guardian. Pecarek's report shot down their motion. Michael Schiavo, it said, had acted "appropriately and attentatively [sic]" toward his desperately ill wife. In 1998, he moved her into the Woodside Hospice. In May of that year, citing what he said had been the express wishes of his wife, Michael Schiavo petitioned a court to have his wife's feeding tube removed so that she could die in peace. Her parents opposed the motion.

The case already had a life beyond the hospice. In 1990, a similar case involving a woman named Nancy Cruzan had galvanized religious conservatives, but they had lacked the media savvy and technological ability to create the political momentum to seriously exploit it. The Schiavo case was different. The right had the means to make its case, and many people were more than willing to listen.

"Unlike in 1990," wrote Damon Linker in *The Theocons,* his memoir of his career inside the religious right, "opponents of the right-to-die now had talk radio and cable news—not to mention a sympathetic president and Congress—on their side to counter the indifference of the mainstream media to their cause."

In 2001, Annie Santa-Maria had been appointed director of inpatient and residence care at the hospice. She walked into the job with her eyes open. One of her duties was to mediate disputes among family concerning a patient that was dying. People argued about money, about the disposition of the body. She felt something familiar in the Schiavo case. Over the intervening year, something was stirring that she remembered from her experience during the early days of the AIDS epidemic. Something was being fashioned out of this case. That other world was close by again, and her world was beginning to wobble in its regular orbit.

"When Terri came, we thought, 'Well, okay, it's going to be a couple of weeks, then we'll get her admitted, and then the judge will assign the date of when actually to remove the tube,'" Annie tells me. "We thought it was just going to be a matter of a few weeks, of getting it on the court docket—that's what Mr. Schiavo expected, and that's certainly what we expected. Well, their attorneys kept throwing out allegations, and that one gets dismissed, so, 'Well, let's file another one.' We had no idea that this was going to be years.

"What's stunning, and what was never really reinforced in the media, was that this happens every day, hundreds of times a day, in each county in every state of this land. People remove a ventilator. People remove a feeding tube. But in this case, people had something new every few months. There was a new allegation. There was a legal proceeding for something wrong with her care that they kept bringing. They had to bring evidence, and then that evidence was dismissed because there really was no evidence, and then it was 'Okay, let's start with the next one.' And they went through many attorneys to do this, to either accuse Michael of being abusive or accuse us of not doing our jobs. They tried every which way to do that. And then when that stopped working, what they did was try the case in the public, you know? That's when the right wing got involved."

On April 24, 2001, after a Florida appellate court upheld an order by Circuit Judge George Greer, the PEG tube was removed from Terri Schiavo. People inside the hospice noticed that a few people with candles had gathered on the other side of the road. Two days later, another court, acting on a motion filed by the Schindlers, ordered that the tube be reinserted. A television truck from CNN arrived shortly thereafter. It was big and boxy and it parked in the dusty lot down across the street from the Cross Bayou Elementary School. More people gathered. More television trucks arrived. The people in the row of machine shops made some money renting space to the media. What Annie Santa-Maria now calls the siege had begun.

* * *

ONE night at the height of the siege, Mike Bell was driving home from the office. It was late and he was tired. He had spent the day trying to coordinate daily life at Woodside, one of several hospices he supervised as director of the Hospice of the Florida Suncoast. By the beginning of 2005, there were checkpoints several blocks away at either end of 102nd Street. You showed your ID and the police checked it against a list provided by the hospice of who was supposed to work that day. Anyone wishing to visit a resident had to notify the hospice in advance so the police could be notified.

"You had to clear that last checkpoint, right before the property, to be cleared," Bell explains. There already had been several attempts—one by someone posing as a produce deliveryman—to smuggle a camera into Terri Schiavo's room. "Once you got inside, it stayed pretty sheltered."

Even past the checkpoints, the hospice workers at Woodside now were running a gauntlet made up of camera crews, radio hosts, ambitious pundits, print reporters, angry monks, people waving crosses, and Jesse Jackson. A group of students from Ohio State came to Tampa over spring break, not to party, but to protest. A man sent his twelve-year-old up the driveway with a cup of water to give Terri. Given her condition, it would have drowned her. It turned out the father was a convicted pedophile from another state and had failed to register with the Florida authorities when he'd arrived to protest outside the hospice. His kid got arrested for trespassing. He didn't. There were police snipers on the roof of the elementary school. One day a hospice cook walking to work was called a Nazi.

At his office, Mike Bell got a steady stream of reports. He heard about the bomb threats, and about one phone call that was traced to Texas and how the FBI had made it to the guy's door almost as soon as he'd hung up the phone. Bell also had to monitor all the cable networks to see what was going on in the world beyond 102nd Street, because he knew that, as soon as something happened in a courtroom, or someone got up in a legislature and made a speech, the impact around the checkpoints would be nearly immediate, as though everyone involved in this case were suddenly standing on the same great fault line.

"What was amazing," says Bell, "was the choreography of it. We would just be learning of the next development and, here we are, the care providers, and we would get a fax or an e-mail, or a phone call and, within two seconds, there would be someone out front from Channel 8 or Channel 10, telling us that there's a new group and this is what their signs say, and it was just a mobilization.

"The thing we kept saying was that we respect your rights to your strongly held beliefs, but we ask that you also try and respect the fact that there are seventy-one other people on a very personal and private journey inside this place, not to mention these other people, coming and going, just doing their job, volunteering, the cook in the kitchen, and they have nothing to do with these decisions."

There was no relief for Bell. His wife's best friend lived next door to Michael Schiavo. Sometimes, when the friend's children were coming home from school, they had to get off the bus up the block so as to avoid the storm of picketers on the sidewalk, calling the besieged husband a murderer. Bell's wife told him that her friend had organized an escape route for Schiavo in case the crowd tried to take his house. Her friend had removed a panel from the fence that separated their properties. If he needed to, Schiavo could slip through the fence, sneak into the neighbor's garage, and escape in a car that had been secreted there for the purpose.

One night, exhausted from another day of the siege, another day of being called a Nazi and an angel of death, Mike Bell drove home in his car, the one whose Florida license plate read "Hospice—Every Day's a Gift." The main roads were clogged with traffic, so he took his usual alternate route, zigzagging along back roads through residential neighborhoods.

"It was one of those days where, in the e-mail, we were all being condemned to hell, and I'm driving home, and this car is just a little too close, and it just seemed to be doing it the whole way. For some reason, at a traffic light, it just very vividly in my mind went, 'I have a hospice license plate.' And it was crazy, I thought, 'They used to bomb abortion clinics, you know, and if they think we have a side in this, and they're out to get us because we're the angels of death—' And it just struck me, and I didn't like it, and I didn't stay in that place. But I was very aware that everywhere I went [my car] said, 'Hospice,' and that I couldn't, even for a minute, turn that off."

It galled them all—Mike Bell and Louise Cleary, who ran the hospice's media relations, and especially Annie Santa-Maria—to see their work being fashioned simultaneously into a weapon of political advantage and an engine of media frenzy. It had become plain that the least important factor in all of this was the health and well-being of Terri Schiavo. There were political and religious agendas. There was apparently a bottomless national desire for a televised freak show. There were advantages to be gained, and money to be made, in the fashioning of "hospice" into the kind of buzzword that is central to the vocabulary of a lunatic national dialogue. In such a dialogue, there is no debate, because debate admits at least the possibility of eventual synthesis between the opposing positions. The manufacture of a buzzword requires the reckless unleashing of a noisy public frenzy that does not so much defeat the opposition as simply exhaust it. There is no more debate present at those times than exists between a rock and a window.

Nobody knew better than did the people inside the hospice the delicate and painful questions that revolve around end-of-life issues. They knew the debate. They'd seen the debate in the eyes of the people who came every day to say good-bye, the people who came up to them now and wondered what would happen to their loved ones, what with hospice being compared daily on national television to Auschwitz. Those people wept with the concern that Woodside would be closed. The real debate was in all the families, grouped in knots in the hallways, talking in low voices, sometimes fiercely, about the decisions that had to be made. The debate was in the people taking long walks out back along the stone paths, in a deep and silent place within them where the murmur of the brook and the music of the wind chimes did not reach. The quiet moments were the real debate, when the room grew still and breathless. Bringing peace to those moments was what hospice was about.

They knew the debate and they knew that what was going on around them in the glare of the lights was not the debate. Instead, it was something that reduced the debate to the counterfeit currency of a performance argument. They knew—oh, God, how they knew—that a lot of the people across the street wouldn't last long doing the kind of work they did every day inside the hospice.

Yet those people were believed. The louder they yelled, the wilder their claims, and the more brutal their rhetoric, the more the outside world seemed to believe them. The people inside the hospice knew the truth, but truth was different now. Truth also was anything anyone was willing to say on television. Truth also depended on how fervently you performed for the cameras, how loudly you were willing to pray, how many droplets of blood you painted on your sign, and how big your papier-mâché spoon was. Enough people believed and were willing to act fervently on behalf of those beliefs, so those beliefs must be as true as any others. The Great Premises of Idiot America were all in play.

Events began to run in a pattern. A court would rule in favor of Michael Schiavo. The Schindlers would appeal. There would be a delay. The appeal would be denied. The Schindlers would file another motion. Another court would rule. The Schindlers would appeal. Some legislature would get involved.

The crowd across the street would grow. The TV lights would grow brighter. At every juncture, there would be new characters introduced into the ongoing drama. A judge to be vilified. A bold legislator with wet eyes and a golden tongue, channeling the thoughts of a woman whose brain was dissolving. The tube would be removed. The tube would be replaced. Someone inside the hospice would have to do it.

On October 21, 2003, at the encouragement of Governor Jeb Bush, the Florida state legislature passed "Terri's Law," a measure specifically giving Bush the unilateral power to replace Terri Schiavo's feeding tube, which had been removed, for the second time during the endless litigation, six days earlier. The law was nakedly, almost hilariously, unconstitutional, in part because it directly contradicted a law the legislature had passed during a less frenzied time several years earlier.

It seemed to Annie Santa-Maria that she had become hostage to a situation detached from any familiar reality. She knew the issues involved in the actual debate, knew them backward and forward. Hell, she'd helped develop the procedures going all the way back to her volunteer days with AIDS patients. But, now, in this one case, it seemed that her life and her work were following a script written by someone else. This was the way she remembered living in Cuba.

"I was watching this"—Annie laughs—"and I'm thinking, 'Surely, they're not going to pass this. They're going to overturn the self-determination act they passed years ago.' And they did. They created a law that was so narrow, that was just for this case, that it was unconstitutional. And when that didn't work, they went to the Florida Supreme Court, and then to the U.S. Supreme Court.

"When they went to the [U.S.] Supreme Court, and they needed other attorneys to help write the briefs, none of the local attorneys would work with Michael Schiavo. So they were forced to go to the ACLU because the president had so much power, and his brother, the governor, had so much power, that the lawyers were afraid it was going to kill their practice if they touched it because this was a political firebomb to promote the Republican and the Christian agenda that the president and his brother had and nobody wanted to get in the middle of that and ruin their career over that."

Annie argued with the lawyers. They were throwing away their own rights to self-determination because they were afraid of politicians and preachers. "I told them, 'Look, you want to be tied to technology against your will because somebody's afraid that their religious views will be damaged?' "

Annie began to monitor the newscasts, as Mike Bell did, trying to discern the outline of the next day's story. She stopped concerning herself with whether the story might have anything to do with what actually was going on in the hospice. "We had things happen here and then the [Schindler] family would come out and tell us something totally different than what had happened and the press would run with it. And whatever story they created that night, that's how we knew what to prepare for the next day. It was always based on whether or not they thought they were doing well. And when they knew the media would be here, there would be more of them doing the carnival circus. You know, it was time for their press releases and their messages of hate and disruption, and yelling at the staff as they drove by, and holding out signs, and calling them murderers, and asking us to repent and not work for hospice, and 'You don't have to do this.' "

Annie turned down police protection, although she'd gotten death threats. "They offered me police, but I didn't need it," she says. "There were so many other people they wanted to kill."

* * *

"**ANNIE?**" says Captain Mike Haworth. "Annie rocks."

It was Haworth's job throughout the siege to coordinate security in the neighborhood of the hospice on behalf of the Pinellas Park Police. It was Haworth whose men had busted the fake deliveryman who'd been bribed to smuggle in a camera. It was Haworth who'd have to tell Jesse Jackson's driver that there was no room nearby in which to park the reverend's limousine. Shortly thereafter, while Jackson was giving a press conference down the block, a man sprinted across the street and made it all the way up to the driveway of the hospice. He was going to rescue Terri Schiavo from the people inside who were killing her.

"He made it right to about here, where he engaged one of my canine officers," says Haworth, pointing to a spot not far from the front doors. "The good news for him was that my canine officer had left his canine in the cruiser. The bad news was that the officer deployed his Taser. And that was our only Tasing out there."

Haworth is a native Floridian, a brawny serious man with a signifying crew cut and a steady gaze. He is the kind of cop who asks you politely to do something, and is willing to do so repeatedly, always politely, but with something formidable there in reserve. The son of a police chief in Dunedin, Haworth went away to Texas for college and did five years in the Air Force before returning to Florida, where he worked his way up through the ranks at the Pinellas Park department from traffic officer, through narcotics, until he was placed in charge of the department's SWAT team. He and his men were sent to the neighborhood around the hospice on three lengthy deployments.

"It was always about Michael, Terri, the legislators, the governor, the president," he says. "It was about everybody but us. We did not want to be the story. We wanted everything else to be the story."

From the start, Haworth was aware that his job was to be at least as much a diplomat as it was to be a policeman. Anything his police did they were going to be doing on national television. " 'Pleasant' is not the right word. But it was accommodating," he says. "We were very accommodating. I mean, my direction to my troops through my lieutenants was 'Look, they [the protestors] have a job to do. We have a job to do. Okay?' It's hot. It's miserable. It's nasty out here, you know? And we're all just waiting, literally, for this woman to pass away.

"From a legal standpoint, we did it in the beginning. We established that this is where we're going to allow you to protest. We're not going to allow you to be on the sidewalk. We're going to keep that clear because we've got a school down there."

Haworth's third deployment to the neighborhood came in March 2005. At the end of February, Pinellas-Pasco County Circuit Court Judge George Greer again had ordered the removal of Terri Schiavo's PEG tube. Absent a successful appeal, his order would go into effect on March 18.

(At this point, Greer had been the judicial point man on the case for over five years, consistently ruling in favor of Michael Schiavo and against his in-laws. Greer's rulings were just as consistently upheld in the state appeals courts. As a result, not only was Greer asked to leave his church but a North Carolina man offered to kill Greer for $50,000. The same man set the price on Michael Schiavo's head at five times that. The FBI arrested him.)

Around the hospice, and out on the police lines, there was a sense that the endgame had been reached. Haworth sensed a desperation among the demonstrators. "They would grasp onto anything," he recalls. "If Jesse Jackson came, maybe he could save the day. If there was a federal subpoena, maybe that could save the day. Maybe, if there was a piece of federal legislation that everybody flies back from [George W. Bush's ranch in] Crawford, Texas, to get done, that'll be it, you know? They kept waiting for it and, you know, our whole position was that she's in the dying process and we were there to keep the peace. That's what our job was." Haworth personally spent several hours on duty in Terri Schiavo's room on Beech Street.

"We always," he says, his voice catching just a bit, "had someone on her."

Haworth struggled for control as much as anyone else did against the heedless momentum of the events around them. The event of the thing seemed totally unstrung. After three years of seeing their children walk a gauntlet every morning, school administrators finally evacuated the Cross Bayou Elementary School. The last straw was a threat that came in through the FBI. A man had warned that he would take the school hostage and kill a child for every ten minutes that nourishment was withheld from Terri Schiavo. The decision to evacuate was made on Easter Sunday. To Marcia Stone, the principal at Cross Bayou, it felt like a surrender.

She'd come to education because being a stewardess had seemed too dangerous. Flying for National Airlines, Stone had broken her foot when the flight she was working had flown through a hurricane. A career in education had seemed like a safe and sane alternative. Now, she was being forced to abandon her school in the face of a threat that she was not allowed to communicate fully to her staff because of security concerns.

"That Saturday night, I sent out the message to my staff that I want you to trust me on this, that we must vacate the school," she recalls. "So, the next day, Easter Sunday, the staff met me here and I still couldn't give them any details even then." On Monday, Stone talked to the parents of her students, and she couldn't give them any details, either.

One thing that Haworth and Stone shared was affection for Michael Schiavo. "I like Mike a great deal," Haworth says. And Stone had a connection to the case because her son-in-law, Patrick Burke, had worked at Palm Gardens Nursing Home, the first place Terri had been taken after her cardiac arrest. Burke had been the first physical therapist to work with her.

"Michael was just incredible, my son-in-law said," Stone explains. "My son-in-law said, 'I can save her,' you know, with the therapy. Eventually, he worked through the reality of 'She's never going to get any better,' and Patrick said that this was the first real incident where he realized, no matter what he did, no matter what anyone did, that there was brain death."

All of these people—Haworth, and Stone, and the people working at Woodside—watched in amazement as the detachment of the coverage from the actual facts reached a mad crescendo. Hospice officials, forbidden by law to discuss the specifics of the case, watched medical professionals with only the most tangential connection to the case trotted out to convince the nation that Terri Schiavo could walk and talk and was demanding to be freed from her captors. They watched as people accused them of letting Terri's lips crack and bleed, as though there weren't an entire protocol for mouth care for people in her situation, and as though the hospice staff weren't following it just as they followed it for every patient. Some of the families of the other residents wanted them to respond, angrily and publicly, to defend hospice care against the slanders of people who didn't care what damage they did. They could not.

"There were people in our community who got a little mad

at us," says Louise Cleary, the hospice's spokesperson. "They wanted us to come out stronger. They wanted us to defend ourselves. They wanted us to say, you know, 'We're the good guys.' But we really did stick to the story that this is not our story to tell, that we just happened to be the hospice where Terri was."

Almost everyone involved inside the hospice was frustrated beyond endurance. Elizabeth Kirkman, whose volunteer work had been so extensive that she had been congratulated personally by both presidents Bush and by Governor Jeb Bush, wrote the governor a scathing letter condemning his meddling. "It was unsettling to us," Elizabeth said. She and her husband went out of their way to make sure their living wills were ironclad.

Annie Santa-Maria had to work harder than most to keep from lashing out. "To have the staff here listen to the Schindler family lawyer, and the Schindler family out there, saying, 'Oh, Terri. We're going to have you home by Thanksgiving. You're going to be eating turkey with your friends and family,' " she recalls. "They would be saying they had these yuck-it-up conversations with someone who's not responding. We'd be aghast. She didn't say a word. She didn't move. She didn't blink. But nobody knows that. But that's what the country's hearing—that we're killing somebody who has limited dialogue ability. And none of it was true."

Ultimately, the *Columbia Journalism Review* published a study that concluded that "coverage of the Schiavo case [has] consistently skewed toward the emotional over the factual. . . . With its performance to date in the Schiavo case, the press is displaying a tell-tale tendency for tabloid-style exploitation in the guise of serious reporting." The Gut, faith-based as always, was in the saddle and driving events.

Bizarre, almost otherworldly slanders flew through the air. A nurse named Carla Sauer Iyer appeared on both Fox and CNN, claiming that Michael Schiavo had poisoned his wife with insulin. She also claimed she'd heard him shout, loudly, "When is the bitch going to die?" Neither network noted that Judge Greer had nearly laughed the woman out of his courtroom almost two years earlier. (On CNN, an anchor named Kyra Phillips breathlessly reported the complete canard that Iyer had come forward for the first time that day.) However, nobody frosted the people at the hospice more than did Sean Hannity of Fox News. "He's a peculiar piece of work," says Cleary. "He's not the kind of journalist who's interested much in the truth, let's say."

At one point, Hannity got caught on camera coaching some of his interviewees to be harsher in their assessment of Michael Schiavo. It was Hannity—along with Joe Scarborough of MSNBC—who brought to the nation the spectacular charlatanism of William Hammesfahr, a doctor who'd been one of many brought in to evaluate Terri Schiavo as part of the seemingly endless litigation over the previous five years. Hannity relentlessly pointed out that Hammesfahr had been "nominated for the Nobel Prize in medicine."

In fact, a Florida congressman once wrote a letter to the Nobel Committee for Physiology or Medicine on Hammesfahr's behalf. That's not how one gets nominated for a Nobel Prize. (If it were, Hannity could "nominate" himself in the category of distinguished letters.) Hammesfahr had told Judge Greer that he could rehabilitate Terri Schiavo. Judge Greer had rejected his findings outright and called him a self-promoter. Previously, he'd been only one of dozens of medical professionals who'd collided with the case, but now he suddenly became useful. He popped up in a number of media outlets, including the *Los Angeles Times* and on CBS. He argued that Terri could be rehabilitated. That she could be speaking within two years. The people working at the hospice gazed in angry fascination. None of them would have been surprised to see Hammesfahr on television claiming that, in no time at all, he could have Terri Schiavo playing linebacker for the Tampa Bay Buccaneers.

"How is it possible," Hannity would intone in meat-headed awe, "we're in this position if you have examined her. You were up for a Nobel Prize. This is mind-boggling to me." Hammesfahr was a television star, an actor in the drama. He had a role to play: presenter of the Other Side of the Argument, to whom fair-minded people were somehow obligated to pay heed, no matter what nonsense he spouted. No place was more fair-minded at that point than the Congress of the United States, which somehow managed to go out of its way to make everything infinitely worse.

"What is really frightening," says Elizabeth Kirkman, that once-beloved Point of Light for the Bush family, "is that we're so gullible that crazy people scare us, and they scare our politicians into foolish, foolish decisions. And that, to me, is just mind-boggling—that our politicians are such wusses that they are so swayed by this kind of thing."

* * *

JUDGE Greer's final order mandated that Terri's PEG tube be removed for good on March 18, 2005. On that evening, Annie Santa-Maria was in her office. A federal marshal was there with her. That afternoon, the U.S. House of Representatives had voted to subpoena Michael Schiavo and several doctors, some hospice personnel, and all the equipment being used to keep Terri Schiavo alive. It also subpoenaed Terri herself to come and give testimony. So the marshal stayed with Annie to make sure that she was there to receive her subpoena, and to take delivery of a subpoena demanding testimony from a woman Annie knew could no longer move or speak or think.

In anticipation of Terri's passing, Annie had contacted a local Catholic priest who was on call to deliver the last rites if necessary to the residents of the hospice. She was unaware that Terri's parents had contacted their own priest. The two men encountered each other in the lobby outside Annie's office. Voices were raised to an unholy volume. It looked very much as if a full-scale clerical hooley might ensue. Annie moved to break it up. The marshal blocked her way. He was sorry. She had to stay in her office. She couldn't go break up a fight between two priests because she had to stay there and wait for a subpoena to be served on a woman who was, for all practical purposes, dead. A few minutes later, the Schindlers were outside, telling the world that the hospice wouldn't let them send a priest to give Terri the last rites.

(Later, Annie tried to explain to her mother what had happened. "I said, 'Mother, that's just not true,'" Annie explains. " 'That woman had last rites many times over.' And my mother said, 'Why would a priest lie about that?' ")

The last-minute intervention by both the Congress and the president reflected the Schindler family's last throw of the dice. They'd lost, time and again, in the state courts. They wanted an act of Congress that would then be upheld in the federal system. Remarkably, and to the astonishment of everyone at Woodside, they got what they wanted. Senate Bill 686 was filed and debated and, improbably, passed into law on a resoundingly bipartisan basis, although the U.S. Senate bravely did so on a voice vote only.

The bill was not merely aimed at one woman in Florida. A memo that circulated on the floor of the Senate described the case as a "great political issue" for Republicans going forward. The bill was aimed at voters in Pennsylvania in 2006, where incumbent senator Rick Santorum, who'd shown up at the hospice to pray with the Schindlers, had a tough reelection fight, and at voters in Iowa who would caucus in 2008 to pick the next Republican nominee. For its Democratic supporters, the bill would serve to blunt future attacks on them from the same quarters, even though every poll consistently showed that the public overwhelmingly wanted the federal government to butt out of the case. To vote for the bill was a careful act of preemptive cowardice.

Senate Majority Leader William Frist of Tennessee was one of the people with serious designs on those Iowa Republicans in 2008. Frist was also a licensed physician and an accomplished cardiac surgeon. After viewing a carefully edited videotape provided by Terri's parents, Frist proceeded to diagnose her from fifteen hundred miles away. She was not in the persistent vegetative state that her doctors claimed. House Majority Leader Tom DeLay agreed: "Terri Schiavo is not brain-dead. She talks and she laughs, and she expresses happiness and discomfort."

March 20, 2005, was Palm Sunday, a fact noted so often on the floor of the House that Tom DeLay should have ridden to work on a donkey. Late that night, flying all the way back from Texas and interrupting a vacation for the first time in his presidency, President Bush signed what was now called, inevitably, the Palm Sunday Compromise. A great roar went up across the street from the hospice. The Schindlers hurried into federal court to apply for a federal order to replace the PEG and to move Terri to another facility.

Federal judge James Whittemore had gone to bed that Sunday night, but a little after three in the morning, his phone rang. His clerk was on the line and she was in tears. "I am so sorry," she told him. The Schindlers' last-chance lawsuit had landed in his court.

The case shook Whittemore so much that he declines to discuss it to this day—unlike Judge Jones, who will talk about the *Kitzmiller* intelligent design case to anyone who will listen. However, the two men shared a panel at a meeting of the American Bar Association that discussed the pressures of working high-pressure, high-visibility cases. Whittemore opened up to that panel about the longest three days of his life. The day they got the case, he and his staff worked all night. At about ten o'clock, somebody sent out for pizza. At that exact moment, Nancy Grace, a CNN legal commentator who combines the nuance of a sledgehammer with the social graces of a harpy, was raging at what she said was Whittemore's delay in ruling on the Schindlers' motion to have the PEG tube reinserted. What's keeping this judge? Grace wondered. He's probably out having a steak with his family.

On the fly, Whittemore and his staff were enveloped by a complex security system. They unplugged all their phones; Whittemore's secretary had gotten physically ill from the abuse. They secured the phones to the point that even Whittemore's mother's phone was routed to the federal marshal's office. Whittemore's sons were placed under protection. (A run-of-the-mill neighborhood arson in St. Petersburg turned into a federal case because it happened behind the house in which one of Whittemore's sons lived.) The person who cared for Whittemore's disabled daughter had to pass a full background check. "It does take its toll on you," Whittemore told the ABA panel.

These were not idle precautions. As mentioned earlier, a man had already been arrested for offering a bounty on Judge Greer. The media was aflame. Michael Savage called Democrats "an army of soulless ghouls," and the former White House aide and presidential candidate Pat Buchanan lumped the removal of the feeding tube with activities of German doctors in the 1930s. He called it a "crime against humanity."

The talk in more respectable quarters was little better. On

the floor of the Senate, Senator John Cornyn of Texas seemed to threaten federal judges with physical harm, and this in a year in which one federal judge, and the spouse of another, already had been killed. Other members of Congress talked darkly of defunding courts whose rulings they did not like.

For all the emotions swirling around him, Whittemore's ruling was simple and direct. The new law did not mandate a stay, so he was not prepared to grant one; and his court lacked jurisdiction in the matter. This ruling was affirmed on appeal. The U.S. Supreme Court refused to hear the case. At 9:05 A.M. on March 30, 2005, Terri Schiavo died.

"I can tell you it was a sacred time," Annie Santa-Maria recalls. "We had a really moving moment where all of the staff just said good-bye and thank you for the privilege of letting us help you." The head of the housekeeping staff came in and cleaned the room up personally. Hospice workers lit a candle. Outside in the hallway, thirty people lined up silently to watch the body go by.

An autopsy revealed that Terri Schiavo's brain had atrophied almost to the point of insignificance. It had been in that condition when the U.S. House of Representatives had subpoenaed her to testify as to how much she wanted to live. The autopsy showed no evidence of abuse by Michael Schiavo, or by anyone else, for example the staff of the Woodside Hospice. She didn't even have any bedsores.

The late Terri Schiavo had a brief afterlife as a political tool. The following April, at a conservative political conference entitled "Confronting the Judicial War on Faith," a reporter for *The Nation* heard one panelist refer to the removal of the PEG tube as "an act of terror in broad daylight aided and abetted by the police under the authority of the governor." Another participant cited a saying of Stalin's that, the speaker opined balefully, suited the situation: "No man, no problem." *The Nation*'s correspondent noted that Stalin coined the phrase as rationale for solving political problems with political murder.

Conservative commentators noisily charged that the memo describing the case as a political godsend to the GOP, which had so engaged the Senate, had been a piece of Democratic disinformation aimed at making the Republican majority look foolish. This conspiracy theory took flight, attaining the giddy heights of briefly being taken seriously in the *Washington Post*. Alas, an aide to Florida Republican senator Mel Martinez confessed that he'd written the memo. In the case of Terri Schiavo, the congressional majority hadn't needed the majority's help to look foolish. Bill Frist declined to run for reelection. His presidential hopes were stillborn. Tom DeLay departed the House under a federal indictment for corruption. In 2006, the voters handed the majority of both houses over to the Democrats.

The bonds forged in the siege are as strong as ever. Captain Mike Haworth and his officers regularly participate in charity fund-raisers—10K runs and the like—to benefit the hospice. Louise Cleary tries to interest the press in them. She now watches CNN only when she wants to watch it; doing so isn't part of the job anymore. Mike Bell had a bad moment when he was told that someone had put what they claimed was Terri Schiavo's PEG tube up for auction on eBay. He checked. The feeding tube was still in the sealed bag it was placed in the moment it came under congressional subpoena. Terri was going to go to Washington and explain how it worked.

The kids are back at school down the street at Cross Bayou Elementary, and Marcia Stone doesn't talk to the FBI anymore. The lots are empty and dusty in the high morning sun. No pundits walk the perimeter. There is no perimeter anymore. Back at work as a volunteer, Liz Kirkman doesn't have to stop at checkpoints anymore. She can walk up the driveway toward the

Woodside Hospice and nobody calls her a Nazi. There are no priests slugging it out in the lobby, and there's a new patient in the room down on Beech Street.

Annie Santa-Maria walks the stone paths out back in the meditation garden. She has been changed by what happened. Her devotion to her patients and their families remains unflagging. But she finds that her faith in her fellow citizens is not what it was. She has seen private suffering coined into public advantage, and she has seen the public, for all its pronounced disapproval, eat up the story as just another television program.

Like the rest of the country, Annie was riveted by the coverage of the massacre perpetrated by a young man named Seung-Hui Cho at Virginia Tech University. She sympathized with the families of the victims. She also sympathized with the other students who, confronted by cameras, tried to explain the inexplicable. She believed in their grief, but that was all she believed. She had lost something she'd brought from Cuba, something very much like faith.

"I knew, okay, that they're probably getting thirty or forty percent of the truth," she says. "The rest? We don't really know what's happening because we're only getting that little piece of the pie that somebody wants them to get.

"And I have to ask you, as a journalist, how do you live with that, in a profession that we're so blessed to have in this country, but you know the truth isn't in there. I don't feel vindicated. I still think the public at large is still very confused about what happened."

The heat of midday doesn't penetrate the trees. Neither does the grinding of the machine shops across the way. The clamor of Idiot America is gone, too, and all that's left is the murmuring of the water and the fluttering of the prayer ribbons. And the wind chimes ring like the songs of ghosts in the trees.

CHAPTER EIGHT

How We Look at the Sea

Mr. Madison, it seems, wanted us to be educated, so that we would not be so easily fooled. In 1810, in the annual message to Congress, he proposed what he called a national Seminary of Learning. "Whilst it is universally admitted that a well-instructed people alone can be permanently a free people," he told them, ". . . the additional instruction emanating from [the seminary] would contribute not less to strengthen the foundations, than to adorn the structure, of our free and happy system of government." Later, not long before his death, he wrote to the Kentucky legislator William Barry that "learned institutions . . . throw that light over the public mind which is the best security against crafty and dangerous encroachments on the public liberty. . . . They multiply the educated individuals from among whom the people may elect a due portion of their public agents of every description."

An educated people is a self-governing people, Madison believed. That was why he and Thomas Jefferson spent so much time developing the University of Virginia, Madison organizing the project after Jefferson's death. "They saw it as the nursery of the future leaders themselves, but also as training the teachers who could then teach the rest of the nation," Ralph Ketchum explains on his porch. "They would never have expected that self-government could work with an ignorant and inattentive citizenry. They would have been disappointed."

* * *

THE Chukchi Sea is a southern child of the Arctic Ocean. The great Pacific storms that barrel through the tropics and then swing north to devastate China and Japan keep coming, roiling and merciless, until they spend themselves in the Chukchi, battering against the hard barrier islands in the far northwest of Alaska. The storms roar themselves hoarse, having finally found a place as implacable as they are. This is where typhoons come to die.

Shishmaref is a village on one of those barrier islands, a flat little comma of land between the sea and a broad lagoon that runs eastward, toward the mountains. There are meadows along the banks of the lagoon where musk oxen roam in the summer. The Inupiaq people have lived on this island for longer than human memory can recall, hunting the oxen in the meadows, fishing in the lagoon, and, in winter, taking long, perilous journeys across the ice that formed on the Chukchi Sea in search of the walrus and the seals that the polar bears were also hunting. Once, hunting season began in the middle of October, when the sea froze, and it wouldn't end until the warm breezes of June broke up the thinning ice and swept it back out to sea.

"I remember that the season would be starting in October," says John Sinnok, a lifelong resident of Shishmaref. "The ship that brought supplies to the village for the winter would come in here in mid-October, leave them off, and then get out before it got frozen in for the winter."

The Inupiaq were already here in 1848, when the first whalers came, following the trail into the Arctic blazed by Thomas Welcome Roys, the master of a ship called *The Welcome,* based in Sag Harbor, New York. Roys had discovered a huge population of bowhead whales living in the Chukchi Sea, and word quickly spread from New York to the whaling centers of New Bedford and Nantucket in Massachusetts. Whalers were fond of the bowhead because it was a slow, docile beast, rich in baleen, far easier to kill and not nearly as deadly as the sperm whale. In addition, the Chukchi Sea formed a smaller hunting ground than the vast South Pacific. The bowheads there were virtually penned for slaughter between the Alaskan barrier islands on one side and the Siberian coast on the other. The whalemen flooded north. Many of the Inupiaq signed aboard the great fleets as what were called "ship's natives." The hunting was so good that hardly any bowhead whales are left today.

However, as safe as it was to stalk the bowhead, it was just as dangerous to sail the Chukchi Sea. The window for a successful hunt was a narrow one. The ships had to hit the killing grounds around the middle of July, because only then would the winter's ice have broken up enough to allow passage. They had only eight to ten weeks to hunt before the ice began to form again. Linger too long in the Arctic whaling grounds, and the merciless ice would trap your ship and, gradually, grind it to splinters.

Some whaling ships wintered in the Arctic at a place called Herschel Island, where a thriving, if rowdy, port city grew. (For a thousand-dollar fee paid to his ship's owners, a captain could have his wife and children join him on the island.) Most of the ships, though, made for San Francisco, where they would lay up for the winter.

Some did not get there. In 1871, thirty-three whaling ships, most of them from New Bedford, were trapped in the ice near Point Belcher at the end of August. The captains ordered their ships to be abandoned, leaving behind an estimated $1.6 million in goods, including an entire season's haul of whale oil and whalebone. All twelve hundred men, women, and children aboard the doomed ships survived after a harrowing journey across the wilderness. The ships were picked clean by the local Inupiaq before being demolished and sunk by the pressure of the ice.

The Chukchi Sea remained a perilous place for sailors even after the whaling industry died. In 1931, a Swedish cargo steamer called the *Baychimo* was trapped in the Arctic pack ice on October 1. For the next three decades, the abandoned *Baychimo* was a virtual ghost ship. It moved at the mercy of the ice. There were sightings of it in different places. The last place anyone saw it was in the Chukchi Sea, near Point Barrow, in 1968. It is now presumed, finally, to have sunk.

In his memoir of the doomed voyage, A. F. Jamieson, the *Baychimo*'s radio telegraph officer, recalled a moment earlier in the voyage when he'd scrambled up on deck to take his first look at the Arctic ice pack. According to Jamieson, he got his first look at solid Arctic ice on July 26.

"I was naturally very interested in seeing this for the first time," Jamieson wrote. "The captain took the ship right up to the pack, had a good look around, and decided there was nothing to be done except to drop anchor and wait. The ice was one solid mass, stretching from the shore as far out as we could see, with no leads in it of any description."

Shishmaref itself was spared the fate of the *Baychimo* and the

New Bedford whaling fleet by the permafrost that is fundamental to the island's geology. Underlying the beaches, the permafrost took the brunt of the dying typhoons. Later in the year, when the ice formed, the permafrost staved off its relentless, grinding power. The formation of the ice allowed the people of Shishmaref to go out on the sea and hunt. The permafrost guaranteed they would have a place to which they could return. Nowadays, though, the ice is late and soft. The permafrost is thawing. And Shishmaref is falling, bit by bit, into the Chukchi Sea.

The estimates are that Shishmaref has lost perhaps as much as three hundred feet of its coastline, half of that in the past decade. With nothing to slow them down, and nothing to dissipate their power, the storms that now rage against Shishmaref have already cost the town so many of its boats that the local economy may never recover. Houses have collapsed into the sea. A school playground has been washed away. And while the storms are catastrophic, even without them, day by day, Shishmaref continues to recede. The ice forms later and dissolves earlier, so the beaches are eroding away beneath the bluffs. There is no permafrost beneath the beaches to hold the land there. Little by little, Shishmaref is being devoured.

John Sinnok remembers great hills, up and down the coastline of the little island. They're all gone now. "We lost them all," he says. "When you're up here on the lagoon now, and you see people, you can recognize them right away. Back then, they were just little specks, because there was a bunch of hills here, then a lowland, then another bunch of hills. That's the way it was."

There is no question about the cause of Shishmaref's whittling away. Global climate change—specifically, what has come to be called global warming—is gradually devastating the Arctic. Alaska's mean temperature has risen five degrees in thirty years and the permafrost is receding everywhere. The Arctic Ocean's ice pack, which so impressed A. F. Jamieson even as it was swallowing his vessel, is shrinking about 10 percent a year, and the pace of that shrinkage is accelerating. In August 2007, scientists in the United States and Japan reported that the ice pack had shrunk that summer to the smallest size ever recorded and that, within twenty-five years, the earth might see the ice pack melt entirely one summer, an event that would have severe repercussions everywhere else in the world. A month later, a German team reported that the Arctic sea ice was 50 percent thinner than it had been in 2001. All over the Alaskan coast, small villages and larger towns are in peril. Point Hope nearly lost its airport's runway to a flood that overwhelmed its seawall. Further north, the city of Barrow has been pounded to the point where its status as a vital oil terminal is seriously threatened.

The people of Shishmaref talk about global warming the way they talk about fishing in the lagoon or hunting seals on the ice. They've lived by internal clocks attuned to the weather and the land, the sea and the ice. The old whalemen learned their ways from them. Now, something has knocked askew the calibrations developed over thousands of years. There is no hunt without the ice, and the ice is not where it should be when it should be there. The land is falling into the sea. A nomadic people came to this island longer ago than anyone can remember and they've been living here ever since. In a very few years, they will be refugees.

" 'Global warming' are new words for us in Shishmaref," says Luci Eningowuk, who has become something of a spokes-woman for this dying place. "We're used to getting spring, sum-mer, fall, and winter. And now this global warming has made our lives unpredictable. We don't know when it is going to be-come winter now."

The evening comes late in the Arctic. The sea goes gray in the dying light. Darker still, almost black against the slowly pearl-ing sky, gulls and geese wheel away inland toward the peace of the lagoon. The sound of the surf is steady and endless, not the thunder that comes when the big storms rage, but the steady dirge of mighty tides, pulling bits of the island away and never bringing them back. It is drowned out by a huge truck, trundling around a battered point, its wheels half in the surf, hauling stone northward to where they're building a seawall. From the cab of his steam shovel, Tom Lee watches the truck round the point, grumbling and splashing down the beach.

He's been there for two or three months, building and reinforcing the island's seawall. On the beach in front of him are piles of mashed asphalt and shattered concrete. These are portions of the earlier seawalls before the storms got them, before the ground beneath them got pulled away. They look like the machines of war left behind by a defeated army long ago.

"They tell us that this wall, this new one, might buy this place ten or fifteen years," Tom Lee says, leaning on the tread of his machine. "Hard to argue with the ocean, though." And, down all along the beach, the Chukchi Sea resounds in its remorseless pulsing power, unfrozen and unbound. It's the first week in November.

* * *

IN December 2007, not long before Christmas, Senator James Inhofe of Oklahoma issued a report declaring that "400 scientists" had announced that they had debunked the overwhelming scientific consensus regarding a human basis for the phenomenon of global warming. Upon closer inspection, the four hundred "scientists" Inhofe cited included a couple of local television weathermen, all consultant-bred and Dopplerized, one short evolutionary step up from the days when they got their forecasts from cat puppets and talking clams. Others were economists, and specialists in fields as distant from climatology as sociology is from astrophysics. Actual relevant expertise did not matter. "Scientists" were talking about other "scientists." The "debate" was all too confusing.

(Sometimes, you don't even need to be a full-time scientist, just somebody who writes about them. The novelist Michael Crichton wrote *State of Fear,* a thriller about bands of eco-terrorists bent on using the global warming "hoax" to capture the world. Inhofe invited Crichton to testify before Congress as an "expert" witness, and he was warmly received at, among other places, the White House. By those standards, poor Dan Brown should have gotten an audience with the pope.)

That global warming—shorthand now for the effects of human activity on the earth's climate—is taking place has been the consensus within the community studying the phenomenon at least since the United Nations' Intergovernmental Panel on Climate Change issued a report in 1995. "The balance of the evidence," said the IPCC report, "suggests that there is a discernible human influence on global climate." This is as loud a clarion as judicious scientists are allowed to sound.

Since then, global warming has lodged itself firmly in the vocabulary of the age and become a pop culture phenomenon. A crack in the Antarctic ice shelf helps cause a new ice age in *The Day After Tomorrow,* a 2004 potboiler in which Dennis Quaid loses a partner who falls through the roof of the atrium section of a glaciated New Jersey shopping mall. And in *An Inconvenient Truth,* the Academy Award–winning documentary made out of Al Gore's traveling PowerPoint presentation, global warming is as destructive a villain as Godzilla ever was. The Arctic ice melts, the seas rise, and whole cities are swallowed up. In one chilling slide, Gore shows the site of the World Trade Center in lower Manhattan being inundated, a perfectly symmetrical collision of manmade catastrophes. We believe global warming is real and dangerous enough to entertain us, anyway.

What we accept in the darkness of the theater, however, is

often not what we accept in the light outside. The reality of global warming, beyond its value as a scary monster, has been fashioned into yet another kind of vaudeville debate, with each side lining up its team like children choosing up sides in a schoolyard, except that, in a schoolyard, the most expert players almost always get chosen first.

If we have abdicated our birthright to scientific progress, we have done so by moving the debate into the realm of political and cultural argument, where we all feel more confident, because it is there that the Gut rules. Held to the standards of that context, any scientific theory is turned into mere opinion. Scientific fact is no more immutable than a polling sample. This is how there came to be a "debate" over the very existence of global warming, even though the considered view among those who have actually studied the phenomenon renders the debate quite silly. The debate is about making people feel better about driving SUVs. It's less about climatology than it is about guiltlessly topping off your tank or collecting contributions for your campaign from the oil companies. Even now that the skeptics accept the reality of global warming, they either dispute the importance of human activity to it, or argue that its origins don't matter as long as we try to ameliorate the effects: the debate is still taking place in the provinces of the Gut.

The journalist Chris Mooney describes how the current debate was created. After the release of the 1995 IPCC report, the ascendant Republican Congress, behind Speaker Newt Gingrich, convened a series of hearings attacking the report's scientific credibility, mostly on the grounds that the IPCC used computer models to predict climate change. These techniques have their shortcomings. Most systems devised to project future trends do, as anyone who's ever been to the racetrack knows. "Obviously," Mooney writes, "computer models cannot perfectly simulate the massively complex climate system." However, computer modeling is used to project future trends in almost every field. "In other words," concludes Mooney, "should policymakers consider the range of possibilities suggested by these highly sophisticated attempts to project future climate change? Clearly, they should."

Nevertheless, the "debate" was joined. The people arguing against the global warming consensus marshaled their own array of experts, drawn from think tanks, and they argued in the syntax of science, but not in its vocabulary. Their words were drawn from the language of sales and of persuasion, a language that appealed to, and drew its strength from, the Gut. It works to keep the debate in those precincts where the Gut can fight on an equal playing field and win.

It was the tobacco companies who drew up the template. In the 1950s, a scientific consensus was growing around the notion that smoking carried a serious risk of cancer. The consensus was reaching so deep into the mainstream that, in 1952, *Reader's Digest,* the best-selling periodical in the country and a mainstay of small-town doctors' offices across America, reprinted an obscure piece from the *Christian Herald* entitled "Cancer by the Carton." This was the decade of *Sputnik,* and of the Salk vaccine that eradicated polio. Americans were proud of their science. They trusted it. It saved lives. It would protect them from the new Russian moon. The building momentum behind a science-based assault on smoking was increasingly perilous to those people who sold cigarettes. The pressure on the tobacco companies to respond to these new studies was overwhelming.

In response, the tobacco companies turned to John Hill of Hill & Knowlton, the most successful public-relations firm of the time. If any field of study was exploding as fast in the 1950s as the physical sciences were, it was the study of how to influence Americans to do what your clients wanted them to do. Hill devised a canny strategy that turned on its head the pride that Americans took in their science. Instead of responding, point by point, to the studies themselves, the tobacco companies created their own Potemkin science almost from scratch. The CEOs of all the major tobacco companies met in New York in December 1953. Allan Brandt, in *The Cigarette Century*, describes the strategy:

> Its goal was to produce and sustain scientific skepticism and controversy in order to disrupt the emerging consensus on the harms of cigarette smoking. This strategy required intrusions into scientific process and procedure. . . . The industry worked to assure that vigorous debate would be prominently trumpeted in the public media. So long as there appeared to be doubt, so long as the industry could assert "not proven," smokers would have a rationale to continue, and new smokers would have a rationale to begin.

Brandt describes the vital role in the strategy played by a biologist named Clarence Cook Little, who agreed to become the scientific director of the Scientific Advisory Board of the Tobacco Industry Research Committee, the group created by the tobacco companies to give a scientific gloss to their sales project. A career eccentric who'd resigned the presidency of the University of Michigan in the face of what was nearly an all-out faculty uprising—he loudly decried the decadent campus life while himself carrying on with a coed—Little believed so strongly in the hereditarian view of biology that he'd become involved in the eugenics movements of the 1930s. In his view, all diseases, including cancer, were traceable to genetic origins. Thus, he was predisposed to reject any evidence of environmental causes, such as smoking. However, his work in cancer research, particularly in the use of experimental mice, of which he'd developed several strains, won him such widespread acclaim that many of his colleagues were shocked when Little took the job with the SAB.

He gave the tobacco industry exactly what it wanted: a thickly credentialed spokesman who could help them sell cigarettes by muddling the scientific evidence. Little argued that cancer was hereditary, and that the research into a link between smoking and cancer was complicated and incomplete, even as study after study piled up outside. As the years went by, Little's hard-won respectability dropped away from him. Nevertheless, the strategy devised in 1953 held, more or less intact, for nearly fifty years.

The echoes of Clarence Little are quite clear when Chris Mooney describes how, in 2002, a Republican consultant named Frank Luntz sent out a memo describing how Luntz believed the crisis of global warming should be handled within a political context. "The most important principle in any discussion of global warming is sound science," wrote Luntz. "The scientific debate is closing [against the skeptics] but not yet closed. There is still a window of opportunity to challenge the science." In short, it doesn't matter what the facts actually are, all that matters is how you can make people feel about them.

Luntz's memo adhered closely to the strategy first used by the tobacco companies. Change the language, Luntz advised. Talk about "climate change" and not "global warming." Call yourselves "conservationists" and not "environmentalists." He also advised them to foster within their campaigns skepticism about the results of the research. His strategy depended completely on an American public easy to fool and on his ability to transfer the issue into those places where the Gut ruled, where the "debate" about global warming could be cast with familiar grotesques from all the other modern morality plays—the Meddling Liberal, say, or the Elitist.

In a sense, Clarence Little had a hard job. The American public was deeply in love with scientific inquiry, and he had to bamboozle them about events that many of them had experienced firsthand, as Dad hacked his way to an early grave across the living room while Arthur Godfrey sang on the television set and sold him more Chesterfields. Luntz had a much easier sell. How many Americans had ever seen polar bears outside of a zoo, let alone cared whether they were drowning in the upper latitudes of Canada? How many of them had seen ice deeper than a hockey rink? *Sputnik* was a dead iron ball in space. The country was accustomed to being told what to think about things like this. They'd listen to anyone. Even the government.

* * *

TRUTH be told, Shishmaref is more rusting than rustic. Along the bluffs behind the beach, old snowmobiles and all-terrain vehicles lie in scattered pieces, like broken teeth, in the long grass by the side of the clotted dirt roads. There's a tread here and a wheel there, and a pile of old engine parts that seems a part of the essential geology of the place. Rows of wooden racks, used for drying sealskins, face the sea. They're pitted by the sand and grit that rides the rising wind; there's no way to tell whether they're still in use. Smiling children ride in carts pulled behind ATVs. In front of his clapboard house, its roof adorned with a cluster of caribou horns, a man guts a seal, its blood reddening the mud of the road.

Shishmaref is not a place anyone but the people who live there will particularly miss. There are two stores and one school. The town's water system is touch and go, and most people catch fresh rainwater in buckets outside the house. In the winter, people chop ice and melt it down, but there's less of that now because of the changes in the ice, which forms later, freezes less thickly, and breaks up sooner than it used to do. Those changes, of course, also affect the winter's hunting, which is still the basis for the subsistence economy on which the town depends. The loss of the permafrost means fewer people use the traditional Inupiaq method of preserving meat for the winter, which is to bury it in the ground. "Even in the summertime, we had our frost that kept our food," recalls Luci Eningowuk. "We didn't have to have freezers years ago; we just put the food underground."

There is a transience about Shishmaref, a vestige of its nomadic origins now exacerbated by time and events into a permanent sense of abandonment. This seems in conflict with the deep attachment of its people to their land. But that attachment has become untenable. Sooner or later, Shishmaref will have to be abandoned. There's not enough of it left to go around, even among the six-hundred-odd people who live there.

"It's eating away at precious little land here," Luci explains. "The main reason that we want to move—that we *have* to move—is for the sake of our children. We don't have any more room to accommodate them. There's no space to make their homes."

* * *

IN 1995, Norman Myers of the Climate Institute estimated that there already were between twenty-five million and thirty million "environmental refugees," and that the number could rise to two hundred million before the middle of this century. Environmental refugees are people fleeing an environmental crisis, either natural or human made. As they move, a ripple effect overwhelms the countries in which they live. They flood the cities, overtaxing the social services which, in many nations, are rudimentary to begin with. A UN study explained that, at least in part because of environmental refugees, Sana'a, the capital of Yemen, has doubled its population every six years since 1972 and that the city's main aquifer may run dry by 2010.

That same study—financed and run by the UN University's Institute for Environment and Human Security—warned that there would be fifty million environmental refugees by 2010, and it argued that they should be recognized in the same way as are refugees from war or political oppression. This would make them eligible for humanitarian aid from a number of governmental and nongovernmental agencies.

Most of the refugees come from sub-Saharan Africa, but there have been similar migrations in the south Pacific, where New Zealand agreed to accept all eleven thousand inhabitants of the Tuvalu atoll, which had been rendered uninhabitable by rising sea levels. According to the journalist Terry Allen, upon arriving in Auckland the Tuvaluans found themselves "lonely and lost, without the support of community and culture, or the skills to survive an urban life based on money." For better or worse, sometime in the next decade or so, the inhabitants of Shishmaref are going to be among the first environmental refugees in North America.

A number of them have come together this afternoon for a meeting in the town's community center. It's a low brown building suffused with what crepuscular light can fight its way through bleary windows. Those present are talking with state highway officials about the early preparations for the evacuation of Shishmaref. The town's elders have determined that the village will be moved twenty miles across the lagoon to the mainland, to a place not far from the town of Tin Creek. It is a peaceful little spot, small and quiet enough for Shishmaref to reconstitute itself according to its traditional culture. "The elders wanted to keep one area as serene as possible because it's a subsistence setting for our lifestyle here," Luci Eningowuk explains.

The process of moving the residents of Shishmaref is complicated and expensive. (The U.S. Army Corps of Engineers estimated that the cost of moving a nearby village half the size of Shishmaref to be approximately $1 million per resident.) In fact, today's meeting is not about moving the village. It's not even about building a road to move the village. It's not even about gathering stone to build a road to move the village. It's about building a road to the place where someone can gather the stone to build the road to move the village.

They're having trouble finding a place with enough gravel to make building a road worthwhile. A spot near Ear Mountain seems promising, but it is logistically difficult to reach, and there are complications in building the road over which the gravel will be carried because the area is located inside protected park land. Patti Miller, an official from the Alaska Department of Transportation, fields questions in the front of the room. Every answer yields another question. Somebody mentions $3 million in government funds already earmarked for assistance in the project.

"Three million dollars," Miller says, "doesn't go very far toward building that road."

Heads nod around the room. Several men get up and pore over the topographical maps that Miller has spread out on the broad tables that, later tonight, will be used for the town's bingo games.

"The reason we're talking about it this way is that we don't really have the funds to move the village," explains Tony Weyiounna, a village official who's been deeply involved in the relocation project for more than five years. "But we do have funding to do some parts of the relocation process. Building the road is one of them.

"In 2002, we developed a strategic relocation plan, along with a flooding and erosion plan, to help guide our community, and we've been trying to follow that along to try and do things symmetrically. Constructing the new seawalls was one of the first things, so that was highlighted, and that's how come we're building so much of the protection piece.

"But the other aspects, like the relocation project, it's slow to gather assistance. You know, in our country, for most people to get assistance, you need a big mass of people that the money will benefit. In our case, we're only six hundred people and the cost of the relocation work is so big, and the benefits to our country are so small, that it doesn't justify getting a lot of assistance."

"Just to move them is going to take twenty years and probably two hundred million dollars," says Patti Miller, after the meeting has broken up. "And the people in the Lower Forty-eight don't understand that. To them, that's like an outrageous amount of money, and it is an outrageous amount of money, but these people haven't got any choices." There was a good turnout for the meeting. After all, the temperature was fifty-eight degrees outside, a nice day for the first week of November.

*　*　*

ON February 18, 2004, sixty-two scientists, including forty-nine Nobel laureates, released a report in which they criticized the administration of George W. Bush for its treatment of the scientific process. The report charged the administration with barbering documents, stacking review panels, distorting scientific information, and forcing science itself into a mutable servility to political ends. In short, the scientists charged that the tobacco industry's approach to science—which is "Science is whatever we can sell"—had become indistinguishable from the government's.

The outrage had been building for a while, and it had become quite general, taking in areas far removed from the study of global warming. At about the same time that the scientists released their report, Dr. Elizabeth Blackburn, whose groundbreaking work on telomeric DNA has revolutionized cancer research, was summarily dismissed from the President's Council on Bioethics. Her firing culminated nearly two years of wrangling with the panel's chairman, Dr. Leon Kass, an outspoken opponent of stem cell research and the man who injected the phrase "the ick factor" into profoundly complicated bioethical debates.

Kass is a true crank, which would be fine if he'd kept his place and carved out a niche among America's rich trove of exotic philosophical and religious fauna, rather than finding himself installed in the government. He has opposed—in no particular order—in vitro fertilization, cosmetic surgery, organ transplants, contraception, and the public eating of ice cream cones. In thundering against the latter, Kass sounds like someone who missed his calling as a member of Monty Python's Flying Circus:

"Worst of all . . . are those more uncivilized forms of eating, like licking an ice cream cone," he writes, "a catlike activity that has been made acceptable in informal America but that still offends those who know that eating in public is offensive. Eating on the street—even when undertaken, say, because one is between appointments and has no other time to eat—displays a lack of self-control: It beckons enslavement to the belly."

This fellow, waving his stick like an Old Testament prophet who'd somehow wandered into Coney Island—this was the man with whom Elizabeth Blackburn was supposed to make national policy on critical issues affecting millions of lives. Actual science played a very limited role in the dispute. The serious debate seemed more suited to a caucus room in Iowa, or a late-night bull session in a seminary, than to a panel aimed at giving policymakers the best advice possible on the way to make policy.

The final crack in the relationship between Kass and Blackburn came over the relative therapeutic benefits of adult stem cells, to which the political right has no objections, and embryonic stem cells, which engage the politics of the abortion issue. Among scientists in the field, these two approaches are complementary. They do not compete with each other. The argument that caused Elizabeth Blackburn's dismissal was a completely political one.

Blackburn did not slink away from the fight. She published quietly outraged articles in the medical journals, and she gave more interviews than she had ever expected to give. "I wasn't maddened, necessarily," she says. "You know, you try to give your input based on what you know about, and what you can find out about the science. And you sort of just do your best. My sense was that all I could do was keep giving my input about what I knew about.

"The idea was to just lay it out and say, 'Here's what we, as scientists, did think of the scientific situation. First and foremost, that stood out to me because, when one looks at the mandate of the federal commission, it is very clear what they are and it's advisory to policy. It struck me that, if you're going to be advisory, you're trying to give the best advice you can give. It doesn't make policy, but it certainly has the function of being a resource for advice."

The dynamic that ensnared Elizabeth Blackburn played out most vividly with respect to climate studies. A report released in December 2007 by the Committee on Oversight and Government Reform of the U.S. House of Representatives stated flatly that the administration "engaged in a systematic effort to manipulate climate change science and mislead policymakers and the public about the dangers of global warming." In the introduction to its report, the committee quotes an internal document from the American Petroleum Institute in which the voice of Clarence Cook Little seems to echo quite clearly.

"Victory will be achieved when . . . average citizens 'understand' uncertainties in climate science . . . [and] recognition of uncertainties becomes part of the 'conventional wisdom.'" The quote marks are what poker players call a tell. At its heart, this is a strategy that depends vitally on its ability to confuse people. Where most science seeks to clarify, this seeks to muddle. This is science turned against itself at the service of salesmen, selling uncertainty. But the strategy is rooted in the confidence that there will always be a market.

According to the House Oversight Committee's report, White House political officials determined which government scientists could give interviews about the subject, and what they could say. All requests were routed through something called the White House Council on Environmental Quality, the operation of which would strike Elizabeth Blackburn as very familiar. For example, on July 20, 2006, Dr. Thomas Karl, the director of the National Climatic Data Center, was scheduled to testify before the committee. The CEQ's editing of his prepared testimony is almost comically piddling. According to the House report, Karl was prepared to testify that "the state of the science continues to indicate that modern climate change is dominated by human influences." The CEQ, at the request of the Office of Management and Budget, changed the word "dominated" to "affected."

Elsewhere, the committee laid out how frantically political appointees at NASA tried to keep Dr. James Hansen, whose outspoken criticisms of the administration's policies toward global warming run throughout the committee's report, from doing a single interview on National Public Radio in 2005. The scramble took almost two weeks, and the paper trail of increasingly agitated e-mails—"If Hansen does interview," reads one, "there will be dire consequences"—is a case study in panicky bureaucratic flop sweat that would have embarrassed the East Germans. None of these frenzied people knew the first thing about climate science, but that hardly mattered. The frenzy wasn't about science. Hansen did not appear on NPR.

Not all of the committee's findings are so petty. Throughout the report, there is a striking sense of how profoundly actual scientific expertise was either sacrificed for political purposes or abandoned entirely. All administrations have a natural tension between their political sides and the outside experts brought in to advise on policymaking. But, on this particular issue, this particular administration seemed to be determined to make the information it rejected simply disappear. Major reports were extensively edited not by experts in the field but by a man named Philip Cooney, the chief of staff at the CEQ. Previously, Cooney had spent fifteen years as a lawyer for the American Petroleum Institute, where his last assignment had been as the "team leader" at the API on issues of climate change. He had been there when the "victory" memo had been written, and he seemed more than willing to apply its principles to his government job.

The committee found Cooney's fingerprints on a number of draft reports—softening the data with adverbs, making statements more equivocal by running them through the passive voice. In a 2003 draft report, for example, model simulations "demonstrated that the observed changes over the past century are consistent with a significant contribution from human activity." In Cooney's hands, the model simulations only "indicated" that the observed changes "are likely consistent with a significant contribution from human activity." Thus do uncertainties become part of the "conventional wisdom." They're put there by lawyers, and by political appointees. The only empirical contribution they can make to the discussion is to muddle it.

James Gustave Speth has been working on the science of global warming for over thirty years. In 2007, he wrote a scathing letter to the *New York Times,* warning against what he called "the suppression of information and the act of disinformation" that he saw in the collision between science and politics over the previous decade. Like Madison and most of the other founders, Speth sees science and self-government as inextricable. What imperils one imperils the other.

"What we have is that the scientific content of public policy issues is increasing," he says. "The difficulty of understanding public policy issues, because of their technological and scientific content, is increasing. And so, what you need is a whole support system that really helps assist the public in understanding this. When you have efforts to cloud up public understanding, to cloud up issues that should be clarified, then you are making a serious problem worse. And I think that's what we've had.

"And what's really at stake is democracy, because the scientific and technical content of public policy issues will continue to increase, I mean, how is the public to understand nanotechnology when the word doesn't mean anything to most people? So there really is a profound issue here. The issue is even more complex now on the environmental front, where I work, where there is a whole range of threats. I mean, nobody wants to believe bad things to begin with, and when you can't see them, and you can't verify them in your own experience, and then somebody tells you they're not happening, well, it's very easy to conclude they're not happening."

In October 2002, a draft copy of a document called the

Strategic Plan for the Climate Change Science Program came across Philip Cooney's desk. It included this sentence: "Warming temperatures will also affect Arctic land areas." Finding the conclusion too strong, Cooney put some mush into the verb. The sentence came out reading:

"Warming temperatures may also affect Arctic land areas."

* * *

THE ocean is not a presence in lower Manhattan, not the way it is in Shishmaref. Walk around Ground Zero, where the iron is rising again, and you hardly remember that the ocean is a few blocks over, just past Battery Park. Its sounds are buried in the noise of traffic and the gabble of conversation. It smells as rank as a dungeon cell, but is overwhelmed by the hydrocarbons in the air. Its tides seem less powerful a hidden force than the subway rattling beneath the sidewalk. And that is how most of us look at the sea—as an afterthought, a secondary, vestigial presence. Its power seems an ancient myth, almost a superstition, like a dragon or a snow beast. We fool ourselves into thinking it's something we've outgrown, when it's really only something we've talked ourselves out of believing in. We have become quite good at mistaking amnesia for wisdom. The sea is something we can spin, and that is how Frank Luntz looks at the sea.

In 2004, a report called the Arctic Climate Impact Assessment was released, showing the devastating ongoing effect of global warming on the Arctic region and its consequences. Almost immediately, a think tank funded by, among other people, ExxonMobil, attacked the science in the report. James Inhofe, then the chairman of the U.S. Senate's Environment and Public Works Committee, cited the latter report to attack the science in the former report. He looks at the sea as something that can't fool him, James Inhofe, who is smarter than the sea will ever be. And that is how James Inhofe looks at the sea.

For centuries, the Arctic seemed an alien place, a place on the earth but not of it. The Canadian archaeologist Robert McGhee summed up that view:

> [This] image of the Arctic as a world apart, where the laws of science and society may be in abeyance, is . . . also moulded by a view of the Arctic that comes down to us from the distant past, when the region was alien and as impossible for most people to reach as another planet. . . . For millennia, this Arctic vision has successfully absorbed the hearsay evidence of travellers' tales, the accelerating flow of scientific information and, in recent years, even the tedium of government reports, while retaining its aura of wonder. The Arctic is not so much a region as a dream: the dream of a unique, unattainable and compellingly attractive world. It is the last imaginary place.

There is an edge to the evening breeze. A vague chill settles in your bones before you know it's there. It is in the hours like this that you can begin to feel how winter could come pressing in on all sides, like the ice that traps a whaling fleet. But it's a shadowy and insubstantial feeling, more an intuition than an instinct. The children walk down the street with their coats open.

A couple of nights a week, the people of Shishmaref gather in the community center to play bingo. The hall buzzes constantly as teenagers wander between the tables, selling extra cards to the players. A sign on the doors warns that nobody even smelling of alcohol will be allowed inside to play. This is high-stakes, competitive bingo. The numbers fly swiftly around the room as the players work four and five cards at once, marking off the numbers in the complicated patterns—"Picture frame!" "Lasso!"—of the game's variations.

John and Emily Weyiounna, Tony's cousins, hunch over a long table near the back of the hall. In addition to their own cards, they are helping a clumsy stranger try to keep up with the play. Emily sees first that the stranger has completed his "picture frame," filling in all the spots around the perimeter of the card. He calls out "Bingo!" too soon, though, and has to split a $300 pot with another player whose timing was better. They laugh as the stranger offers to share his winnings with them.

"What?" John Weyiounna says to him. "Do you think we are poor people?"

They have taken upon themselves the aspect of refugees. They have made provisions within themselves to maintain the community they have built here wherever they eventually go, the way the European immigrants came to the great cities in the Lower Forty-eight and re-created in their neighborhoods the old places they'd left behind. They have no illusions about what is happening to them. There are some local conspiracy theorists who believe that someone, somewhere, wants this land for some nefarious purpose, but most of the people have seen the ice come later and later in the year, and they've felt the permafrost soften beneath their feet, and they know there is no argument they can make against what is happening to them.

The bingo game runs late. When it finally breaks up, the people scatter down the clotted, muddy streets. It is dark and the sky is alive with stars. Moonlight ripples across the waves. Come to the seawall in the Arctic, where now nobody knows when winter will come again. Come and dispute cleverly those things that the people of Shishmaref have known for thousands of years. The sea feeds, but the sea also devours. And that is how they look at the sea.

CHAPTER NINE

The Principles of Automatic Pilot

In 1912, the Sperry Corporation developed the first automatic pilot system for airplanes. Two years later, Lawrence Sperry, the son of Elmer Sperry, a famous inventor and founder of the company that bore his name, took an airplane up and flew it around for a while with his hands spread wide and away from the controls. Spectators on the ground gasped in not inconsiderable alarm. Modern autopilots do occasionally fail. Some crashes occur when the human pilot fails to disengage the automatic pilot before attempting to fly the plane manually. All delicate mechanisms fail most catastrophically through human error or, especially, through human neglect.

The country was founded by people who considered self-government no less a science than botany. It required an informed and educated and enlightened populace, or else all the delicate mechanisms of the system would come apart. The founders provided no mechanism for a government to run on automatic pilot.

"Public opinion sets bounds to every government," Mr. Madison wrote in an essay that the *National Gazette* published in December 1791, "and is the real sovereign in every free one." Later in the same essay, though, he warned: "The larger the country, the less easy for its real opinion to be ascertained, and the less difficult to be counterfeited; when ascertained or presumed, the more respectable it is in the eyes of individuals. This is favorable to the authority of government. For the same reason, the more extensive a country, the more insignificant is each individual in his own eyes. This may be unfavorable to liberty."

Mr. Madison, whose scientific curiosity was piqued more by agriculture than by mechanics—John Quincy Adams once referred to him as "the best farmer in the world"—was most acutely conscious of how easily any government, even a republic, could slip into war and find itself wrecked before anyone knew it had been damaged in the first place. "In war," he wrote in 1795, "the discretionary power of the executive is extended; its influence in dealing out offices, honors, and emoluments is multiplied, and all the means of seducing the minds, are added to those of seducing the force, of the people. . . . No nation could preserve its freedom in the midst of continual warfare."

He ended up, of course, with a war of his own, a picked fight with Great Britain in 1812 out of which the United States gained Andrew Jackson, Old Ironsides, and its national anthem, but which was ruinously expensive and was highlighted by Madison's fleeing the White House a few steps ahead of the Royal Marines, who burned the place. Not even he could resist wholly the temptations he saw as inherent in any executive. However, he did try, as hard as he could, to maintain control over the delicate mechanisms he'd designed. The war was properly declared by Congress and when, late in the hostilities, delegates from New England convened in Hartford to discuss seceding from the Union, Madison did not march on the hall.

"Because he was worried [about the use of his war powers] is the reason, I think, that the French ambassador [Louis Serurier] said it was a triumph because the country got through the war and accomplished at least a standstill, without compromising or destroying its republican institutions," Ralph Ketchum says. "Madison really stuck to it. He repeatedly refused to whip up a kind of hysterical intolerance around the war. And when it looked darkest, and some New England leaders were gathering for the Hartford Convention—it looked like they might try to make an alliance with the British and with Canada—he did nothing more than warn a good loyal militia unit in New York, 'Stand by on the border. If these characters in Hartford do anything that's treason, you go.' "

In fact, the Hartford Convention's resolves didn't get to Madison until after the Treaty of Ghent had ended the war. Madison received them with a silence that Jefferson said, "showed the placid character of our Constitution. Under any other their treasons would have been punished by the halter. We let them live as the laughing stocks of the world and punish them by the torment of eternal contempt." Idiot America has no gift for that.

* * *

IN August 2001, an official of the U.S. government dropped by Louise Richardson's office at Radcliffe College in Cambridge, Massachusetts. Born and raised in rural Ireland, Richardson had been steeped in the revolutionary history of that country. "The extremism I imbibed came from school, books, popular history, and songs," she once wrote. "It came from the air around me." She had friends from home—and, later, friends from Trinity College—who took the oath and joined the Irish Republican Army. Having watched as their politics gravitated toward the gun and the bomb, Richardson was struck by how poorly understood the subject of terrorism was.

She made it her field of expertise. She sought out terrorists and listened to them. Gradually, there developed a network of experts on the subject. They even once held a conference, at an undisclosed location, where "activists," as she put it, critiqued the academic papers presented by Richardson and her colleagues. Working with a cell of Chechen rebels in a kind of war game, Richardson discovered that, when the decision came about targeting women and children, it was the academics who embraced the option first. "I mention this not to make light of a serious issue," she writes, "only to make the point that terrorists are human beings who think like we do."

Richardson had taken it upon herself to develop and to teach courses at Harvard on the subject of terrorism. She'd achieved some renown in what was still an orphan specialty among political scientists. When the government man showed up at her office, he wanted to know why no terrorist group had ever used an airplane like a guided missile, flying it into a target on the ground. Richardson told him that it had occurred to people, and that somebody was likely to do it sooner rather than later.

A month later, after terrorists of the Al Qaeda network had flown planes into the towers of the World Trade Center and the Pentagon, and after a third hijacked plane had crashed into a field in Pennsylvania where today people are arguing about the shape of the memorial, Richardson and her colleagues around the country e-mailed each other furiously, trying to bring their expertise to bear on what had happened. Not long afterward, Richardson went to another undisclosed location, this time at the invitation of the Pentagon.

"They wanted me to go somewhere in Virginia and talk with some people," she recalls. "And I walked into the room and my heart soared. Because if you had asked me who were the twenty people in America who knew the most about terrorism, I'd have named the twenty people in that room. And nobody has ever heard of them. You never see them on TV. We are talking about people who have been working in this field for years, and we spent several days there, and they were asking us questions constantly. We sat around a table and debated points.

"Afterwards, the people who'd invited us were extraordinarily complimentary and grateful and asked if we'd come back again, and we, of course, said yes. None of us ever heard a word again."

Over the next seven years, when the response to the September attacks morphed inexorably into a "war on terror" that produced the invasion and occupation of Iraq, Richardson was on the outside looking in at problems she'd spent twenty years analyzing. "The people [who had been] in that room, they sat back and watched these newly minted experts pontificate," she says, "and those experts were dismissive of us for failing to predict that this would happen. It was apparent to me at the time that we were doing this wrong, that there was a lot we could derive from the experience of other countries, but the people who were saying that were obscure academics like me.

"From my prism of being a terrorism expert, it was apparent to me that there were absolutely no links between Saddam Hussein and bin Laden. They hated one another. People like me knew that. This information was readily available to the decision makers in Washington. They must have known it. So that legitimization of the war, I felt, was preposterous. For someone as notoriously paranoid as Saddam Hussein to give weapons of mass destruction to terrorists is preposterous.

"I think most Americans are not terribly interested in foreign policy. They are interested in paying the bills and the rest of it.

And then, you have your leadership telling them the simple story of good and evil. We're good. The other guys are bad. And the media, I think, have really let us down insofar as they haven't sought out—not necessarily me, but contrary voices. They've gone for the easy spokespeople."

The "global war on terror"—and the war in Iraq that it spawned—is a real war with real casualties. It began, as all our wars now do, without the constitutional nicety of a formal declaration of hostilities. However, after the initial shock of the September 11 atrocities wore off, and the United States slid almost dreamlike toward the catastrophe in Iraq, it was clear that war nonetheless had been declared. Through millions of individual decisions, through the abandonment of self-government, through the conscious and unconscious abandonment of the obligations of citizenship, it had been declared by Idiot America.

The war was Idiot America's purest product. It was the apotheosis of the Three Great Premises. People believed what they were sold, not what they saw. Before the invasion of Iraq, the White House chief of staff, Andrew Card, admitted that the administration would push for war in the autumn of 2003 because everybody knew that the fall was when you rolled out your new product line. Later, after so much had gone to ruin, Paul Wolfowitz, one of the war's architects, explained that the administration had settled on pitching the war on the basis of Iraq's alleged nuclear weapons program because that was the easiest case to sell. Those weapons, of course, were as faith-based a fiction as saddles on a dinosaur.

Americans chose *not* to believe those people who really knew what they were talking about. They chose to believe those people who seemed most sure of everything about which they had no clue. Expertise became a liability, a form of softness in the face of an existential threat. Expertise was not of the Gut. In the months and years after September 11, the worst possible thing was to know what you were talking about. People who knew too much were dangerous; on this the country largely agreed.

It was a huge and expensive demonstration of Hofstadter's argument:

> The case against intellect is founded on a set of fictional and wholly abstract antagonisms. Intellect is pitted against feeling, on the ground that it is somehow inconsistent with warm emotion.
>
> It is pitted against character, because it is widely believed that intellect stands for mere cleverness, which transmutes easily into the sly and diabolical. It is pitted against practicality, since theory is held to be opposed to practice. It is pitted against democracy, since intellect is felt to be a form of distinction that defies egalitarianism. . . . Once the validity of these antagonisms is accepted, then the case for intellect . . . is lost. ·

Inside the government, things were little better. On September 11, 2001, nobody in that government knew more about Al Qaeda than did Richard Clarke. He'd watched it grow. He'd watched it strike—in New York, in Africa, and in the harbor in Yemen. He'd spent the summer trying to get people to hear his warnings that an attack might be imminent. That morning, in the Situation Room at the White House, Clarke watched the Twin Towers burn and fall, and he recognized the organization's signature as well as he'd recognize his own. Instead, in the ensuing days, a lot of people around him—people who didn't know enough about Al Qaeda to throw to a cat—wanted to talk about Iraq. What they believed trumped what Clarke knew. He left the government.

"In the 1970s and 1980s, when the key issue became arms

control, the traditional diplomats couldn't do the negotiating because that negotiating involved science and engineering," Clarke explains. "Interagency decision papers were models of analysis, where assumptions would be laid out and tested.

"That's the world I grew up in. The approach still applied to issues, even terrorism. Then these people come in, and they already have the answers, how to spin it, how to get the rest of the world on board. I thought, 'Wait a minute, that isn't analysis. It's the important issues where we really need analysis.'

"In the area of terrorism, there's a huge potential for emotional reaction. The one thing I told my team [on September 11]—they were mad and they were crying, the whole range of emotions—was that we didn't have time for emotion that day."

It ought not to have shocked anyone that a government that deliberately put itself at odds with empirical science would go to war in the way that it did and expect to succeed. The Bush administration could sell anything. Remember the beginning, when it was purely about the Gut, a bone-deep call for righteous revenge for which Afghanistan was not sufficient response. (Donald Rumsfeld lamented that there wasn't enough in the country to blow up.) In Iraq, though, there would be towering stacks of chemical bombs, a limitless smorgasbord of deadly bacteria, vast lagoons of exotic poisons. Nukes on the gun rack of every pickup in Baghdad. Our troops would be greeted with candy and flowers. The war would take six months—a year, tops. Mission Accomplished. "Major combat operations are over."

"Part of the problem was that people didn't want the analytic process because they'd be shown up," Clarke says. "Their assumptions would be counterfactual. One of the real areas of expertise, for example, was failed-state reconstruction. How to go into failed states and maintain security and get the economy going and defang ethnic hatred. They threw it all out.

"They ignored the experts on the Middle East. They ignored the experts who said [Iraq] was the wrong target. So you ignore the experts and you go in anyway, and then you ignore all the experts on how to handle the post-conflict."

The worst thing you could be was right. Today, there are a lot of shiny Washington offices housing people who got it right and got left behind. They form a kind of underground. Some of them failed to press their case as hard as they could have. Some of them did press their case, and were punished for doing so. They were ignored, many of them, because they knew too much. They were punished, many of them, because they knew too much and spoke out about what they knew. They see where the country went on automatic pilot. They're a government in exile representing the reality-based community.

Four thousand lives later, they remember the beginning. A career neoconservative ideologue named Michael Ledeen made himself famous by espousing a doctrine by which, every few years or so, the United States should "throw a small nation up against the wall" to prove that it meant business in the world. And Idiot America, which was all of us, was largely content to put the country on automatic pilot and, cheering, forgot to disengage the mechanism.

Goddamn right. Gimme another. And see what the superpowers in the backroom will have.

* * *

THE office is neat, which is to say that the books are arranged in an orderly fashion as they overwhelm the shelves, and the great stacks of paper are evenly stacked, one next to another, on the desk and on the various tables. Tucked into a brick rowhouse in the Georgetown section of Washington, D.C., the office is every bit as full as the usual academic's landfill, but it is nowhere near as chaotic. It is a busy place, but there's nothing random about it. Every pile has its purpose.

In 2002, Paul Pillar was working for the Central Intelligence Agency as its national intelligence officer for the Near East and South Asia. One of Pillar's duties was to assess and evaluate intelligence regarding, among other places, Iraq. In October 2002, the CIA produced two documents in which Pillar had had a hand. The first was a National Intelligence Estimate that the agency presented to Congress regarding what the Bush administration argued was the overwhelming evidence that Iraq had stockpiled a vast number of dangerous weapons. There were mobile biological laboratories: a captured spy codenamed Curveball said so. There was a deal to buy uranium from the African nation of Niger. There were documents that said so, produced by the Italian government and vetted by British intelligence. There were aluminum tubes that could only be used for building centrifuges for the production of nuclear bombs.

The NIE also contained within its fine print the information that a number of government agencies thought the whole case was a farrago of stovepiped intelligence, cherry-picked data, wishful thinking, and utter bullshit. For example, the State Department's Bureau of Intelligence and Research thought the tale of the aluminum tubes was a bunch of hooey. The Air Force pooh-poohed the threat of Iraqi "drone aircraft" that could zoom in through U.S. air defenses, spraying anthrax. The whole Niger episode read to the people who knew the most about Niger, uranium, Iraq, or all three like comic-opera Graham Greene. "There were so many ridiculous aspects to that story," says one source familiar with the evidence. "Iraq already had five hundred tons of uranium. So why would they bother buying five hundred tons from a country in remote Africa? That would raise the profile in such a high way."

According to the investigative journalists David Corn and Michael Isikoff, one staffer for the Senate Foreign Relations Committee read the NIE for the first time and determined, "If anyone actually takes time to read this, they can't believe there actually are major WMD programs." The staffer needn't have worried. Hardly anyone in the Congress read the NIE.

Instead, two days later, the CIA released a white paper on the same subject. The white paper was produced with congressional lassitude in mind. It was easy to read. It had color maps and charts and it was printed on glossy paper. All the troublesome caveats in the NIE were gone. In their place were scary skull-and-crossbones logos indicating where the scary weapons were. The thing looked like a pesticide catalog. Seven months after the release of the NIE and the white paper, the United States launched the invasion and occupation of Iraq.

Ever since, Pillar has written and spoken about the climate within which those two documents were produced—an environment in which expertise was devalued within government for the purpose of depriving expertise of a constituency outside government. "The global question of whether to do it at all," he muses. "There never was a process that addressed that question. There was no meeting in the White House or in the Situation Room. There was no policy options paper that said, 'Here are the pros and cons of invading. Here are the pros and cons of not invading.' That never happened. Even today, with all the books that have been written, and with some great investigative reporting, you still can't say, 'Ah, this is where the decision was made.' "

In the years since the war began, more than a few people have said that the invasion of Iraq was a foregone conclusion the moment that the Supreme Court ruled on the case of *Bush v. Gore* in 2000. The incoming administration was stacked to the gunwales with people who'd been agitating for over a decade to "finish" what they believed had been left undone at the end of the first Gulf War. Lost in the now endless postmortems of how the country got into Iraq as a response to the attacks of September 11 is the fact that the country had been set on automatic pilot years earlier.

Madison warned at the outset how dangerous the war powers could be in the hands of an unleashed executive. "War," he wrote in 1793, "is in fact the true nurse of executive aggrandizement." As the years went by, and the power of the presidency grew within both government and popular culture, Madison looked even more prescient. Writing in the aftermath of the Lyndon Johnson presidency, which collapsed like a dead star from the pressure of an ill-conceived war, Johnson's former press secretary George Reedy limned the perfect trap that a president can set for himself:

"The environment of deference, approaching sycophancy, helps to foster an insidious belief: that the president and a few of his trusted advisors are possessed of a special knowledge that must be closely held within a small group lest the plans and designs of the United States be anticipated and frustrated by enemies."

Reedy cites the decisions that were made regarding the bombing of North Vietnam. As he concedes, "it is doubtful that a higher degree of intelligence could have been brought to bear on the problem"; the flaw lay in the fact that "none of these men [Johnson's pro-bombing advisers] were put to the test of defending their position in public debate." Even then, President Johnson solicited the opinion of Under Secretary of State George Ball, who thought the whole Vietnam adventure a bloody and futile waste. Johnson wanted Ball's opinions even when those opinions sent him into paroxysms of rage. Pillar sees inevitable, if imperfect, parallels in the meetings he sat through during the period between September 11, 2001, and the invasion of Iraq. He recalls walking face-first into a foregone conclusion.

"The only meetings and discussion were either, How do we go about this? or, most importantly, How do we sell this, and how do we get support for this?" he says. "It was a combination of a particular bunch of people who were really determined to do this thing, with a president who seized on the post-9/11 environment and thought, 'Oh, I'm going to be the war president.' That's my thing, after sort of drifting theme-less for a while. There was a synergy there. They came into office with even greater contempt for the bureaucracy and for all the sources of expertise beyond what they considered their own.

"I look at the work of the people who would have been my counterparts . . . during the Vietnam era, and I admire the courage of some of them. On the other hand, they had it a lot easier than people like me in Iraq, because they were asked and their opinions were welcome. In Iraq, our opinions were never asked. Your opinion clearly wasn't welcome."

Elsewhere, the country had become accustomed to confronting self-government through what the historian Daniel Boorstin called "a world of pseudo-events and quasi-information, in which the air is saturated with statements that are neither true nor false, but merely credible." The effect on the country's leaders was that they began to believe their own nonsense. The effect on the country was that citizens recognized it as nonsense and believed it anyway. A culture of cynical innocence was born, aggrieved and noisy, nurtured by a media that put a premium on empty argument and Kabuki debate. Citizens were encouraged to deplore their government, ridicule its good intentions, and hold themselves proudly ignorant of its functions and its purposes. Having done so, they then insisted on an absolute right to wash their hands of the consequences.

Cynics bore even themselves eventually. However, as a land

of perpetual reinvention and of many frontiers, and founded on ideas and imagination, America had a solution within its genome. It could create fictions to replace the things from which cynicism had drained its faith. It could become a novelized nation.

Novelizations are so preposterous an idea that they only could have been hatched as an art form here. They are based on the assumption that people will read a book that fills in the gaps of the screenplay of a movie they've already seen. A novelization is pure commerce, a salesman's delight. Few writers brag about writing them; one online critic referred to them memorably as "flipping burgers in someone else's universe."

The very first one, written by Russell Holman in 1928, was aimed at promoting a Clara Bow film called *Follow the Fleet.* Since then, science fiction fans have come to dote on them as treasure troves of previously unknown arcana, the movies themselves having spent little time on Han Solo's childhood bout with Rigellian ringworm. The most successful of the genre was William Kotzwinkle's best-selling rendition of Steven Spielberg's *E.T.: The Extra-Terrestrial,* which sold more than a million copies on top of the tens of millions of people who saw the actual movie, but in which, as the film writer Grady Hendrix pointed out in a piece for *Slate,* Kotzwinkle grafted onto the story a genuinely creepy obsession on the part of the lovable little alien with the mother of the children who take him in. Some gaps are best left unfilled.

As art, novelizations are almost completely worthless. As commerce, they make perfect sense. They are creatures of the First Great Premise, by which anything has value if it moves units. And their principles are ready to be applied to almost every endeavor in a country dedicated to using whatever raw material is at hand to create vast vistas of abject hooey.

Once, when there were still actual frontiers, novelizing the country helped explain the new parts of the country to the old. Now, though, all frontiers in America are metaphorical, and the novelization of the country serves to give the national cynicism an America it can believe in. In this, the presidency came to represent a comforting counterfeit. If you sold a presidency well—and it was all about selling—the easy cynicism about "government" could be abandoned with respect to the president, who was the one part of "the government" over whom citizens seemed proud to claim common ownership.

All the way back to Parson Weems, presidents have been in some way fictionalized, but the modern presidency now takes place in the place where art is defined almost solely by commerce, and a place where the president is the only fungible product. In a way that would have shaken Madison down to the buckles on his shoes, the presidency became the government's great gravitational source, around which every other part of the political culture orbited, and it became the face of government in the popular culture.

Actual presidents—and people who wanted to be the actual president—caught on quickly. The pursuit of the presidency is now a contest of narratives. Create your own and get it on the market fast, before someone—possibly your opponent, but probably the media—creates one for you. Poor Al Gore learned this lesson far too late. The successful narrative is judged only by how well it sells. Its essential truth becomes merely a by-product. The Third Great Premise now dominates the marketplace of narratives, which is not necessarily the same as the marketplace of ideas. If enough people believe that Gore said he'd invented the Internet, or that George Bush is a cowboy, then those are facts, even though Gore never said it and Bush is afraid of horses. If people devoutly hate Gore for saying what he never said, or profoundly like Bush for being what he isn't, then that becomes the truth.

In 1960, Nixon had lost to the first thoroughly novelized presidency, that of John F. Kennedy. The New Frontier was a fairly conventional political narrative; nothing sells in America like the notion that we have to pick up ourselves and start anew. But, like William Kotzwinkle cobbling together E.T.'s libido, historians and journalists and other scribbling hangers-on fell all over themselves to fill in the elided details of the television photoplay. The idea of the cool and ironic Jack Kennedy, who used to run with the Rat Pack in Vegas, turning mushy over a piece of treacle like *Camelot* is on its face preposterous. But it sold well enough to define, in shorthand, everything from Pablo Casals playing in the East Room to the Cuban missile crisis, which was decidedly not a time for happy-ever-aftering.

The apotheosis of the modern novelized presidency was that of Ronald Reagan. He and his people created a remarkable and invulnerable narrative around him, so complete and whole that it managed to survive, relatively intact, until Reagan's death in 2004, when what was celebrated in lachrymose detail was not his actual biography but what had been created out of it over the previous forty years. To mention his first marriage, to Jane Wyman, during the obsequies was not merely in bad taste, but seemed irrelevant, as though it had happened to someone else besides the deceased.

Reagan's people maintained their basic story line even through the perilous comic opera of the Iran-Contra scandal. The country learned that Reagan had arranged to sell missiles to the people who sponsored anti-American terrorism in the Middle East, in order to finance pro-American terrorism in Latin America, and that on one occasion, he sent an important official to Teheran with a Bible and a cake. The country learned this without laughing its beloved, befuddled chief executive out of office. Ol' Dutch, what a card.

When Karl Rove (or whoever) talked to Ron Suskind about the contempt he felt for the "reality-based community," and how his administration would create its own reality for the rest of us to study, he wasn't saying anything groundbreaking. People in his job had been doing that for years. What he had was a monumental event to act upon. When September 11 happened, and it was clear that events moved whether people wanted them to or not, the country swung radically behind a president who, somehow, was not a part of "the government," but a quasi-official king and father. It was said that irony died on September 11; but cynicism was what fell most loudly.

Suddenly, "the government" was us again. Of course, "the government" largely was defined as the president, whom we were accustomed to treat as our common property. Dan Rather told David Letterman that he would "line up" wherever George Bush told him to line up. This attitude of wounded deference obtained for nearly three years. The Iraq war happened because the people who'd wanted it all along were uniquely positioned to create a narrative about why it should happen, and seized the right moment for its release date.

In short, all the outside checks on what Paul Pillar saw within the government were gone. Events were becoming novelized, and the wrong people were filling in the elided details; the relationship between Al Qaeda and Iraq, which didn't exist in fact, existed within the prevailing narrative. The Iraqi nuclear program was an established threat, as real as Jack Kennedy's love for the scores of Lerner and Loewe. Public opinion, which Madison said "sets bounds for every government," was in no condition to set any limits whatsoever. It needed a narrative, and the people who were selling the war gave the country what screenwriters call a through-line, from Ground Zero through Kabul to Baghdad.

"We are talking here about national moods," says Paul Pillar. "And, of course, 9/11 was the big event here in suddenly bringing about a change in the national mood. It became far more belligerent, far more inclined to strike out somewhere, and so it was the perfect environment for something like going to war on automatic pilot in Iraq to work. Politically, it wouldn't have been possible without 9/11 at all.

"We are talking about people who had a basis for thinking they were smarter than just about anyone else they met. So, sure, if we're going to manipulate an issue like the weapons thing, or even distort things about the terrorist connections, if it helps bring about a result I believe with all my intellectual firepower is right for the country, then so be it. If there are a few misrepresentations along the line, that doesn't matter."

* * *

THE fact is," Carl Ford, Jr., says, leaning across a round, cluttered table in an office in another part of Washington, "there were all kinds of opportunities to speak up. The fact was that—those people in CIA and in the DIA [Defense Intelligence Agency]? I didn't hear them, and there were plenty of opportunities for my analysts who were out there among them, just among the leaders like I was, and they didn't hear [the CIA and DIA people speak up], either. The fact was we felt like we were just spitting into the wind.

"There were those like Paul Pillar who, if he talks about weapons of mass destruction, I said, 'Paul, where were you?' Because he was in a position where he could have spoken up. It's not a case in which the intelligence community has a significant impact and they want to cry about the fact that policymakers don't listen to them. They want to say, 'Well, I tried and they wouldn't let me do it.' Bullshit. The fact is that they couldn't convince anyone that they were right simply because they were smart. Because that's not the way the world works."

Ford is an intelligence lifer. He'd worked at CIA and in the Pentagon. He was a good friend and a longtime admirer of Vice President Dick Cheney. As events moved toward war, Ford was working at the State Department as the director of its Bureau of Intelligence and Research (INR). A short and fiery ex-Marine who served in Vietnam, Ford had a reputation of being a very hard sell, the kind of person who flourished in cold-shower briefings like the ones Richard Clarke recalled from his time at State, in which people who brought in badly researched reports or half-baked proposals found themselves leaving the meeting room through a meat grinder. Ford felt this intellectual rigor reverse itself when it came to Iraq. The facts were whatever was malleable enough to fit into a salable narrative. The truth was sent through the meat grinder.

"On the case of the internal Iraq issues," recalls Ford, "the policymakers really didn't listen at all. My point is that, if we had said, 'There are no weapons of mass destruction,' it might have slowed them down, but I don't think it would have had any impact on most of the people who were deciding on the war. I think that it would have made it more difficult for them to sell that war. In fact, one of the things that disturbed me the most, that eventually led to my leaving, was the sort of view that, 'Well, okay, but if we tell the people that, if we don't focus on weapons of mass destruction, we might not be able to sell the war.'

"That's what a democracy is all about. You haven't got the evidence, even if you passionately believe that they [the Iraqis] have them [WMDs], then it's up to you to make that case. But there was a sense that they were so certain that it didn't really matter."

In his job at INR, Ford was intimately involved with one of the crucial elided details in the narrative that was concocted to justify the invasion of Iraq. And because this detail fit so perfectly into the story that was being developed, all the people developing the story believed it—or so effectively pretended they did that the difference hardly mattered. It became the source of a series of the noisiest subplots of the ongoing narrative, and it was a moment of utter fiction, a passage of the purest novelization.

A little more than a month after the September 11 attacks, the Italian intelligence service handed over to the CIA's station in Rome a sheaf of documents that had been kicking around intelligence circles for a couple of years. They involved a visit by Iraqi officials to the African country of Niger, an impoverished nation planted atop some of the finest uranium in the world. The Italians passed the same documents to British and French intelligence, as well.

One of the documents was a letter, written in French, in which the president of Niger, Mamadou Tandja, offered to sell Saddam Hussein five hundred tons a year of uranium "yellowcake," suitable, if enriched, for use in the manufacture of nuclear weapons. This letter was why the CIA dispatched a former diplomat named Joseph Wilson to Niger in February 2002. Wilson reported back that there seemed to be no basis for the story. Nevertheless, the letter later became the basis of the famous "sixteen words"—"The British government has learned that Saddam Hussein recently sought significant quantities of uranium in Africa"—in George W. Bush's prewar 2003 State of the Union speech. Watching the speech today, it is striking how Bush reads the last two of those sixteen words. He drops his voice to a lower register. He speaks . . . very . . . slowly. All that's missing are some ominous minor chords from a moviehouse pipe organ. There seem to be bats hanging on every syllable. The war was launched three months later.

"Remember," Ford says, "the argument for years was whether or not they had reconstituted their nuclear program. That was the single most important issue and, when that changed, the time line changed. All of a sudden, you say they've reconstituted their nuclear weapons program, not only do they have chemical and biological weapons, but the clock has started on when they're going to have nuclear weapons and, if we don't do something, they are going to build one. But, before that, if they're not reconstituting their nuclear program, you can't argue that you need to go in there and kick their ass."

In July 2002 Wilson published an op-ed in the *New York Times* reiterating what he'd earlier told the CIA—that, as far as he could determine, the transaction between Niger and Iraq was the purest moonshine. In retaliation, the White House political apparatus leaked the name of Wilson's wife, Valerie Plame, who was a covert CIA operative working on issues of nuclear proliferation, to a series of Washington journalists. A lengthy investigation ensued, concluding with the conviction of I. Lewis (Scooter) Libby for perjury. His sentence was then commuted by President Bush. His trial opened a window into the novelization of the process by which Idiot America had taken itself to war.

And the letter that helped start the war was a clumsy, obvious fake. Skeptics with a firsthand knowledge of Niger—such as Wilson—found the whole transaction as described in the letter implausible. An international consortium strictly monitored Niger's uranium production. There was simply no way to move five hundred tons of uranium a year around the country discreetly. It would tie up the entire nation's trucking capacity, and shipping these loads down the rudimentary roadways from the mines to the port cities would paralyze the country's traffic. It was probably the most consequential forgery since the publication of the *Protocols of the Elders of Zion,* and people all over the United States government, like Carl Ford, knew it.

"This one was not a hard one," Ford explains. "This was one of those easy cases. You have a fragment of information that is accompanied by a couple of older fragments, and all it suggests is that somebody from Iraq may have talked to the Nigerien government about buying some yellowcake. The reports don't say they did. They don't say exactly when or how, and that, alone, for a long time, at least through the NIE [in 2002], became the basis for people—everybody; CIA, DIA—saying they are in fact buying yellowcake from Africa."

The narrative had triumphed. Reality had been richly novelized with details that people made up to fill in the inconvenient gaps in the actual story. A forgery had been used to reinforce untruth and wishful thinking, and the people selling it had been able to do so with full confidence that the people they were taking to war by and large hadn't been paying attention to their government closely enough over the previous two years. Shell-shocked, the country had put itself on automatic pilot and hadn't remembered to turn the equipment off in time. The crash came, and it was bloody and ongoing.

"Remember," Ford muses, "this was a time in which people were doing and saying things in response to 9/11 that not only seemed to me at the time to be outrageous, but were clearly the majority positions. My argument isn't that there weren't substantive issues. What bothered me was the rationale that we know better than Congress, that we know better than the American people. The problem is that it takes leaders who are willing to say, 'This is going to be painful, folks, but we got a crisis here between our Constitution and the threat and we've got to work together to find a solution to it.' I have great faith that the American people can learn. They do believe in our Constitution and they'll fight to keep it."

Carl Ford left government and now works in one of those Washington offices just out of the gravitational sphere of the official city. The same dynamic that enabled a clumsy forgery to remain part of a casus belli was at work throughout the war and everything that came after it. The endless occupation. Secret prisons. Torture. All of it came as reflex, unthinking and automatic.

* * *

IN *Imperial Life in the Emerald City,* his account of the first two years of the American occupation of Iraq, Rajiv Chandrasekaran describes the hiring process by which young Americans— undeniably brave and in many cases admirably idealistic—were hired to go to work for the Coalition Provisional Authority, the governing body cobbled together for the purpose of bringing some semblance of order to the postwar chaos. According to Chandrasekaran, applicants were vetted on, among other things, the fervor of their opposition to *Roe v. Wade,* the Supreme Court decision that had legalized abortion years before most of them had been born. Qualified people in fields like the production of electricity were passed over in favor of the offspring of Republican campaign contributors. Prospective employees were treated during their interview process to lengthy grilling as to their opinions on capital punishment and the Bush domestic agenda—which is to say, the Bush domestic agenda for the United States, not for Iraq. When, in desperation, the CPA sent an actual headhunter back to Washington to get control of the process, the civilian leadership tried to have the man thrown out of the Pentagon. Thus was the essential dynamic of the *Hardball* green room grafted onto a massive foreign policy experiment in the most volatile part of the world, the Marx Brothers working from a script by Graham Greene.

In retrospect, some of what was said during the run-up to the war about the postwar period in Iraq sounds fantastical. Paul Wolfowitz was "reasonably certain" that the U.S. troops would be "greeted as liberators," and that Iraqi oil revenues would pay for the reconstruction. Richard Cheney expected "candy and flowers" to be tossed from every balcony from Mosul to Basra. The looting of priceless antiquities from the Baghdad museum was greeted with "Stuff happens" by Donald Rumsfeld, channeling every teenager who ever cracked up the family sedan. The looting of tons of ammunition, which would have more serious immediate consequences, was greeted in much the same way. The liberation of Iraq by force, it was said, would set off a wildfire of democratization that would remake the Middle East as it had Eastern Europe after the fall of the Iron Curtain. It was as though the people in charge of the enterprise went into Iraq expecting to be rescued from the consequences of their own decisions by the sword of Gilgamesh, or the timely intervention of Baal.

And, just as was the case with the intelligence that led to the war in the first place, experts within the government who were dubious about the prospects of a short, easy occupation were ignored, marginalized, or, in several cases, attacked and forced to resign. One of those people was David Phillips, a consultant who once headed up what was called the Future of Iraq Project for the State Department, a program that involved seventeen federal agencies. It spent $5 million and it developed plans for everything from rural electrification to political reconciliation.

Perhaps its most important element was the Democratic

Principles Working Group, which took upon itself the considerable task of devising a workable plan for democratic reforms on a country that had been cobbled together in the aftermath of World War I to include various ethnic and religious sects, most of whom did not like one another. Phillips was deeply involved in that particular element of the project.

Phillips was not a softhearted bureaucrat. He was a hardheaded realist who earlier had helped reconstruct the Balkans after that region had spent a decade tearing itself apart in a spasm of genocidal lunacy. Phillips was a partisan of the Kurds, in the northern part of Iraq. The United States had sold this embattled people down the river at least twice over the past thirty years; their history is the living definition of being only a pawn in the game. Phillips believed in regime change in Iraq and, if military action was absolutely necessary to achieve it, he would support that, too.

Phillips's project was torn apart largely through infighting between the State Department and those elements elsewhere in the government—particularly in the Department of Defense, the National Security Council, and the Office of the Vice President—who were trying to sell the country on the war.

"I had an evolving sense that we were being set aside," Phillips says. "It was clear that they were approaching this work from a different ideological perspective than were the professionals at State that I was in touch with, and that they were much more interested in lining up Iraqis so they could present a united front to American public opinion as opposed to working substantively through the kind of problems that had to be addressed." Gradually, but inexorably, Phillips says, the center of gravity for the reconstruction of Iraq shifted away from the State Department and toward a group of people engaged in what seemed to Phillips to be magical thinking.

"They were engaged in a discussion, actively engaged," he

says. "But they wanted the discussion to reach conclusions that were consistent with their prejudgment, which was that the Iraqis were desperate to be liberated, the Iraqi exiles could be parachuted in, that the U.S. could decapitate the Ba'athist hierarchy, install the exiles, and be out of Iraq in ninety days. Because the administration was dominated by ideologues, ideology trumped pragmatism."

Phillips knew what he knew. He just didn't believe what the ideologues believed. "You can just as easily have a faith-based, or ideologically driven, policy," he says. "You start with the presumption that you already know the answer prior to asking the question. When information surfaces that contradicts your firmly entrenched views, you dismantle the institution that brought you the information.

"We went in blindfolded and believed our own propaganda. We were going to get out in ninety days, spend $1.9 billion in the short term, and Iraqi oil was going to pay for the rest. Now we're deep in the hole, and people are asking questions about how we got there. It's delusional, allowing delusions to be the basis of policymaking. Once you've told the big lie, you have to substantiate it with a sequence of lies that's repeated. You can't fix a policy if you don't believe that it's broken."

Frustrated that all his work had been ignored—in April 2003, when American ambassador L. Paul Bremer III suspended the handover of sovereignty to the Iraqis, the members of Phillips's Democratic Principles Working Group were infuriated at what they saw as a betrayal—Phillips resigned in protest on September 11, 2003. He did not, however, go quietly. He gave speeches and appeared on television. He wrote a book, *Losing Iraq: Inside the Postwar Reconstruction Fiasco*. He found himself tangled in the thickets of deception that still surrounded the war and its aftermath, and in the complete inadequacy of those institutions whose job it was to cut through them. Once, when he was consulting for NBC News, a young producer asked him to come on television to comment on something Hans Blix was going to say to the UN Security Council. Blix was speaking at five P.M. They wanted Phillips on the air at four.

"They said, 'Just assume, guess what he'll say, and comment upon it,' " Phillips reports. "I told him that I couldn't comment on a statement that hadn't been made yet."

* * *

IN Falls Church, deep in the Virginia countryside outside Washington, parkways wind gently between the gleaming offices set back among the trees. Consultants work here, ex-military types who wear their expensive suits like uniforms. Other people still in uniform come out to meet with them, jamming the food court of a Marriott hotel. One man in fatigues eats a salad holding a fork in his prosthetic hand. A soft rain mottles the glass of the windows.

Anthony Zinni works in one of the quiet office towers. He is a security consultant, one of the non-uniformed men with whom the uniformed men come to do business. But he is still a soldier, a Marine, built like a bullet, with the unwavering gaze that makes it look as though he sees everything through a gunsight. For ten years, Zinni was the general in charge of keeping Saddam Hussein in a box. He is now an outcast in the circles within which he once worked. He's an outcast because the strategy that he helped create was abandoned and Zinni objected, forcefully. He objected to the war and he objected to what he believed was the meretricious grounds on which the war was launched. He is an outcast mostly because he was right.

"We value theory over experience," he says. "We've come

to that. That's relatively new. This town is full of bright young twenty- to thirty-something Ph.D.s who all have a new strategy, a new theory that fits over a page and a half about how the world should be run. There's no balance between theorist and practitioner anymore. We like short, snappy, quick answers to things, and the world is much more complex.

"You know, the most boring thing you could imagine is a politician standing up and giving a complex, strategic view of the world. Which is necessary, but it's soon put off. We judge the political debates by who has the snappiest little phrase that can be put out there. We live in a world of spin. So we don't look at reality and truth."

Zinni got smacked in the face with this revelation one day in August 2002. He was in Nashville, attending the national convention of the Veterans of Foreign Wars, at which he was to be given an award. He'd recently retired after thirty-five years in the Marines, in no small part because his expertise had been marginalized in the new administration, which he'd supported during the 2000 campaign.

The keynote speaker at the VFW convention was Vice President Dick Cheney. In his speech, Cheney said, flatly, "There is no doubt that Saddam Hussein now has weapons of mass destruction. . . . There is no doubt that he is amassing them to use them against our friends, against our allies, and against us." It was a call for war. Sitting behind Cheney on the platform, Zinni was gobsmacked.

"I said, 'You have to be kidding me. Where is that coming from?' " he says. "The situation wasn't even anything remotely like that. I'm listening to this case for war based on faulty or— and I'm being kind—embellished intelligence.

"I couldn't believe they were doing this. And it became clear to me that the neocons were selling this idea that had been from the mid-nineties—some of them even called it 'creative destabilization'—that you go in and do something like this and Iraq's the right place, and you're going to light the fire of democracy in the Middle East and change the equation. All of us who knew that area and had been out there said, 'You're going to light a fire, all right, but it's not going to be one of democracy and stabilization. It's going to be destabilizing and destructive. You do not understand the forces you were about to unleash.' "

Zinni's opposition was not simply geopolitical. He saw with a grunt's eye view what the American soldiers were going to face in Iraq. "We don't appreciate the lessons of history," Zinni says. "There's a difference between failures based on arrogance and incompetence and ignorance, and mistakes that everybody makes in the course of very involved and complex undertakings like this one."

Zinni had one last chance to make his case. He was called before the Senate Foreign Relations Committee in February 2003. Four months earlier, Congress had given the president the authority to use military force against Iraq, and Bush had made it quite plain that he planned to do so. Having already surrendered its war powers, Congress was putting on something of a bipartisan dumb show. Administration officials were stupefyingly vague about plans for dealing with the problems of postwar Iraq, and Zinni knew why: They didn't have any plans, because some of them didn't really care. He saw in these officials not merely a lack of expertise, but a contempt for those who had it.

Zinni's expertise was in devising ways to keep as many soldiers as possible from getting killed in pursuit of a specific objective. He gently chided the committee for its lack of curiosity and its passive acceptance of the gruel it was being fed. He continued to oppose the war in public appearances, but the war came anyway, because nobody who could have stopped it stood up and tried.

That was what stayed with Anthony Zinni as the war was launched, and Saddam fell, and Iraq exploded, as more than three thousand Americans died over four years during which everything he thought would happen did happen, over and over again. The country had wandered into this war, eyes half closed, stunned and shocked and too willingly sold. The people had left the country on automatic pilot too long to pull out of the crash.

"The problem comes on this sort of ideological notion that's presented, and it discounts all those with experience in the region, despite what they're saying. There's no hearing for the other side. As a matter of fact, what it becomes is for those of us who voiced our concerns to be called traitors. You were losing this war from the day you crossed the line of departure. . . . Taking down the regime was not a difficult task. Doing it with too few troops, not having a plan for reconstruction, doomed you from the start.

"I was talking awhile back to a citizens group in Richmond and almost everybody in the audience was a conservative. There were a couple of Democrats there and, at the end of my spiel, a young man got up and he was really angry and he said, 'I'm a Republican and I'm very conservative and I support this war." Then he pointed at one of the Democrats, and he said, 'But, you, as the opposition party, you had the obligation to create the debate on this war and you failed.' I mean, we had the failure on one side to stand up and be counted and we had the failure on the other side of bullying and using patriotism to stamp out any debate and now both sides regret that more and more."

The rain falls more steadily on the trees outside. A low, wet fog rolls in along the parkway. The men in uniform shake hands outside the Marriott with the men who don't wear uniforms anymore. It is a loose summer's day in a nation at war, a country full of easy marks, blinking in the ruins and soggy now with futile buyer's remorse.

* * *

IF everything, even scientific discussion and even questions of an individual life and death, is going to be dragged into politics, then the discussion there at least ought to exist on a fairly sophisticated level. The founders thought it should. They considered self-government a science that required an informed and educated and enlightened populace to make all the delicate mechanisms run. Instead, today, we have the Kabuki politics and marionette debates exemplified by cable television, creating its own events to argue about. Every discussion, even discussion of who should be president, ends up in a bar fight.

(And even that standard is imprecise. If his two terms as president prove nothing else, it proves that George Bush was the kind of guy who comes with you to the bar, disappears into the gents' when it's his turn to buy, and ducks out the back door, after starting a fight with the defensive tackle of the football team that you have to finish.)

A year after that famous Zogby poll was released concerning the nation's preference to toss back a brew with George W. Bush— August 19, 2005, to be precise—it was a beautiful day in Idiot America. In Washington, William Frist, the Harvard-educated physician and majority leader of the U.S. Senate who from the well of that chamber had recently diagnosed Terri Schiavo as fit to dance the merengue, endorsed the teaching of intelligent design in the nation's public schools. "I think today a pluralistic society," Frist explained, "should have access to a broad range of fact, of science, including faith."

That faith is not fact, nor should it be, and that faith is not science, nor should it be, did not elude Dr. Frist. He simply wanted to be president, and he was talking to the people who believe that faith is both those things, and he believed that those people would vote for him simply because he talked this rot, and that everyone else would understand him as an actor reciting his lines. In Idiot America, nonsense can be a no-lose proposition.

On that same day, across town, Larry Wilkerson, a top aide to former secretary of state Colin Powell, told CNN that Powell's pivotal presentation to the United Nations, in which the general described Iraq's vast array of deadly weapons, was little more than ten pounds of manure in a five-pound bag. "It was," said Wilkerson, "the lowest point in my life." By August 19, 2005, it had proven to be an even worse moment for thousands of American families and God alone knew how many Iraqis. This apparently was trumped by Wilkerson's tender conscience.

Powell's speech was the final draft of the novelized Iraq saga. The war's proponents needed a narrator with gravitas, and they had found him. "You can afford to lose some points," Dick Cheney reportedly told Powell, sending him off to befuddle the UN and concluding with breathtaking cynicism that the sparkle of Powell's public image would be enough to dazzle the rubes out in the country. And on August 19, 2005, long after it could have made a difference, Larry Wilkerson looked into his hemorrhaging conscience and said that that was precisely what happened. The successful sale of the Iraq war was a pure product of Idiot America.

But Idiot America is a collaborative effort, the results of millions of decisions made and not made, to reduce everything to salesmanship. Debate becomes corrupted argument, in which every point of view is just another product, no better or worse than all the others, and informed citizenship is abandoned to the marketplace. Idiot America is the development of the collective Gut at the expense of the collective mind. It's what results when we abandon our duty to treat the ridiculous with ridicule. It's what results when politicians make ridiculous statements and we not only surrender our right to punish them at the polls but also become too timid to punish their ideas with daily scorn— because the polls say those ideas are popular, and therefore they must hold some sort of truth, which we should respect.

Idiot America is what results when leaders are not held to account for mistakes that end up killing people, and that's why, after Frist and Wilkerson had their moment in the spotlight, August 2005 went on to become a seminal month in Idiot America. With complete impunity, George W. Bush, the president of the United States, wandered the landscape and talked like a blithering nitwit.

First, he compared the violence surrounding the writing of an impromptu theocratic constitution in Baghdad to the events surrounding the Constitutional Convention in Philadelphia in 1787. Undaunted, he later compared the war he'd launched in Iraq to World War II. And then he compared himself to Franklin D. Roosevelt. One more public appearance, and we might have learned that Custer was killed by the Hezbollah.

Then, we saw the apotheosis of the end of expertise, when New Orleans drowned and then turned into a Hieronymus Bosch painting in real time and on television. As the city was virtually obliterated as a functional habitat for human beings, the country discovered that the primary responsibility for dealing with the calamity lay with a man who'd been dismissed as an incompetent from his previous job as the director of a luxury show-horse organization. And the president went on television and said that nobody could have anticipated the collapse of the city's levees.

In God's sweet name, engineers anticipated it. Politicians anticipated it. The poor bastards in the Ninth Ward anticipated it. Hell, four generations of folksingers anticipated it. And the people who hated the president went crazy and the people who liked him defended him. But where were the people who heard this incredible, staggeringly stupid bafflegab, uttered with conscious forethought, the people who realized that, whatever they thought of the man, the president had gotten behind a series of podiums and done everything but drop his drawers and dance the hootchie-koo? They were out there, lost in Idiot America, where it was still a beautiful day.

Oh, he paid for it. His poll ratings cratered and his party lost its congressional majority in 2006. He became the subject of tinny mockery. But the dynamic that created Idiot America remained in place. In 2007, on the question of habeas corpus for prisoners the U.S. military had detained, the Congress could muster only six Republicans to vote essentially in favor of the Great Writ, but twenty-two Democrats were willing to vote to condemn an antiwar newspaper advertisement. Habeas corpus had less of a constituency in 2007, in the Congress of the United States, than it had in the field at Runnymede in 1215. The disorder remains.

None of these episodes was inevitable. Terri Schiavo's death did not have to become a media circus. The country could have rejected, now and forever, the media culture that made it into one, and the people who even now are shining up the green room in anticipation of the next. The facts and the science surrounding the global climate change that is slowly eating away at the lives of the people of Shishmaref could have been kept out of the cheap and tawdry disputation that passes for political debate; it shouldn't matter that "liberals" are on one side of the issue while "conservatives" are on the other. The land is still being pulled away into the Chukchi Sea. There were opposing voices speaking out in the aftermath of September 11 and in the run-up to the war in Iraq that was devised from the shock of it, but those voices were marginalized and ignored, and the media that did so acted with the tacit approval of its audience. We leave ourselves on automatic pilot and realize, too late, what happens when we do.

"There was no plan except 'Defer to us,' " explained Andrew Bacevich, Sr., a retired Army colonel who teaches history and international relations at Boston University. He is a blade of a man with unsparing eyes. His is the last of the cluttered offices to visit, the ones where the people who knew work now. A CNN crew has just packed up and left. People are listening to Bacevich, seven years into the war, because the war has gone bad, and some important people are pretending that, glorioski, they can't imagine how it all happened.

"They said, 'We will cut your taxes and we will not have a draft. Don't worry. The U.S. military is unbeatable, so go to Disney World,' " Bacevich said. "And I think that's the inclination of the American people anyway, and we were all encouraged to do that. Had the president said at the time, 'This requires an all-out national effort. I'm going to increase your taxes. We're going to pay for this. Expand the Army'—in that moment, I think the Congress would have said, 'You got it, Mr. President.' As Americans, we would have said, 'Okay, if that's what it takes.' He said, 'Go to Disney World,' and the moment passed.

"The guys who were so smart that thought they knew how to exploit the window of opportunity were, actually, stupid. I think that's where the historians will puzzle."

Real people get used up in the transactions of Idiot America. None of these people live in Idiot America. Their lives are hijacked there. Annie Santa-Maria finds doing God's work made infinitely harder by people who think they've divined God's thoughts. Faith is sold as science, and a town is torn apart. Spin is treated as fact, and Shishmaref comes apart. Propaganda is indistinguishable from truth, and thousands die. On June 4, 2008, the Senate Intelligence Committee released a report that stated, flatly, that the president and vice president had sold the Iraq war to the country on the basis of claims that they knew were false.

By then, more than four thousand Americans, and God alone knows how many Iraqis, had died. One of those people was First Lieutenant Andrew J. Bacevich, Jr., of the U.S. Army, who had been killed in Iraq on May 13, 2002. Six years after his death, his father wrote a book in which he quoted Reinhold Niebuhr: "Those who think there is little difference between a cold and hot war are either knaves or fools."

"Between 2002 and 2003," his father wrote, "the knaves and fools got their war."

The book you are reading was almost called *Blinking from the Ruins*. But that would have been dishonest and wrong, because there's an innocence between the lines there that none of us deserve. Nothing happens in Idiot America by accident. It is a place that we will into being.

"I got to go meet a guy for lunch," Andrew Bacevich said.

He has not followed us all into the bar, where all opinions are of equal worth, where everyone's an expert, where the Gut makes everyone so very sure. No voice is more authoritative than any other one; some are just louder. Of course, the problem in the bar is that, sooner or later, some noisy bastard always picks a fight. The next day, in the cold light of the morning, everybody's too embarrassed to remember how it all began.

Part IV

✱

MR. MADISON'S LIBRARY

CHAPTER TEN

Torture in New Hampshire

They weren't made of marble. Years after the Constitutional Convention, William L. Pierce, a delegate from Georgia, published his impressions in a Savannah newspaper. Many of them detailed the work of the convention, but Pierce also took the time to write down his personal impressions of his colleagues which, owing to the enforced secrecy of the convention's deliberations, made the sketches something of a sensation. Reading them today is a blessed, gossipy relief from what has become the Founder of the Month Club on various best-seller lists.

Pierce found that William S. Johnson of Connecticut had "nothing in him that warrants the high reputation he has for public speaking." Johnson's colleague Roger Sherman was "the oddest shaped character I ever remember to have met with." Alexander Hamilton sometimes showed "a degree of vanity that is highly disagreeable" and Benjamin Franklin "is no speaker, nor does he seem to let politics engage his attention. He is, however, a most extraordinary man and he tells a story in a style more engaging than anything I ever heard."

Pierce sized up "Mr. Maddison" as "always . . . the best informed man of any point in debate. . . . Mr. Maddison is about 37 years of age, a Gentleman of great modesty—with a remarkable sweet temper. He is easy and unreserved among his acquaintance and has a most agreeable style of conversation."

This is shrewd, intelligent gossip, but gossip nonetheless, and it serves as a deft counterpoint to what Mr. Madison was about, sitting in his chair closest to the front of the room, taking down with almost preposterous precision the specifics of the great debates going on around him. But the works are not interchangeable, and they ought not to be. Neither Madison's notes nor Pierce's sketches ought to define fully any of the people in them. But there seems little question that, had there been cable television news shows in 1787, Pierce would have been booked solid for a week, while you'd have had to scan CSPAN during whiskey hours of the poker game to catch a glimpse of James Madison.

For example, Roger Sherman, of Connecticut, was a ferocious defender of the rights of the smaller states. He threatened to pull all of them out of Philadelphia if his concerns were not addressed. He was not bluffing. (Thomas Jefferson said of him that Sherman had never said a foolish thing in his life.) Luckily for all concerned, Sherman's great gift was compromise. Without him, the Constitution might not have passed at all. That he also was odd-looking is both beyond question and beside the point. Define him by the latter, and everything is out of place, an eighteenth-century equivalent of John Edwards's hair, or of the many voices screaming lines from old movies that seem to echo in the head of Maureen Dowd.

Why not apply the most precisely loony of modern standards

and ask with which of the founders you'd most like to have had a beer? Franklin's the obvious answer, although the ferocious dipsomaniac Luther Martin, from Maryland—"he never speaks without tiring the patience of all who hear him," according to Pierce—might have been entertaining for an hour or so. Pennsylvania's James Wilson would have been no fun at all. He was pedantic, and he was always talking about how much he knew. (Pierce admired how Wilson could run down all the stages of "the Greecian commonwealth down to the present time.") Sure, we might not have had a Bill of Rights without him, but how much fun would he have been?

It's good that there was gossip. There is a place in our understanding for Madison's meticulous note-taking on the great questions being decided, and for Pierce's loose-limbed assessment of the men who came to decide them. It's good that they were not made of marble. Reality demands that they not be cast as figures from Olympus. But reality also demands the acknowledgment that they were not the cast of *My Man Godfrey*, either.

* * *

FOR a brief moment in 2008, reality disappeared from American television because there was nobody around to write it.

A trend as deeply rooted in Idiot America as anything else is, reality television shakes out as little more than the creation of a context in which one set of connivers is set against another. The ur-program *Survivor* was meant to set a number of contestants against one another in an every-person-for-themselves free-for-all. Within a week, one set of contenders was conspiring against another. The "tribal council" became a venting of boundless suspicion, some justified and some not, but all with the essential integrity and suspense of a professional wrestling match. We had, after all, already seen the actual plotting as the series went along.

Televised sports and the media attendant on them had already broken a lot of ground, and the creation of a television reality as an arena went back even further than that, all the way to the rigged quiz shows of the 1950s and to forgotten classics like *Queen for a Day* and *You Asked for It*. In the former, a woman with a terrible tale of sorrow and woe would share it with an adoring public and be rewarded with a new stove. In the latter, people wrote in asking to see a man break a board with his head, or to watch a Tahitian fertility rite, and the host would obligingly share it with a grateful, if baffled, nation. Sooner or later, a country that could so invest itself in Charles Van Doren, or in a housewife from Kansas with ulcers, or in dancing South Sea islanders was bound to start arguing about reality.

The essential dynamic of reality programming is the creation of teams through which Americans can vicariously compete against one another, whether in rooting for the personal trainer in the loincloth on *Survivor*, the Shania Twain wannabe on *American Idol*, or the harried mom and dad trying to win the daily battle of getting the sextuplets off to school in the morning. It is the creation of profitable vessels in which to invest whatever we find unsatisfactory in our own lives. In every real sense, we buy the people and their problems. The essential truth of reality shows lies in how fervently we involve ourselves in them.

"All reality shows," Craig Plestis, an NBC executive, told Forbes.com, "should have a visceral reaction for the viewer. You need to feel something."

Even *American Idol*, Fox television's star-making phenomenon, is shot through with the notion that the panel of demi-celebrities doing the judging is conspiring against one contender and in favor of another. (The charges gained a little credibility early on, when a judge, Paula Abdul, was discovered to be dating one of the contestants.) Now, the cable dial is dotted with reality shows involving huge families, dangerous jobs, messy garages, and really big tumors. There are even reality shows about unreality, people going off in search of Bigfoot or the Jersey Devil. Ignatius Donnelly, alas, died much too soon.

After all, there is very little that's real about a reality show. In them, the imagination is tamed by a re-created reality, as in a zoo. These shows create what looks like an actual habitat for actual human beings, but, since the habitat is designed to be lived in by characters designed to prompt a vicarious involvement on the part of the audience, no less than were Rob Petrie's suburban home or the precinct house in *The Wire,* the whole thing might as well be a cage. Nobody goes to a zoo to dream of dragons.

Today, though, the dynamic present in the reality shows also drives too much of the more serious business of how we govern ourselves as a country, and how we manage ourselves as a culture, and it pretty plainly can't stand the power of it. We've chosen up sides on everything, fashioning our public lives as though we were making up a fantasy baseball team. First, I'll draft a politician, then a couple of "experts," whose expertise can be defined by how deeply I agree with what they say, or by how well their books sell, or by how often I can see them on TV. Then, I'll draft a couple of blowhards to sell it back to me, to make me feel good about my team.

One of the remarkable things about fantasy baseball is that it provides a deeper level of vicariousness in that it enables its participants to cheer for players who are in no way real people, simply columns of statistics and variables. There are no human beings playing in the games of fantasy baseball, only columns of figures. In our politics and our culture, there often seem to be no human beings running for office, or making art, or singing songs. There are only our opinions of them, crammed into the procrustean uniform of Our Side. Winners and losers are judged by which side sells the best.

The most revelatory moment of all came in 2008, when the reality shows had to go off the air because the Hollywood writers had gone on strike and there was nobody to write the reality. Deprived of their vicarious lives, the fans of the shows went into a funk not unlike that which afflicted baseball fans in 1997, when a labor dispute canceled the World Series. It seemed to strike very few people as odd that reality had to go off the air because nobody was left to write it. After all, if you've already made reality a show, what's the point in making a reality show at all?

* * *

THE rain came down in torrents, sluicing through the campus of St. Anselm College in Manchester, on a night in June 2007. Ten Republicans came with the rain, all of them seeking the presidency of the United States in what was supposed to be a transformative election, a chance to reorder the country, to separate fiction from nonfiction, faith from reason, that which sold from that which was true: a chance to put things back where they belonged. It was the first election to be held among the people who were blinking from the ruins.

They were a remarkable bunch. Former New York City mayor Rudolph Giuliani was running against the nineteen hijackers in the September 11 attacks, while Congressman Tom Tancredo was running against ragged immigrants who were sneaking across the Rio Grande. Congressman Ron Paul plumped for pure libertarianism, while Congressman Duncan Hunter seemed to be trying to slice away the moderates among Paul's voters—the people who did not necessarily dive behind the couch after mistaking the sound of their blenders for approaching black helicopters. Paul was also the only one of the bunch firmly against the war in Iraq, which gave him some cachet among young voters who did not know that Paul also would like us to return to the gold standard.

Senator Sam Brownback of Kansas was an out-and-out theocrat, albeit a charitable one. Former governor Mike Huckabee of Arkansas was just as amiably Jesus-loopy as Brownback was. Outside of Giuliani, the two most "serious" candidates seemed to be former governor Mitt Romney of Massachusetts and Senator John McCain of Arizona. As it turned out, Romney spent tens of millions of dollars to prove that he was little more than the Piltdown Man of American politics. McCain would end up as the nominee almost by default, and by virtue of the fact that he was able to allay the fears of the Republican base while maintaining a grip on that dwindling element of his party that can fairly be described as Not Insane. That grip did not hold.

* * *

FOR a time, briefly, it seemed that the country was coming to realize that it had poisoned itself with bullshit and nonsense for nearly a decade. It seemed ready to act upon that realization in its 2008 presidential election. Barack Obama's rise to the Democratic nomination on a nebulous concept of "change" seemed to be based, at least in part, on the idea that we would all stop conning ourselves.

But no.

In August, in what was the first major event of the general election campaign, both Obama and John McCain went out to California to a "forum" organized by Pastor Rick Warren at his Saddleback Church. The very notion that an affluent God-botherer like Warren should be allowed to vet presidential candidates was in itself a sign that the opportunity that twinkled briefly in the election was largely lost. At one point, Warren turned to Obama and asked, "At what point does a baby get human rights?"

The only proper answer to this question for anyone running for president is "How in the hell do I know? If that's what you want in a president, vote for Thomas Aquinas." Instead, Obama summoned up some faith-based flummery that convinced few people in a crowd that, anyway, had no more intention of voting for him than it did of erecting a statue of Baal in the parking lot. Subsequently, Warren gave an interview in which he compared an evangelical voting for a pro-choice candidate to a Jewish voter supporting a Holocaust denier. And the opportunity went a-glimmering.

While Obama merely bowed clumsily in the direction of Idiot America, John McCain set up housekeeping there. Desperate to disassociate himself from the previous administration, which had spent seven years crafting policies that it could sell to Idiot America while the actual America was coming apart at every seam, McCain instead wandered deeply into Idiot America himself, perhaps never to return. He embraced the campaign tactics used to slander him in 2000, even hiring some of the people who had been responsible for them. He stated that he couldn't now vote for his own immigration reform bill. He spent a long stretch of the campaign in violation of the campaign finance reform bill that bore his name. He largely silenced himself on the issue of torture.

He really had no choice. The Republican party, and the brand of movement conservatism that had fueled its rise, had become the party of undigested charlatans. Some of them believed the supply-side voodoo that so unnerved Jonathan Chait. Some of them believed in dinosaurs with saddles. Movement conservatism swallowed them all whole, and it valued them only for the raw number of votes they could deliver. The cranks did not assimilate and the party using them did not really care whether the mainstream came to them. It simply hoped there were enough of them to win elections. The transaction failed the country because it did not free the imagination so much as bridle it with conventional politics. It niche-marketed the frontier of the mind so rigidly that, by 2008, you couldn't run for president as a Republican without transforming yourself into a preposterous figure.

To win the primaries, you had to placate the party's indissoluble base. (This is what ate poor Mitt Romney alive. He went from being a rather bloodless corporate drone to being a rip-roaring culture warrior and ended up looking like a very big fool.) Having done that, you then had to tiptoe away from those same people without alienating them completely. The more successful you were at this delicate fandango, the more preposterous you had to become, especially if, like John McCain, you'd tried to avoid the cranks for most of your public career.

Once McCain got the nomination, he was denied his first choices for vice presidential candidates because neither of them passed muster with the base he had so debased himself to woo. He ended up with Sarah Palin, the governor of Alaska, whose hilarious lack of qualifications for the job was interpreted at the Republican nominating convention as the highest qualification of all. She said so herself.

Palin's nomination was an act of faith in Idiot America almost unsurpassed in political history. Her speech to the Republican National Convention was one prolonged sneer. In what was perhaps the most singularly silly thing ever said of a national candidate of a major party, Republican surrogates up to and including McCain himself argued that Palin's foreign policy bona fides were established because Alaska is so close to Russia. By McCain's own standard, then, Sarah Palin could have run for vice president as an astronaut because she comes from the planet closest to the moon.

She then gave a series of interviews that slid precipitously from the merely disastrous to the utterly catastrophic, including one session with CBS anchor Katie Couric in which Palin, lost amid her talking points, simply abandoned verbs entirely. In another segment of the Couric interviews, Palin brought McCain along for help, and she looked like a middle-schooler who'd been asked to bring her father to a meeting in the vice principal's office.

If the country took its obligations to self-government at all seriously, the presence of Sarah Palin on a national ticket would have been an insult on a par with the elevation of Caligula's horse. However, the more people pointed out Palin's obvious shortcomings, the more the people who loved her loved her even more. She was taken seriously not merely because she had been selected to run, but also because of the fervor she had stirred among people in whose view her primary virtue as a candidate was the fact that she made the right people crazy. Their faith in Idiot America and its Three Great Premises was inviolate. Because the precincts of Idiot America were the only places where his party had a viable constituency, John McCain became the first presidential candidate in American history to run as a parody of himself.

You could see it all coming that rainy night in New Hampshire, when all the Republican candidates were alive and viable. They were faith-based and fully cognizant of the fact that they were not running for office so much as they were auditioning for a role, trying for a chance to do their duty on behalf of people who were invested as vicariously in their citizenship as baseball fans are in their teams, or as the viewers of *American Idol* are in their favorite singer. So that was how it happened that, at one point in the debate, the contenders were asked whether they believed in evolution.

And, in response, three of the Republican contenders for president of the United States, in what was supposed to be one of the crucial elections in the country's history, said that, no, they didn't believe in evolution. And the people in the hall cheered.

It was a remarkable moment in that it seemed so unremarkable. There was no doubt that the three of them—Tancredo, Brownback, and Huckabee—were sincere. However, since admitting that you don't believe in evolution is pretty much tantamount to admitting that you plan to eradicate the national debt by spinning straw into gold, it should immediately have disqualified the lot of them. In fact, it should have given people pause about the entire Republican party that a third of its presidential field was willing to admit that their view of the life sciences had stalled in the 1840s. Instead, it was a matter of hitting the right marks, and delivering right on cue the applause lines that the audience expected.

Within both the political and popular culture, as the two became virtually indistinguishable, the presidency itself had changed, and not entirely for the better. Gone were the embattled, vulnerable presidents, like Fredric March in *Seven Days in May,* who fretted out a military coup that sought to batter down the doors of the White House with Burt Lancaster's bemedaled pectorals. No modern president could be as humble as

Raymond Massey's Abe Lincoln, riding that slow, sad train out of Illinois, martyrdom already clear in his eyes.

Even the gooey liberal pieties of *The West Wing* made way for this kind of thing. The show abandoned its original mission, which was to somehow make speechwriters into television stars. (Hey, that's CNN's job!) It gradually found itself drawn into orbit around the character of President Jed Bartlet, who originally was supposed to be a presence standing somewhere out of frame. The show became as much a cult of personality as any genuine White House ever has. One more scene of the staffers in the Bartlet White House intoning that they "served at the pleasure of the President of the United States," and Gordon Liddy might have sprung, giggling horribly, from behind the drapes on the Oval Office set. Even our fictions ceased to portray the president as a constitutional officer who held his job only at the informed sufferance of the voters.

That's how Andrew Card, George W. Bush's chief of staff, could get up in front of a group of delegates from Maine during the 2004 Republican National Convention in New York and tell them that the president looked upon the people of the United States—his nominal employers, after all—the way all of "us" looked at our children, sleeping in the night, and nobody mentioned to Card that there isn't a single sentence proceeding logically from what he said that doesn't include the word "Fatherland."

The important thing about running for president was to make sure that people were willing to cast you as president in their minds. Be smart, but not so smart that he makes regular people feel stupid. Handsome, but not aloof. Tough always, but a good man to toss a few back with after the bad guys were dispatched. The presidency had conformed itself to the Great Premises of Idiot America. Anything could be true, as long as you said it loudly enough, you appeared to believe it, and enough people believed it fervently enough.

Expertise, always, was beside the point, and the consequence had been both hilarious and dire: a disordered nation that applied the rules of successful fiction to the reality around it, and that no longer could distinguish very well the truth of something from its popularity. This election, which was said to be one that could reorder the country in many important ways, did not begin promisingly.

The byplay concerning evolution in New Hampshire had been preceded by an even more remarkable conversation in South Carolina on the subject of torture. Surely, there have been few more compelling issues in any election than the question whether the president of the United States may, on his own, and in contravention of both domestic and international law, order the torture of people in the custody of the United States, and in the name of the people of the United States. That the president could do so had been the policy of the U.S. government for nearly five years by the time that the ten Republicans gathered in Charleston for their first ensemble debate. A question concerning the efficacy of torture—couched in a melodramatic, post-apocalyptic hypothetical by the moderator, Brit Hume— was posed to the various candidates.

Speaking from his experience, which was both unique and not inconsiderable, John McCain argued that, in addition to being basically immoral, torture doesn't work. He was quickly shouted down by Giuliani, who was once tortured by the thought that his second wife wouldn't move out of the mayor's mansion in favor of his current girlfriend, and by Romney, who once was tortured by the fact that gay people in Massachusetts were allowed to marry each other, and who announced his desire to "double Guantanamo."

This was not a serious discussion of the reality of torture, any more than the discussion about evolution had anything to do with actual science. It was an exercise in niche marketing. Evolution and torture were not being discussed in the context of what they were but, rather, in the context of what they meant as a sales pitch to a carefully defined group of consumers. They were a demonstration of a product, as when those guys at the home shows show you how the juicers work. Suddenly, the Republicans all seemed to be running for Sheriff of Nottingham. But it took Tom Tancredo to drag the whole thing over the vast borders of Idiot America.

"We are talking about this in such a theoretical fashion," Tancredo fumed, ignoring the fact that the whole colloquy was based on a hypothetical. "I'm looking for Jack Bauer."

The audience exploded. The 2008 presidential election was not beginning well. It did not get appreciably better.

* * *

THE bomb is always ticking.

In 2001, Fox television launched *24*, an impeccably crafted thriller in which a federal agent named Jack Bauer races against the clock—each episode is one "hour" in a day—to thwart a massive terrorist attack somewhere in the United States. The show has the velocity of a rifle bullet. Storylines ricochet off each other with dizzying, split-screened abandon. Its craftsmanship, at least through its first four seasons, was beyond reproach, and no television show in the history of the medium so completely captured the zeitgeist. Besides reflecting considerable theatrical craftsmanship, however, *24* was something unique in the history of the country. It was the first attempt at successfully mass marketing torture porn.

Over and over again, to get the information he needs, Bauer

cuts up his suspects with knives. He suffocates them. He electrocutes them. He beats them to a pulp. According to a survey by the nonpartisan Parents Television Council, there were sixty-seven scenes of torture in the first five seasons of 24. Some of the torture was performed by the show's bad guys, and these scenes mainly served only further to justify what Jack Bauer found himself doing later. The torture always works. The country is always saved.

In a nation thirsting for revenge, vicarious or otherwise, operating from those parts of the Gut most resistant to reason, 24 provided a brimming reservoir of vengeance. The show sold. The show was a hit. It was not a reality show. Instead, it was a show that made its own reality out of the desires of its audience. The co-creator of 24, a self-described "right-wing nut-job" and former carpet salesman named Joel Surnow, explained to Jane Mayer of *The New Yorker* that the show landed right where he aimed it. "There are not a lot of measures short of extreme measures that will get it done," Surnow told Mayer. "America wants the war on terror fought by Jack Bauer. He's a patriot."

For all its whiz-bang action and pinballing plotlines, 24 is as resolutely and deliberately free of actual expertise in interrogative techniques as *F Troop* was of actual conditions on the American frontier. There are actual experts in interrogation, and most of them agree that the "ticking bomb" scenario is largely fantastical and, anyway, even in that situation, torture probably won't yield the information you need to foil the plot. Significantly, Mayer reported, when a team of experienced Army and FBI interrogators flew to California to meet with the people behind 24, and to explain their concern that the show was mainstreaming torture in a dangerous way, Surnow blew off the meeting to take a call from Roger Ailes, the president of the Fox News Channel.

According to Mayer, an Army general named Patrick Finne-

gan told the people behind 24 that the show was complicating
his job teaching the laws of war to his students at West Point.
"The kids see it," Finnegan later told Mayer, "and say, 'If torture
is wrong, what about 24?' "

Finnegan's students are not alone in this. The show's reach
has extended into some extraordinary places. Surnow was the
guest of honor at a dinner party thrown at Rush Limbaugh's
house by U.S. Supreme Court Justice Clarence Thomas. The
Heritage Foundation, the de facto headquarters of respectable
conservative opinion in Washington, threw a laudatory panel
discussion on the show that included, among other people, Michael Chertoff, then the secretary of Homeland Security. On
that same trip, Surnow and some other people from the show
got to have lunch at the White House with Karl Rove and with
the wife and daughter of Dick Cheney.

The show was cited in a book by John Yoo, the Justice Department lawyer whose memos justified much of the actual torture that was being carried out by the United States. The talk
show crowd inferred support for torture from the show's ratings. In 2007, attending a panel on the subject in Canada, U.S.
Supreme Court Justice Antonin Scalia argued that torture can
be justified: "Jack Bauer saved Los Angeles. . . . He saved thousands of lives. Are you going to convict Jack Bauer? Say that the
criminal law is against him, is any jury going to convict Jack
Bauer? I don't think so."

And perhaps the apotheosis of the show came when it was
revealed by an international lawyer named Philippe Sands
that, during high-level administration meetings regarding the
treatment of detainees, "People had already seen the first [sea-
son]. . . . Jack Bauer had many friends at Guantanamo. He gave
people lots of ideas."

"I am quite pleased to report," says Colonel Steve Kleinman, an Air Force intelligence officer, "that I have never seen that show."

Kleinman has spent his career in what is called human intelligence, and specifically, in the interrogative techniques best suited for getting actionable information out of people reluctant to give it up. "I was reading Jane Mayer's piece this morning and she's got Chertoff, who's described as a big fan, and all these other people, and I'm thinking, 'Wait a second. That's the way we're conducting ourselves? Our senior people are being informed by Hollywood, by a guy who was a former carpet salesman? They're just making it up as they go.'

"I guess we are informed by the mass media and this very silly show, where interrogation is a very visible means of revenge. So we have this person and, if we have to shake him up to get information, well, that's just part of the process, and I say, 'Wait a second. Interrogation is not punishment. Interrogation is not supposed to be some form of retribution. Interrogation is a very sophisticated and very critical intelligence platform, and it's a methodology that needs to be employed with some foresight, with care, and with diligence. It's not to wreak revenge. What your gut tells you to do, what your gut says the other person is thinking, is almost always wrong.' "

* * *

IN February 2008, Forbes.com noted that reality programming might have topped out. The genre's initial shock value had worn off, and attempts by the networks to push the boundaries of the form further were greeted with at best apathy and, at worst, public revulsion, as was the case with CBS's *Kid Nation,* an extraordinarily bad idea that went even more wrong in the execution. Children left on their own to go feral on camera in

New Mexico turned out to be nothing anyone wanted to see, and there weren't enough William Golding fans left in America to save the project. At the end, the network reality shows that maintained their large audiences were mainly those most clearly descended not only from *Queen for a Day,* but also from the old *Hollywood Palace*—most notably, *American Idol* and *Dancing with the Stars.* Thus did reality shows bring the variety show back to prime time.

Around the same time, the producers of 24 gave an interview to *The Wall Street Journal* in which they explained that their show was in trouble because torture didn't seem to be as popular as it had been a few years earlier. News reports about the Bush administration's predilection for Jack Bauer solutions to real-world problems had soured the audience on Jack Bauer solutions to Jack Bauer's problems. (The *WSJ* piece tracked the slide in 24's ratings as almost perfectly paralleling the decline in George W. Bush's approval ratings.) Actors declined to appear. Jane Mayer's piece in *The New Yorker* made the show's producers sound like braying jackasses and thumbscrew salesmen. "The fear and wish-fulfillment the show represented after 9/11 ended up boomeranging against us," lamented the show's head writer. The problem with torture, it seemed, was not that it had proven to be ineffective and immoral and illegal under any conceivable circumstance, but that it couldn't hold an audience anymore. The producers took the show off the air for some extended retooling.

But torture remained, a shadowy issue on the edges of the presidential campaign, which was just hitting its stride as the reality shows came back and 24 went into the shop. Jane Mayer's *The Dark Side,* a book about how, slowly but quite willfully, the United States had established forms of torture as a national policy, sold well, but the issue was strangely absent from the political news of the moment; most of *that* concerned the election of the next president, for whom torture was going to be a fait accompli whether he wanted it to be or not.

Writing in Salon.com, Rosa Brooks noticed that torture was becoming the new abortion, a litmus test among conservative Republicans to measure a candidate's fealty to a unilateral and aggressive approach to a war on terror, and among Democrats a measure of a candidate's commitment to constitutional guarantees. In her acceptance speech to the Republican National Convention, Sarah Palin got a big hand when she said, "Al Qaeda terrorists still plot to inflict catastrophic harm on America and [Barack Obama's] worried that someone hasn't read them their rights." So, of course, torture is an issue like all the other issues, a way of measuring one's commitment to the team in which people vicariously invest themselves.

Torture turned out to be no more or less important, as the campaign went on, than John Edwards's hair, Hillary Clinton's laugh, or John McCain's age, and far less important than the crazy things that emanated from the pulpit of Barack Obama's church. In April 2008, the blogger Glenn Greenwald put "torture" through a Nexis search along with the name of John Yoo, the Justice Department lawyer who drafted the memos that gave the administration cover for what it was doing. Greenwald came up with 102 entries over one two-week period as the story of Yoo's opinions was first breaking. In that same period of time, Greenwald's search rang up more than three thousand entries containing both Obama's name and that of his controversial pastor, Jeremiah Wright. There were more than a thousand stories about Obama's public ineptitude as a bowler.

"Torture" was now just another political product, a brand name, a trademark issue among dozens of others involved in an extended national transaction that was not going the way it was supposed to go but, rather, the way it always did—according to the Great Premises of Idiot America, where anything can be true if enough people believe in it.

* * *

THE problem is not that America has dumbed itself down, as many people believe. (Reality shows are often cited as Exhibit A for the prosecution here.) It's that America's gotten all of itself out of order, selling off what ought never to be rendered a product, exchanging (rather than mistaking) fact for fiction, and faith for reason, and believing itself shrewd to have made a good bargain with itself. Real people get ground up in these transactions. Sell religious fervor as science, and Annie Santa-Maria's checking the rearview mirror as she drives home in the dark. Sell corporate spin as science, and the people of Shishmaref watch their homes get eaten by the sea. Sell propaganda as fact, and hundreds of thousands of people die. For real. None of these people lived in Idiot America. They were shanghaied there.

In 2007, a man named Scott Weise was in a bar in Decatur, Illinois, watching his beloved Chicago Bears play the Indianapolis Colts in the Super Bowl. Perhaps well lubricated, perhaps not, Weise made a bet with the assembled fans in the bar that, if the Bears lost, he would change his name to Peyton Manning, the name of Indianapolis's star quarterback. Weise even signed a pledge to that effect, which his fellow patrons duly witnessed.

The Bears were pretty awful that day, and Indianapolis won from here to there. Manning was voted the game's Most Outstanding Player. Weise stood by his pledge. However, a judge subsequently ruled that Weise couldn't legally change his name to "Peyton Manning" because to do so would be to violate the quarterback's privacy.

"I had told the judge that I was not doing this because I

wanted to change my name, but I was doing it because I was honoring a bet," Weise told the local newspaper. "I think she understood that."

There are people who will believe that a man named Scott Weise represents Idiot America. But they would be wrong. He was merely a crank, making a crank's wager and accepting the consequence when he lost. And when the court ruled against him, he accepted the ruling because he didn't really want to be "Peyton Manning" anyway. It was an honorable transaction all the way around. There was nothing out of order about it. By comparison, though, consider Antonin Scalia, associate justice of the U.S. Supreme Court, citing a fictional terror fighter as a justification for reversing literal centuries of American policy and jurisprudence, and citing that fictional character, furthermore, on a panel that had gathered to discuss international law. Consider the highest level of the U.S. government, gathering in the White House in order to set American law back to a point ten minutes before Magna Carta was signed, and tossing around ideas they'd heard on the same television show. And people are worried that this country pays too much attention to *American Idol*? That's just a reality show, which is more show than reality, because somebody has to write it. That meeting in the White House is what happens when you've already made reality a show.

Idiot America is always a matter of context, because it is within the wrong context that things get out of order. Idiot America is a creation of the mind in which things are bought and sold under the wrong names and, because some of those things sell well, every transaction is treated as though it had a basis in reality. Put things back in order and it becomes plain. Scott Weise is an American crank who did something any American crank would be proud of. Antonin Scalia, and the people at that White House meeting, are representatives of Idiot America. The sad irony is that they think everyone else lives there.

CHAPTER ELEVEN

Mr. Madison's Library

The flat heat of early summer floats, shimmering, just above the asphalt of the parking lots. The Creation Museum has been open for just over a year now, and the parking lots are respectably crowded for a Monday in June. The cars are from Mississippi, and from Wisconsin, and from Minnesota. There's a minivan from West Virginia with a vanity license plate: "JE-SUSROX."

They really have done it well. The hilltop in Hebron contains not only the museum itself, but a petting zoo, a picnic area, and a nature walk around the perimeter of a small lagoon alive with perch and echoing with the low sound of croaking bullfrogs. Like any other museum, the kids are entertained for a while by all the bells and whistles, but by the time everyone gets to the picnic area, everyone's pretty hot and sweaty and praying, not for guidance, but for Coca-Cola.

Inside, of course, the museum is cool and shady, dark in many places and in many different ways. It shrewdly mimics other museums with its exhibits and interactive diversions for the younger crowd. The walls are filled with small signs explaining what the visitor is looking at. Of the respectable collection of fossils, none, the visitor is told, can be older than four thousand years. The museum has animatronic people and animatronic dinosaurs. Dinosaurs are almost everywhere you look; walk in the front door, and the neck of a huge herbivore looms over you, chewing away on plastic grass. In fact, dinosaurs are a lot more visibly present in the place than anything else. There's more Jurassic than Jesus here.

The Creation Museum is also a richly appointed monument to complete barking idiocy, from start almost all the way to the finish.

Anyone who'd visited while it was under construction came away thinking to themselves, "Well, a lot of what they say is basically to flush the rubes to raise money." But, no, they actually believe it. The planetarium show is fairly conventional, although the narrator occasionally reminds people who might be overly awed by Alpha Centauri that "all these worlds are marred by the Curse," which is to say that Adam's sin dropped the hammer on some Venusians who never did anything to anyone.

The museum is organized as a scientific walk through Genesis. Poor Adam likely is still dickless, but in his two appearances he's lounging in the Garden with shrubbery in front of his naughty bits, and standing hip-deep in a pond with water lilies around his waist, so a firsthand examination is impractical. Eve still has the long hair, arranged conveniently so as not to scandalize the faithful.

"Hey, come on down here," yells a young boy who has gotten ahead of the story. "Eve's pregnant!"

Walking through the exhibits is an airless, joyless exercise. Among other things, you learn that there were no poisonous creatures, nor any carnivores of any kind, until Adam and Eve committed their sin. Then, it seems, velociraptors developed a taste for hadrosaur tartare, and we were off. Things get a little dicey when an exhibit tries to explain why it was all right for Cain to have married his sister. (The answers seem to be, in order: (1) there weren't many women around; (2) everybody was doing it; and (3) who are you to be asking these questions, you infidel bastard?) Out of that room, past a grumpy robot Methuselah, and you come to a huge exhibit depicting the construction of the Ark.

Noah and his sons are milling about, moving their arms and heads like mechanical Santas and talking about the upcoming disaster. Now, it would be unkind to point out that there probably weren't many Jewish people involved in the construction of the Creation Museum. So let's just say that the people who built it can possibly be excused for believing that every Jew since Abraham has sounded like Tevye in *Fiddler on the Roof.* Noah himself seems to favor Topol from the movie, rather than Zero Mostel's broader performance in the original stage musical.

The flood is central to the museum's "science." The exhibit contends, quite seriously, that Noah took two of everything, including two of every species of dinosaur, and that he was able to load up the latter because he took baby dinosaurs rather than the full-grown kind. The flood is vital not only to the museum's paleontology, but to its geology and topography as well. As the tour goes drearily on, you wander half-awake through the Hell in a Handbasket sections depicting the modern world. (Poor Darwin comes in for a real hiding here.) But what's startling you is their theory that, if dinosaurs got on the Ark, then they must have gotten off it as well. Which means that they survived into human memory.

That compelling notion—catnip for kids, no matter what

age they are—illuminates the museum's collection of fossils. As wretchedly Stalinist as the explanatory cards are—one refers to "the false idea" that birds are descended from dinosaurs, reflexively couching scientific disagreement in the clumsy language of doctrinal dispute—the fossils are quite good, and the room is bright and alive with the sounds of children released from those parts of the museum that warn them that evolution is the gateway to sin, death, graffiti, and eternal damnation. The place almost seems like fun.

At the end, over by the snack bar and just short of the gift shop, there is the Dragon's Theater, where a film explains that, not only did dinosaurs survive the flood, they may well have lasted long enough to account for the multiplicity of dragon legends that exist in all the cultures of the world. Absent its obvious religious filigree, this notion is a blessed piece of pure American crankhood amid the religious eccentricity of the museum. The impulse behind it is the same that compels secular cryptozoologists to go haring off to the Congo to look for Mokele-mbembe, or all those film crews haunting the Himalayas trying to capture the Yeti for the History Channel. People seeing dinosaurs in dragons are no different from people going off their heads looking for the Templar gold.

This little film places into stark relief what is truly depressing about the place—its conventionality, its unseemly lust for credibility in the wider world. In Dealey Plaza, for example, there are dozens of independent crackpots who will gladly take a couple of bucks to explain to you who shot John Kennedy, and from where, and who was behind them. They work their territories by themselves and for themselves, and none of them is demanding that the country's historians take their theories seriously. (The Sixth Floor Museum inside the Texas School Book Depository is resolutely agnostic on the big questions.) Counternarratives are designed to subvert conventional ideas, but there is nothing at all subversive about the Creation Museum. The ideas in it are not interesting. They're just wrong. It's a place without imagination, a place where we break our dragons like plow horses and ride them.

The dinosaur with the saddle (still English) is tucked into the end of the tour now; but you can almost miss it as you come around the corner. The kids spot it, though. They climb up and smile and wave for the camera. Something is there that's trying to break out, but it never really does, God knows.

* * *

OUT where the broad lawn meets the road, workmen are digging a series of holes in the ground, looking for the place where the carriages once turned around, stopping briefly to disembark the ladies and gentlemen who had come to have dinner with the little old fellow who ran the place. The carriages would come up the twisting, narrow paths from the main road, rattling between the long white rail fences until they came to a spot somewhere right along here, right at the edge of the lawn. A house slave would greet them there, and bring them up to the main house for dinner.

On a hot day at the end of August, the high whine of power tools cuts through the low hum of the bees and drowns out the birdsong in the shrubbery. On their knees, two workers cut the earth away in a series of precise squares, down just far enough until they find some more of the old brick. They are gradually pulling the history from the earth, one square at a time.

James Madison was nine when his father built the plantation that would come to be called Montpelier, tucked into a green valley below the Blue Ridge Mountains in Orange County in Virginia, now two hours by car southeast of Washington, D.C.

Madison lived there the rest of his life, and he died there, on June 28, 1836. He and Dolley had no children—Dolley's son from her first marriage, Payne Todd, was a profligate drunk who ran up $20,000 in debts that Madison paid off secretly, in order to spare his wife the heartbreak—so, in 1844, Dolley sold the estate. Eventually, in 1901, it passed into the hands of some members of the DuPont family. In all, the DuPonts added thirty-three rooms. They built a racetrack on the grounds. They also did up the exterior of the main house in flaming pink stucco. The DuPonts built on, added to, and refurbished the place until the original Montpelier disappeared like Troy vanishing beneath a strip mall.

In 1983, the last remaining DuPont owner bequeathed the place to the National Trust, and the effort then began to free Montpelier from the encrustations of Gilded Age plutocracy. The process is nearing completion on this breathless summer afternoon, as the old turnaround out front is unearthed. The garish pink stucco is surrendering at last to the original red brick. The mortar being used is mixed the same way that it was in the eighteenth century, and a fireplace is being rebuilt of red sandstone from the same quarry as the original. A piece of Madison's personal correspondence was found as part of a rat's nest inside one of the walls. In June 2007, a reunion was held on the grounds for the descendants of the plantation's slaves.

Madison was never a superstar, not even among his contemporaries. His home never became a shrine, not the way Washington's Mount Vernon did, or Jefferson's Monticello. The ride out from Washington takes you through three major battlefields of the Civil War. It seems as though you are driving backward in time through the inevitable bloody consequences of the compromises born in the hallways of Montpelier. Madison is an imperfect guide, as all the founders were.

But he felt something in his heart in this place. (And he did have a heart, the shy little fellow. He never would have won Dolley without it.) He studied and he thought, and he ground away at his books, but it wasn't all intellect with him. Not all the time. He knew the Gut, as well. He knew it well enough to keep it where it belonged.

Madison amassed more than four thousand books in his life, and the people working at Montpelier are not altogether sure where he kept them. Some people believe the library was on the first floor, in the wing of the house where once lived Madison's aged mother, Nelly. A better candidate is a room on the second floor, at the front of the house. It has broad, wide windows, and it looks out on the sweeping lawns and off toward the Blue Ridge beyond. It is a place to plan, but it's also a place to dream.

"You know what's nice about Madison in contrast to Jefferson," says Will Harris, who runs the Center for the Study of the Constitution on the grounds of Montpelier. "Jefferson has this debate with himself with his heart and his head. Madison doesn't split the two up. He can be very angry, and he can be very motivated, in the sense of emotion and sentiment. But what that does, it engages his intellect. So when his emotions are running strong, his intellect is running strong. He wouldn't say, 'Well, my heart tells me this but my mind tells me this.' He puts the two together. And, in some ways, it's a more progressive understanding of the relationship."

In this room, with the mountains going purple in the gathering twilight, you can see all the way to the country where Ignatius Donnelly felt free to look to Atlantis, the country where a thousand cranks could prosper proudly. But also to a country in balance between the mind and the heart, as Madison was when he walked these halls in blissful retirement. A country where the disciplined intellect and the renegade soul could work together to create a freedom not merely from political tyranny, but also from the tyrannies of religion and unreason, the despotism of commercial success and brute popularity. A country where, paradoxically, the more respectable you become, the less credible you ought to be.

Whatever room the restorers finally decide is the one where the old fellow kept all his books, it turns out we are all Mr. Madison's library. He and his colleagues, who were not made of marble, gave us the chance to learn as much as we could learn about as much as there was to learn, and to put that knowledge to work in as many directions as the human mind can concoct.

But we were supposed to keep things where they belonged, so their essential value would be enhanced and not diluted. Religion would remain transcendent, and not alloyed cheaply with politics. The entrepreneurial spirit used to sell goods would be different in kind from the one used to sell ideas. Our cranks, flourishing out there in the dying light, would somehow bring us around to a truth even they couldn't see.

We need our cranks more than ever, but we need them in their proper places. We've chained our imagination because we've decided it should function as truth. We've shackled it with the language of political power and the vocabulary of salesmanship. We tame its wilder places by demanding for them conventional respectability, submitting its renegade notions to the banal administrations of school boards and courthouses. We build museums in which we break our dragons to the saddle.

That's why that room on the second floor of the mansion has to have been the library, because you can see the mountains from there. It's a room meant for looking forward, for casting your imagination outward into the outland places of the world. The nation had a government of laws, but it was a country of imagination. From that window, where you can see the mountains in the dying light of the afternoon and feel their presence as a challenge in the night, you can imagine the wild places beyond the mountains, in the vast country into which John Richbourg once had enough faith to beam his music. You can imagine the wild places in yourself. You can imagine the great things crazy notions can accomplish, if we can only keep them out of the hands of the professionals.

He designed a government, Mr. Madison did, but he dreamed himself a country. It's time for us to get ourselves in order, to set out and find that place again. Or else we will stay where we are, like that statue of Adam, before they covered his nether parts with water lilies so you wouldn't notice what was missing, lounging around, brainless and dickless, in an Eden that looks less and less like paradise.

Acknowledgments

This book started as a magazine article—in the November 2005 edition of *Esquire*—and the article started as a three-line pitch that read, "Dinosaurs with saddles." So the first toast goes rightfully to David Granger and to Mark Warren, who saw everything there was to see in those three words, and who saw the length and breadth of the story even before I did. There is no possible way to explain how much their faith in this idea meant to me, so I won't really try except to wish upon every writer in the world the chance to work with people like them.

The best way to thank all of the people who found themselves dragooned into this project is chronologically through the text, so the first ones are Ken Ham and the staff at the Creation Museum in Hebron, Kentucky. Then comes Ralph Ketchum, who sat on his porch with me as a morning thunderstorm broke over Lake George and talked about James Madison, the great subject of his life. The conversation was too short in that it ended at all.

Ed Root shared his experience with the Flight 93 Memorial in Pennsylvania, and Kit Hodges explained why scientists don't explain themselves very well. My local Masons—and perhaps, shhh!, Templars—were gracious hosts, most notably Larry Bethune. Sean Wilentz was generous enough to spend an hour on the phone talking about anti-Masons. Thanks also to Jack Horrigan, my local UFO host.

Michael Harrison and the staff of the New Media Conference in New York gave me the run of the place, and I thank Steve Gill, Tom Peace, and Patrick Blankenship at WLAC in Nashville for doing the same. Thanks also to radio guys Cenk Uygur, John Parikhal, and Holland Cooke, as well as Sgt. Todd Bowers. Andrew Cline took time to explain in detail his laws of modern punditry. Also thanks to Keith Olbermann for chatting over breakfast in the days before he became an authentic TV star, thereby confounding one of the central tenets of this book—and, as a wise man once said, that's if you're scoring at home, or even if you're not.

Judge John Jones gave me the better part of a day, and was not in any way banal, but especially not breathtakingly so. Thanks also to Liz O'Donnell in Judge Jones's office. And thanks to Pastor Ray Mummert for his patience and his honesty.

It's not possible to measure the admiration I feel for the people at the Woodside Hospice. Their graciousness in talking about the worst few weeks of their lives was nothing short of a gift. This starts, of course, with Annie Santa-Maria, a very formidable and brave soul, but includes no less Mike Bell and Louise Cleary. Thanks also to Captain Mike Haworth and the Pinellas Park Police Department, and to Marcia Stone and the staff of the Cross Bayou Elementary School, as well as to Elizabeth Kirkman, who's still a Point of Light.

Thanks to everyone in Shishmaref, especially the folks at the Fire and Rescue-cum-journalists' hostel, but also to John Stenik, Luci Eningowuk, Tom Lee, Patti Miller, and all the Weyiounnas—Tony, John, and Emily. Special thanks to Emily for noticing that I'd won at bingo, or else there might have been one more ironic twist to Idiot America. Thanks also to James Speth and Elizabeth Blackburn for their insights into politicized science.

There are a number of people who were willing to talk about their roles in what happened as the United States went to war in Iraq. All of them were painfully honest about it. Thanks, then, to Richard Clarke, Paul Pillar, Carl Ford, David Phillips, Anthony Zinni, and Eric Rosenbach. Louise Richardson—and her book, *What Terrorists Want*—was essential in understanding the roads not taken. Steve Kleinman's clear-eyed assessment of torture was just as essential in understanding the roads that were. And finally, my profound gratitude to Andrew Bacevich, who found time to talk during what must have been a period of nearly insupportable sorrow. People like him need a nation worthy of them.

I advise everyone to visit the ongoing restoration of Mr. Madison's place, Montpelier, down in the hills of Orange County in Virginia. Thanks especially to my tour guide, Elizabeth Loring, and to Will Harris at the Center for the Study of the Constitution. And, finally, thanks to Gary Hart, for a long conversation that informs almost every part of this book.

Three libraries were vital to portions of the book. My gratitude to Greg Garrison and the staff of the John Davis Williams Library at the University of Mississippi, the staff of the Minnesota Historical Society in St. Paul, and to the staff of the Oral Histories Project at Columbia University. Special thanks to Matt Kane (Columbia '07) for expert emergency aid.

I bounced the idea of this book off a number of people and I am grateful for the way they bounced it back. Thanks, then, to Bob Bateman and also to the two Doc Erics—Alterman and Rauchway—for their help and support.

As always, I had a wonderful pit crew for this trip around

the track. Mulberry Studios in Cambridge again provided the transcriptions, and I thank again the Benincasa family of Watertown, Massachusetts, for their submarine sandwiches and for the use of the hall. David Black is my agent and my friend and, most of all, a conjurer of the first rank. Almost on the fly, he made a book out of a lot of amorphous notions. Everyone else at the giddily pinwheeling empire that is the David Black Literary Agency knows that I love them madly.

For about seven months, I was absolutely unable to explain what I wanted this book to be about. This did not faze Bill Thomas at Doubleday, who knew what it was supposed to be about and patiently waited for me to figure the damn thing out. My debt to his patience and deft way with the editing blade is huge and ongoing. (He got promoted while working on this project. I have not yet asked for a kickback.) Thanks also to Melissa Danaczko for her forbearance with my utter ineptitude at the task of sending electronic mail, and for her odd idea of what Pierce Brosnan should look like. Thanks also to the folks at my day job at the *Boston Globe Magazine,* especially editor Doug Most, for his understanding of why I one morning happened to be calling from arctic Alaska.

There is no explaining my family, and no measuring the debt I owe to them, especially to my wife, Margaret Doris, who is the strongest and bravest person I know, and who lived this project through a year in which she needed all of her strength and courage. Abraham, Brendan, and Molly know what I'm talking about, because there is so much of her in them. I am so damned blessed.

Charles P. Pierce
Autumn 2008

Notes on Sources

The author is grateful to the authors and journalists whose work is cited directly herein. Some of these works also served as resources for this book's spirit as well as its text. The ur-text was probably Richard Hofstadter's *Anti-Intellectualism in American Life,* which produced several invaluable offspring. These include: *The Assault on Reason* by Al Gore, *The Age of American Unreason* by Susan Jacoby, and *The Closing of the Western Mind* by Charles Freeman. The passages about James Madison and his work would not have been possible without Ralph Ketchum's magisterial biography of the man, the Library of America's collection of Madison's writings, and Madison's *Advice to My Country,* which was edited by David Mattern. I was able to make Ignatius Donnelly Madison's curious doppelganger partly through a biographical piece in *Minnesota* magazine written by my friend and NPR quizmaster, Peter Sagal.

The chapter on WLAC in Nashville first gestated while I was reading the work of Peter Guralnick, especially *Sweet Soul Music* and *Feel Like Going Home.* The account of Michael Savage's brief career as a host of a television program on MSNBC is drawn largely from James Wolcott's hilarious *Attack Poodles and Other Media Mutants.* The author also acknowledges a debt in his treatment of talk radio to the proprietors of Media

Matters for America, and to Eric Alterman's *What Liberal Media?* and *Sound and Fury.* The discussion of the treatment of presidential candidate Al Gore would not have been possible without the work of the redoubtable Bob Somerby at www.daily howler.com.

In addition to Gordy Slack's *The Battle Over the Meaning of Everything,* my account of the Dover intelligent design case, and of the intelligent design controversy in general, also depended on *Before Darwin* by Keith Thomson; *The Creationists: From Scientific Creationism to Intelligent Design* by Ronald Numbers; *Monkey Trials and Gorilla Sermons* by Peter J. Bowler; Margaret Talbot's contemporaneous reportage in *The New Yorker;* and P. J. Myers's work at his blog, www.science blogs.com/pharyngula.

The account of the death of Terri Schiavo was aided immeasurably by *The Case of Terri Schiavo,* a collection of essays edited by Arthur Caplan, James McCartney, and Dominic Sisti. The story of Elizabeth Blackburn's experiences on the President's Council on Bioethics can be found most completely in *Elizabeth Blackburn and the Story of Telomeres* by Catherine Brady. Also immensely helpful were Michelle Goldberg's *Kingdom Coming: The Rise of Christian Nationalism* and Esther Kaplan's *With God on Their Side.*

The brief account of the history of whaling in and around the Chukchi Sea is drawn from the work of NASA's Jeremy Project (http://quest.arc.nasa.gov/arctic/explore/ship_history.html) and the online resources of the New Bedford Whaling Museum (http://www.whalingmuseum.org/library/amwhale/am_arctic .html). A. F. Jamieson's account of the *Baychimo* comes from www.theoutlaws.com/unexplained8.htm. The author also acknowledges a debt to the previous reporting on Shishmaref done by Margot Roosevelt of *Time* magazine.

A number of accounts have been published concerning how the Iraq war came about. The author is especially indebted to *Hubris* by David Corn and Michael Isikoff, *Fiasco* by Thomas Ricks, *Losing Iraq* by David Phillips, *The Limits of Power* by Andrew J. Bacevich, *Imperial Life in the Emerald City* by Rajiv Chandrasekaran, and *The Italian Letter* by Knut Royce and Peter Eisner. The Report of the Select Committee on Intelligence on Prewar Assessments about Postwar Iraq is available online at http://intelligence.senate.gov/prewar.pdf, as is the report concerning the political interference with government scientists produced by the House Committee on Oversight and Government Reform. The strange history and influence of 24 were ably set out first by Rebecca Dana of the *Wall Street Journal,* and, most notably, by Jane Mayer of *The New Yorker.*

The American Bar Association was kind enough to send along a transcript of the panel it conducted on the subject of high-profile cases that included both Judge Jones and Judge Whittemore. A précis of the event can be found at http://www.abanet.org/media/youraba/200702/article08.html.

Ignatius Donnelly's papers, including his vast diaries, are stored in the archives of the Minnesota Historical Society, and those of John Richbourg are part of the Blues Collection at the Williams Library of the University of Mississippi. The Reminiscences of F. C. Sowell, p. 30, are in the Oral History Collection of Columbia University. David Sanjak's study of postwar popular music was published in *American Music* (vol. 15, no. 4, winter 1997, pp. 535–62). William Butler Pierce's impressions of his fellow delegates was published in *The American Historical Review* (vol. 3, no. 2, January 1898, pp. 310–34). All material from these archives is used by permission.

Portions of this book previously appeared in other forms in *Esquire* and in *The American Prospect Online.*